A MAN OF THREE WORLDS

PUBLISHING FOR THE WORLD
125 Years

THE JOHNS HOPKINS UNIVERSITY PRESS

A
MAN OF
THREE WORLDS

Samuel Pallache, a Moroccan Jew
in Catholic and Protestant Europe

Mercedes García-Arenal *&* Gerard Wiegers

Translated by Martin Beagles

With a foreword by
David Nirenberg *&* Richard Kagan

THE JOHNS HOPKINS UNIVERSITY PRESS
Baltimore & London

© 1999 Siglo XXI Editores, S.A., and the authors
Originally published as *Entre el Islam y Occidente:*
Vida de Samuel Pallache, judío de Fez
English Translation © 2003 The Johns Hopkins University Press
All rights reserved. Published 2003
Printed in the United States of America on acid-free paper
2 4 6 8 9 7 5 3 1

The Johns Hopkins University Press
2715 North Charles Street
Baltimore, Maryland 21218-4363
www.press.jhu.edu

Library of Congress Cataloging-in-Publication Data
García-Arenal, Mercedes.
[Entre el Islam y occidente. English]
A Man of Three Worlds: Samuel Pallache, a Moroccan Jew in Catholic and
Protestant Europe / Mercedes García-Arenal and Gerard Wiegers ; translated by
Martin Beagles.
p. cm.
Includes bibliographical references and index.
ISBN 0-8018-7225-1
1. Pallache, Samuel, d. 1616. 2. Jews—Morocco—Fáes—Biography.
3. Sephardim—Morocco—Fáes—Biography. 4. Jews, Moroccan—Spain—
Madrid—Biography. 5. Jews, Moroccan—Netherlands—Amsterdam—
Biography. 6. Jewish businesspeople—Biography. 7. Spies—Spain—Biography.
8. Fáes (Morocco)—Biography. 9. Madrid (Spain)—Biography. 10. Amsterdam
(Netherlands)—Biography. I. Wiegers, Gerard Albert, 1959– II. Title.
DS135.M9 P35413 2003
964'.004924'0092—dc21
2002008122

A catalog record for this book is available from the British Library.

CONTENTS

FOREWORD

Samuel Pallache was born in Morocco circa 1550 and grew up in interesting times. His grandparents were refugees, expelled from Spain in 1492 along with all other Jews. For him, as for many of his people, the memory of that year remained a vivid one, mourned in every generation. His Muslim neighbors surely reminded him of another milestone marked by 1492: the Spanish Christian conquest of Granada, Islam's last outpost in Western Europe. Since then the struggle between Christendom and Islam had only grown sharper, and although he was a Jew, much of Samuel's life would be spent in its trenches, serving powers on both sides simultaneously. As a child, he would doubtless have learned that Christendom, too, was being transformed, though he could not have known that his life would eventually depend upon navigating the emerging enmity between Protestants and Catholics. And, of course, Samuel could see for himself the consequences of yet another of 1492's events. The "discovery" of America's riches had opened an era of colonization and transoceanic empire. Samuel grew up in this "new world order" of global powers and grand alliances and built his career around its geopolitics. At one time or another, he would offer his skills to all the key players: the Catholic Spanish and the Muslim Ottoman empires, as well as the monarchies of France and England. For the most part, however, he served two smaller powers struggling to survive the dance of giants: Morocco and the United Provinces (roughly the modern Netherlands).

These pages are in large part an account of Samuel's career and those of his sons and nephews. What careers they were! We first meet Samuel in 1603 in Catholic Spain, buying jewels for his master, the sultan of Morocco, and attempting to sell his master's "secrets" to the king of Spain. Not until the eve of his death thirteen years later did he succeed in signing a contract with that monarch: 200 escudos a month in exchange for information on diplomatic relations between the Dutch and North Africa. In between, Samuel worked as a trader and translator, diplomat and informant, naval general and privateer. His schemes had a way of going awry. As a businessman he lost his ships to privateers, and as a privateer he lost his fleet to storms and enemies. Trusted by none and selling his services to all, he died just out of prison and in penury. Yet over the course of this calamitous career, his name and his business became familiar to many of the princes of Europe and the Muslim world: Philip III of Spain, James I of England, Louis XIII of France, Prince Maurice of Nassau and the States General of the United Provinces, as well as sultans both Ottoman and Marinid, all concerned themselves with the doings of this wandering Jew.

How is it that such a marginal man came so often to the attention of the powerful? The answer to that question tells us a great deal about the early modern world, and about the place of Jews and converts from Judaism in that world. There is irony in the fact that, at the very moment that the European sense of the world became global, it also became national. Early modern Europe arose out of the fragmentation of Christendom precipitated by the Reformation and the struggle between Catholic Spain and its many, mostly Protestant opponents. It was a Europe composed of states demanding increasingly exclusive religious, economic, linguistic, and political loyalties. It was also an age of hardening frontiers, of passports and embargoes, of new theories about citizenship and international law, and escalating war. In this new world, Jews and converts from Judaism became both more problematic and more useful. On the one hand, the mobility of a figure like Samuel Pallache, and the malleability of his loyalties, made him suspect in a world of increasingly high-pitched political antagonisms. On the other, more than ever, such a world needed people capable of moving across its borders.

In this world, the Pallaches functioned above all as mediators between Europe and North Africa. No matter where they migrate in the pages that follow, their primary service is always to the sultan of Morocco. Gripped often by civil war, the Morocco of their day was a minor Mediterranean power whose survival depended upon playing Protestant against Catholic against Ottoman. Jews like Pallache and his nephew Moshe were ideally suited for this task. To begin with, they were fluent in the languages and cultures of both Islam and Europe, a skill as rare then as it is now. Furthermore, Jews and *conversos* (baptized Jews and their descendants) often had family connections scattered throughout Europe by means of which they could communicate across borders. Finally, precisely because their religious identity marked them as despised and disloyal, they could be trusted. A Dutch, French, or English adviser might be suspected of putting his "natural" loyalties to cult and homeland ahead of those of his Moroccan master. A Jew, on the other hand, was treated by Christians and Muslims alike as the enemy of all nations, citizen of none. He had by definition few loyalties and few rights. As Christians and Muslims saw it, the Jew was unique in that his services were governed entirely by a market logic of self-interest. That was what made him so useful.

All of the Pallache family's employers, whether in Fez or The Hague, in Madrid or London, shared these assumptions. At Pallache's trial for "piracie, spoyle, and outrage at sea" in London, for example, both his accuser (Spain's ambassador at the Court of St. James, the count of Gondomar) and his defender (Noel de Caron, the Dutch ambassador) agreed that he was a Barbarian Jew, deserving no better treatment than a dog. But, Caron argued, he was an employee and ambassador of the sultan of Morocco, and as such should be accorded respect for reasons of state. Gondomar disagreed bitterly. Not to hang Pallache, he argued, was to give Judaism a triumph over Christianity. But once the trial ended in Pallache's acquittal, the count was enthusiastically advocating that Spain recruit him into her service.

Were the Pallaches' loyalties really so flexible? The authors cannot help but ask this question, and we readers want to know the answer. Often it seems that, even in their most duplicitous actions (such as attempting to sell the king of Spain information about Morocco), the Pallaches were playing a double game on behalf of their Moroccan masters. But in the end, we have no way to judge the loyalty of an individual whose status is defined by a society's logic as disloyal. We find ourselves in something like the Cretan paradox: in a world that defines all Jews as changeable and duplicitous, it becomes impossible to establish the Jews' true identity. The Pallaches, like many other Jews and converts from Judaism, sometimes benefited from this paradoxical status: it made possible their movement across cultures and frontiers. But they also paid a high price for it. Defined as chameleons, they were never allowed the possibility of choosing their own allegiances, whether of nation or of cult. Their conversions and political commitments were by definition expedient and insincere. If they converted to Islam, Catholicism, or Protestantism, it could only be for convenience, not out of conviction. In 1633, for example, Samuel Pallache's nephew Isaac, son of his brother Joseph, converted to Protestantism. The family clearly understood the conversion to be total: Joseph not only disinherited his son but sued for custody of one of his grandchildren. Yet from a Christian point of view, the conversion meant little. Business rivals in the Dutch East India Company did not hesitate to accuse Isaac of apostasy when it suited their purposes, and even Christian houseguests whom Isaac had helped to free from captivity in Morocco thought nothing of calling him a Jew. Isaac's reply to his accusers is as moving as it was fruitless: "How could I pretend to be a Jew, when I have abandoned my father and my mother and my belongings and my home country, all for the love of the Christian religion?" The world needed the Pallaches and their coreligionists to be "pretenders," and regardless of their own intentions, it would always classify them as such.

For all of its importance for the history of early modern Jewry, this remarkable study of Samuel Pallache and his family grows out of the common interest of its authors—one Spanish, the other Dutch—in the history of another of Spain's beleaguered ethnic and religious minorities: the moriscos. The moriscos were Spanish Muslims who, like the conversos, had converted to Christianity, but who were nevertheless expelled from their Iberian homeland at the orders of King Philip III in 1609. Mercedes García-Arenal, a research professor in the Department of Arab Studies in the Institute of Philology at the Higher Council of Scientific Research, one of Spain's premier research institutions, is internationally acclaimed for many books and articles on the moriscos, and, more broadly, on the status of ethnic and religious minorities in the early modern Mediterranean world. She shares many of these interests with her co-author, Gerard Wiegers, an associate professor in the Department for the History of Religions and Comparative Religion in the Faculty of Theology at Leiden University. Specializing in the study of Arabic literature and in *aljamiado*, an amalgam of Arabic and Spanish found among the moriscos, Wiegers has published widely in this area, and his books include a notable bilingual edition of the diaries of Ahmad b. Qâsim al-Hajarî, a morisco physician who traveled throughout Europe and North Africa after having been forced out of Spain in 1609.

That a common concern with the history and culture of the moriscos should lead these two scholars to Pallache is not altogether accidental. Prior to 1609, Spain's moriscos had long-standing ties with North Africa, and after the expulsion, those who found their way to Morocco, siding with the sultans, were actively involved in raids upon Spanish shipping and even in plots against the Spanish king. Samuel Pallache's knowledge of the moriscos, their culture, and of Morocco in general rendered him an invaluable resource for the Spaniards, and it was largely for this reason that he made his appearance in Spanish diplomatic and military dispatches relating to North Africa. If these letters and memoranda, many unpublished, served as the starting point for this study, García-Arenal and Wiegers found additional nuggets in other sources they already knew, among them, the rich archives of the Spanish Inquisition in Madrid and the *Sources inédites de l'histoire du Maroc*, an invaluable but underutilized documentary collection relating to the history of North Africa and its relationship with various European countries, including Spain, England, and the Netherlands. Further digging turned up more about the Pallaches and their various activities, but ultimately it was the authors' skill and experience, and a combined linguistic expertise allowing for the use of sources in Arabic, Dutch, French, Spanish, and Hebrew, that enabled them to transform what must have initially seemed like random tidbits of information into the fascinating, multifaceted study that appears in the pages ahead.

The present edition owes much to the translating skills of Martin Beagles, a historian in his own right. His detailed knowledge of early seventeenth-century European history has served to enrich this study, just as his writing skills have made it accessible to a broad, English-reading audience. Readers are advised, however, that the original documents published (in Dutch, French, and Spanish) in the appendix included in the original Spanish edition are not reproduced here. Those interested in these materials should therefore consult *Entre el Islam y Occidente. Vida de Samuel Pallache, judío de Fez* (Madrid, 1999).

David Nirenberg
Richard L. Kagan

PREFACE

This short book has taken a long time to write. Preparing it meant spending many hours in archives looking for items of information that often turned out to be minute and were always widely dispersed. As this search went on, we accumulated numerous debts of gratitude, but particular mention must be made of Isabel Aguirre, the excellent *jefe de sala* of the Archivo General de Simancas. All those who frequent the archive at Simancas are well aware of the extent to which her knowledge and kindness contribute to the work of researchers. We are also grateful to Luisa Isabel Álvarez de Toledo, duchess of Medinasidonia, for allowing us access to her family archive, as well as helping to guide us through that magnificent collection. The doors of another private archive, the former Mozes Heiman Gans Collection of Amsterdam, were opened to us by the courtesy of its current heir. The members of staff at the Archivo Histórico Nacional and the Biblioteca Nacional de Madrid, the Arquivo Nacional da Torre do Tombo in Lisbon, the Amsterdam University Library, the Leiden University Library, and the Archives Générales du Royaume in Brussels have all responded to our requests for help and photocopies. They all displayed great kindness and understanding when faced with the occasional impatience of one who is working for a few brief days at an archive far from his or her home city. We wish to express our gratitude to them all.

The idea for this book first arose out of discussions between the two authors about the possibility of a joint research project after Gerard Wiegers had come across some intriguing records on the Pallache family at a time when we were both involved in research at the Archivo General de Simancas. Using these documents as a starting point, Mercedes García-Arenal went on to find a large amount of clearly fascinating material, and we started to lay down the basis of the present study. From that moment on, the research was divided in accordance with our respective home bases of Madrid and Leiden: Mercedes García-Arenal took responsibility for the archives and libraries within the Iberian Peninsula, and Gerard Wiegers worked at those in Holland and Belgium. As the years went by, we were able to match our findings and discuss our ideas and interpretations during meetings at various international conferences. Drafts of the book later traveled back and forth by Internet, which has so greatly favored international cooperation. Looking back, it must be said that the greatest part of the writing was done by Mercedes García-Arenal. However, the text has been entirely rewritten and revised by the two of us, and we are both equally responsible for its contents.

During the years in which we were working on the book, Gerard Wiegers's research was financed by the Royal Netherlands Academy of Arts and Sciences (KNAW). A *cátedra* from the Fundación Banco de Bilbao-Vizcaya (FBBV) permitted him to spend the fall 1997 trimester at the C.S.I.C. in Madrid.

As it will not be hard to imagine, our families and close friends have had to hear a great deal about Samuel Pallache over the years, and have even been required to read chapters at various stages of the writing process. Their comments, their amazement, and their misunderstanding have all been extremely useful to us; their moments of boredom have also led us to lighten our most cumbersome chapters.

Our colleagues Maribel Fierro, Manuela Marín, and Fernando R. Mediano of the Department of Arabic Studies at the C.S.I.C. in Madrid, Sjoerd van Koningsveld of the University of Leiden, and David Wasserstein of the University of Tel Aviv read versions of this book in manuscript, and their comments and criticisms were tremendously important. We also wish to thank Alistair Hamilton and Wim de Baar for their help in deciphering some of the documents. Driss Mansouri, Abdelilah Benmlih (University of Fez), and José María Viñuela provided illustrations for the original Spanish edition.

Esperanza Alfonso translated the Hebrew articles cited in the Bibliography. Aernold van Gosliga, Welmoet Boender, and Hanny Slootman, students at the History of Religions Department at the University of Leiden, and Cristina de la Puente of the C.S.I.C. provided technical assistance in the final phases of our work.

In addition, we are particularly grateful to our colleague Herman Prins Salomon (State University of New York) for his extensive critical comments on the Spanish version of the text and for bringing to our attention the records kept in Brussels. Finally, special thanks are due to Martin Beagles, not only for his translation of this book into English, but for pointing out certain errors and inconsistencies in the Spanish original.

NOTE ON TERMINOLOGY

This book is based on documentation in several different languages, and individuals' names are generally spelled as those concerned would themselves have written them, except where a well-established English alternative exists. An exception has been made for members of the Pallache family, who have been given standard English versions of their names for reasons of clarity. The man we call "Moses" Pallache, for example, was commonly known as "Moisés" in Madrid, "Mozes" in Amsterdam, and "Musa" when residing in Morocco. To have chosen any one of these names over the other two would have misleadingly implied the predominance of one element in the makeup of his multiple identity, whereas to have used all three names interchangeably would probably have created unnecessary confusion.

It is also worth pointing out that the family name was written both "Pallache" and "Palache" in the early seventeenth century, and that "Palache" is the form most commonly used by the family today. We have chosen to use "Pallache" throughout for the simple reason that it was the spelling favored by Samuel Pallache himself.

Moroccan Arabic names are spelled in accordance with standard English usage. The term "Dutch Republic" is used to refer to the state composed of the seven united northern provinces, and "Flanders" for the provinces of the south. "Holland" generally refers to the actual province of that name and "The Netherlands" to the entire region, including the southern provinces dominated by Spain.

INTRODUCTION

There are individuals whose life stories can be read as epitomes of the great conflicts of their times. We are not referring to major figures who made decisions that marked an epoch, but to the "minor lives" of people forced to contend with economic and political developments beyond their own control. The personal dramas of such individuals can serve to exemplify the lives of thousands of anonymous human beings. It can be immensely rewarding to examine how they challenged or evaded the constraints of their circumstances, and also to dwell on the peculiarities that made each of them deviate from the norm. Occasionally, such lives will have the uniquely vivid potential to evoke a specific political or social situation for us—to summon up, in other words, an entire lost world.

The problem is that, almost by definition, the lives of such obscure minor figures are very hard to document or to reconstruct in their entirety. It is perhaps precisely for this reason that we, the authors of this book, have come to feel such fascination for the ambiguous and complex life of Samuel Pallache.

PALLACHE WAS BORN IN FEZ to a Moroccan Jewish family of Iberian origin. He worked in Amsterdam and The Hague for several years as a commercial and diplomatic agent of the Moroccan sultan Muley Zaydan until his death in 1616. During his time in the Dutch Republic, Pallache was a practicing Jew and an important member of Amsterdam's burgeoning Jewish community. But before that, Pallache had lived in Madrid, where he worked for the Spanish crown, and had been willing to convert to the Catholic faith as part of an official attempt to settle permanently in Spain with his family. To complicate matters further, Pallache never quite gave up his home base in Morocco, and at one time, he even flirted with the idea of serving the Ottoman government in Istanbul. The specific nature of his professional career was equally unstraightforward: at various times in his life, Pallache worked as a spy, a businessman, a double agent, and even as one of the Barbary corsairs, often finding it possible to combine these activities with his work as an official representative of the Moroccan state.

It will be immediately clear that Pallache's life was far from exemplary in the Plutarchian sense of the term. In the course of his extraordinary career, Pallache repeatedly showed himself to be an accomplished dissimulator with a talent for deceit who was adept at tailoring versions of himself to suit his ever-varying circumstances. His most outstanding personal qualities were perhaps flexibility and adaptability. He combined these traits with the risk-taking, enterprising spirit of a man who was constantly being forced to negotiate and to improvise ad hoc survival strategies. Like other men of his stamp, the sinuous and elusive Pallache lived on the margins, making constant use of his ability to straddle the borders between two worlds in conflict with one another. Pallache's talents were exceptional up to a point, but they were by no means unique and were certainly not exclusive to post-Expulsion Iberian Jews. In this book, we shall meet other men who were just as complex and just as adaptable as Samuel Pallache, such as the Frenchman Jean Castelane and the English brothers Robert and Anthony Shirley.

At the same time, the authorities who employed Pallache, and especially the authorities in Spain, demonstrably chose to make use of his skills even when they were fully aware of his disloyalty to them (or, to be more precise, of his loyalty to several conflicting parties at the same time). As we shall see, there were even occasions when such duplicity seemed to work in his favor rather than counting against him. This forces us to ask ourselves difficult questions about the possibility of widespread acceptance of a positive side to "treachery" in the seventeenth century—known to Spaniards as the century of the baroque.

Samuel Pallache is not a complete unknown. Previous studies have tended to present him as a leading member of the Sephardic community in Amsterdam and as a famed and active enemy of the Spanish nation. Thus, when we started working in the Estado section of the Archivo General in Simancas (each of us alone and in search of different data), we were considerably surprised when we came across documents describing Samuel and his brother Joseph's work in Madrid. The evidence revealed a much more complex and inconsistent individual than the Samuel Pallache of the specialized monographs. It also threw fascinating light on the changeable, piecemeal nature of Pallache's identity, and on the contradictory ways in which he constructed this identity for himself. Our subsequent fascination with Pallache has since taken us to other European archives in an effort to fill the gaps in his story, but this book is not the result of a comprehensive search for all those documents that might make some reference to him. To give just one example, we decided to deal only briefly with economic aspects of his career, which meant, as far as the documents in the Public Record Office in The Hague were concerned, that we limited ourselves to those published in the *Sources inédites de l'histoire du Maroc* collected and edited by Count Henry de Castries (*SIHM*). To do otherwise would only have produced a wealth of data that might have confused the general thrust of the book.

One of our greatest difficulties has been how to write an account that would allow for the apparent inconsistencies in Pallache's career. In addition, how could we make sense of Pallache when there were so many gaps and insuperable obstacles in the evidence? What could we say for certain about the behavior or psychology of such a man? We wanted to do more than lay down a mere chronological sequence of events, and one of the ways in which we have tried to cover the gaps and address the inherent paradoxes is by presenting as many as possible of the people with whom Pallache came into contact. We have tried to improve our understanding of his milieu by looking at other members of the Pallache family, several of whom played important roles in diplomatic relations between Morocco and the Dutch Republic throughout the seventeenth century. (Samuel's brother Joseph became the Moroccan ambassador in The Hague, and his nephew Moses was employed as a translator and interpreter to Sultan Muley Zaydan and several of Zaydan's successors.) As well as studying the Pallache family, we examine contemporaries whose careers ran parallel or convergent to Samuel Pallache's own. These are mainly other Jews from Fez who also emigrated to Spain, Portugal, or the Dutch Republic, or who pursued similar professional careers to Pallache's. Some of them were brought before the Inquisition in Spain or Portugal and required to give full accounts of their backgrounds and the "discourses of their lives," thus providing us with fascinating information on their upbringing and professions.

The differences between these individuals turn out to be as significant as the similarities. Marginalized and faced with various kinds of adversity, Jews from Fez invented a wide range of strategies for survival or social promotion, often resorting to conversion to another religion, plus either simultaneous or serial employment by warring states. The evidence reveals that the religious commitments of these Jews were often variable and even negotiable, and this inevitably forces us to question traditional essentialist notions of a united Jewish nation or people. Not only did such Jews serve different religious and political causes, but they can often be found switching allegiance throughout their lives from one master to another. Samuel Pallache was by no means unique in this respect.

Nor was it only Jews who acted in this way. As we seek to show, faced with the same sorts of difficulties as their Jewish compatriots after expulsion from Spain, the moriscos (Muslims who had been baptized as Christians) adopted similar solutions. In fact, alliances even came about between exiled Jews and moriscos, which had only occurred very rarely when the two minority groups had lived together on Iberian soil. The Jewish and morisco experiences of expulsion suggest that there are many ways of "belonging" to a religion, and that such belonging cannot be reduced to a mere belief system. In any case, we shall try to show that individuals "belong" first and foremost to a culture, in the anthropological sense of the term, and that an individual's identity can be an extremely variable sum of numerous cultural elements. This mixture is what makes Pallache and contemporary Jews of his kind so fascinating. In the multiplicity and complexity of their allegiances, they seem to anticipate by several generations a mental shift more usually associated with the Enlightenment.

THIS BOOK IS SET MAINLY IN THREE PLACES, one of which is the city of Fez, where Samuel Pallache was born and brought up in the second half of the sixteenth century. The Pallaches descended from Jews expelled from Spain who had retained their Iberian character over successive generations. Fez had been an important place of refuge for Iberian Jews since the persecutions of the late fourteenth century, and it received especially significant numbers of Spanish Jews after the Expulsion of 1492. During the sixteenth century, the Jewish quarter of Fez became a renowned place of return to Judaism for crypto-Jews from both Spain and Portugal. However, conditions worsened considerably in the first third of the seventeenth century, which saw the outbreak of a bloody civil war in Morocco. This conflict persuaded a number of Moroccan Jews to attempt a "return" to the Iberian Peninsula. In Chapter 2 of this book, we look at the life and characteristics of the Jewish community of Fez, paying particular attention to the duties performed by Jews at the Moroccan court and in Morocco's diplomatic and commercial relations with other nations.

The second locale is Madrid. The least well-known phase of Samuel Pallache's life is the time he spent there between 1603 and 1607, covered here in Chapter 1. It is surprising to discover the presence of Jewish agents, informers, and traders in Madrid during this period, but Pallache was not the only Moroccan Jew to take up residence in the very center of a country that had gone to such great lengths to have Jews expelled and that did not admit their legal presence within its borders. We examine Pallache's dealings with his various Spanish employers and his attempts to settle permanently in Spain with his family, until problems with the Inquisition forced him to leave the country.

After Fez and Madrid, the third city to feature prominently in Pallache's life was Amsterdam. This is the longest and best-documented period in his career. Pallache was a diplomatic and commercial agent (but never, as has often been claimed, an ambassador) of the Moroccan sultan in the Dutch Republic. In Chapter 3, we record his many travels between Morocco and the Netherlands and his participation in the lives of the Jewish communities that were taking shape in the Dutch Republic. The end of the sixteenth century had seen the beginnings in Amsterdam of what would grow to be the most important of all the post-Expulsion Jewish communities, and we consider the true extent of Samuel Pallache's involvement in this community, casting some doubt on traditional interpretations of his role.

Chapter 4 deals with Pallache's imprisonment and trial in London in 1614–15, and with the little-known attempts he made in the last year of his life to work for the Spanish government again. In 1614, Pallache had been returning to the Dutch Republic in command of a corsair ship laden with booty from Spanish ships taken near the Azores when a storm sent him off course and forced him into harbor in the English port of Plymouth. At the request of the Spanish ambassador in London, Pallache was arrested and, after a series of lengthy judicial wranglings, placed on trial for piracy. After being found not guilty and released, he then, somewhat ironically, spent the final months of his life secretly negotiating to return to the service of the Spanish crown, but died in The Hague in February

1616. The final chapter of this book continues the story after Samuel's death, when his brother and nephews performed important diplomatic services for the Moroccan state.

All in all, one is tempted to apply to Samuel Pallache a reflection of Jorge Luis Borges's about one of his own ancestors: "Le tocaron, como a todos los hombres, malos tiempos en que vivir"—"He was destined, as all men are, to live in hard times."

A MAN OF THREE WORLDS

Samuel Pallache's World

CHAPTER 1

FROM FEZ TO MADRID

*Muley Sidan, king of Morocco, aggrieved that King Philip III of Spain would
not return to him the Arabic books taken from him by the Spaniards off a ship
[sailing] from the port of Zafi to that of Santa Cruz, sent Samuel Pallache as
his ambassador to the States of the United Provinces to prepare pirate ships, of
which Joseph Pallache, brother of the ambassador, was made commander, [to
be used] against Spanish coasts and vessels. The said ambassador of Morocco
had the best of a martial engagement with the Spanish ambassador when
their carriages met on a street of the Hague, capital of Holland. Then
Ambassador Pallache died in the year 1616. Maurice, prince of Orange,
and the nobility of the Hague accompanied his corpse, which was
interred in the burial ground of the Jews of Amsterdam.*
—Miguel de Barrios, *Historia universal judayca*

This paragraph by Miguel de Barrios, also known as Daniel Levi de Barrios, a distinguished Jewish writer born in Spain in the early seventeenth
century, is the first known reference to the brothers Samuel and Joseph
Pallache in a historical work. Barrios lived in Amsterdam half a century
after the Pallaches and published numerous verse and prose writings there.
His books have been widely used by historians as source material, and they
continue to be cited even today, but Barrios's general unreliability has now
been established beyond all doubt.[1] Thus the *Historia universal* presents
both Samuel and Joseph Pallache as leading members of the Amsterdam
Jewish community in the year 5357/1597, adding that Samuel's house was
used for prayer meetings, a claim Barrios repeated in his *Triumpho del
govierno popular judayco* (Triumph of Jewish Popular Government), where

he lists sixteen leading Jewish citizens, one of whom was "Semuel Pay-ache, with the merit that his house was frequented for prayer."[2] This is misleading, however, because the Pallaches did not even arrive in Amsterdam until 1608, and it is unlikely that they were ever prominent members of the Jewish community.[3]

For all its unreliability, Barrios's outline of Samuel Pallache's career contains the seeds of a romantic and heroic biographical legend, and his imaginative rendering laid the basis for further mythic versions of Pallache's life. In the brief passage quoted from the *Historia universal*, Pallache is firstly shown being sent to Holland as the Moroccan ambassador by Sultan Muley Zaydan on a mission especially dear to his master: a bid to recover books stolen by Spaniards from the sultan's private library while it was being transported by sea. Later, Samuel and his brother Joseph work together with the States General, the government of the Dutch Republic, to fit out ships for a revenge attack on Spain. Then, in an encounter in their carriages on the streets of the Dutch capital, Pallache succeeds in defying and humiliating the Spanish ambassador. Pallache is presented throughout as a close and esteemed friend of both Maurice of Nassau and Muley Zaydan, and after his death, the body of this distinguished figure is accompanied by leading members of the States General to the Jewish cemetery of Ouderkerk aan de Amstel, a beautiful baroque cemetery near Amsterdam immortalized by the painter Jacob van Ruysdael, where Samuel Pallache's grave can still be found today.

Barrios's sketch has served as a basic design upon which modern writers have continued to elaborate.[4] Pallache has been portrayed as an important political figure in both Morocco and the Netherlands, where he is also supposed to have played a leading religious role in the Jewish community. He is invariably described as a noble, pious, and prominent Jew who never balked at confronting the Spaniards. According to this conventional view, Pallache's career was driven mainly by anti-Spanish motives, which united the Dutch and the Moroccans, and also by the personal rancor felt by descendants of those who had suffered expulsion from Spain, the land of Inquisition.

This legend has prospered to such an extent, and been so embellished in secondary sources, that it comes as a shock to discover that it originates entirely in this one short paragraph from the *Historia universal*. Of course, other convenient textual evidence has been produced for the purpose of bolstering Barrios's original claims. But the problem is that the whole legend is based on very shaky foundations. As we shall show, even the most central incident in Barrios's passage turns out to be historically inaccurate: the episode of Muley Zaydan's stolen books, which Barrios presents as the reason for Pallache making his first journey to Holland, did not actually occur until several years later, and it was not Samuel Pallache who was sent on this mission, but his nephew Moses (see Chapter 3 below).

In order to understand the development of the Pallache legend, one has to consider the historical context that favored its production and survival. The New Jews of sixteenth- and seventeenth-century Amsterdam had suffered painful and traumatic experiences in the Iberian Peninsula, which later led them to deny or suppress their collective memory of a "marrano" past. This denial of memory, or "collective amnesia," resulted in a general refusal to acknowledge the fact that generations of Jews had ever been forcibly converted to Christianity; and this refusal clearly made it difficult to admit to the notion of a later "return" to Judaism.[5] The topic of past conversions was strictly taboo among the Jewish community and could not even be mentioned as a way of exalting Inquisition victims in one's own family. The family chronicle of Isaac Pinto and the works of Miguel de Barrios himself are good examples of genealogical memoirs illustrating the extent to which Amsterdam Jews had suppressed disquieting aspects of their Iberian past: the theme of Jewish descent and of a return to a religion that their forebears had been forced to abandon is quite simply never broached.[6] The reason for this silence is clear—these authors had great difficulty in accepting the Christian conversions of ancestors who had been born, and might have been brought up as, Jews. The emotional effect of this denial was kept alive by many factors, and can still be detected even in the work of some contemporary historians.

In recent years, Spanish archives have yielded interesting new evidence about Samuel Pallache, but the general view of his career has remained stubbornly unaltered. Thus Jonathan Israel's study of Spain and the Dutch Sephardim presents Samuel as a man who served the Spanish crown for a time but soon joined forces with a deeply committed group of Dutch Jews. According to Israel, this group contrasted sharply with another faction that had rejected Judaism and remained on the margins of Jewish community life. It was only members of this marginal group who were prepared, in this view, to take money from the Spaniards in exchange for providing information on the activities of Jews outside the Peninsula and of conversos within it.[7] In our opinion, this standard, clear-cut view of events becomes unsustainable after a careful reading of all the available evidence. We propose a more complex interpretation of Pallache's activities.

To make our position clearer, let us start by examining the earliest evidence relating to Samuel Pallache's extraordinary career.

MADRID

The earliest references that we have found in Spanish records seem to indicate that Samuel and his brother Joseph Pallache first went to Madrid in 1603.[8] Although their names are not at first used in the official correspondence about them, it should be remembered that this was common practice in European records of the period, which often refer to "Jews" as such, rather than as named individuals. As we shall see, later developments seem to show that the two "Jews" concerned can only have been the Pallache brothers.

In January 1602, the Moroccan sultan Ahmad al-Mansur, who sought to buy precious stones in Lisbon, had obtained Philip III's permission to send two of his Jewish servants to broker the deal. The sultan also requested permission to bring to Spain an amount of between 800 and 1500 *quintales* (8,000–15,000 lbs) of beeswax—essential in the making of candles and seals—to pay for the jewels.[9] That autumn, Alonso Pérez de Guzmán, the seventh duke of Medina Sidonia and previous commander of the ill-fated "Invincible" Armada sent by Philip II to England in 1588, requested a passport to be used by two Moroccan Jews who had by then reached Ceuta. As *capitán del mar océano* for the Andalusian coast and captain-general of the armies of Portugal, the duke was responsible for all Moroccan business. Medina Sidonia informed the king that the Moroccan Jews intended to travel to Spain, not only to buy jewels for the sultan, but also to provide the Spaniards with information on Moroccan public affairs, as the two men claimed to have "an *arbitrio* [informative report] of considerable importance." Medina Sidonia suggested that the Jews be granted a hearing.[10] Philip III acquiesced and granted the Moroccans the passports they sought, on condition that they be received and interviewed.[11] It seems reasonable to conclude that the two "Jews" in question were the same two servants first mentioned by the sultan in January.

After they had arrived in Spain, the two Jews requested permission to travel on to Lisbon, but one of the king's advisers, the marquis of Castel Rodrigo, warned that "if those who come from the Sharif and must go there [Lisbon] to buy stones are Jews, they will do much harm among those of their nation, as experience has taught us on other occasions."[12] Castel Rodrigo's fear was that the Barbary Jews might entice some of Lisbon's conversos to return to a faith they were supposed to have forgotten. The king therefore wrote to Medina Sidonia instructing him to tell the sultan not to send Jewish servants to Lisbon for this purchase.[13] Medina Sidonia replied by saying that he saw no inconvenience in granting passports to these particular Jews, but that the main problem lay in the large numbers of Barbary Jews already living in Lisbon, who deserved to be expelled because they were "very intelligent"—that is, involved in espionage.[14]

The first document that actually refers to one of the "Jews" by name dates from 1605. This document, a *consulta*, or dispatch, issued by the Spanish Council of State, identifies Samuel Pallache as an individual who had volunteered to help Philip III in future dealings with Muley al-Shaykh, one of the warring sons of Ahmad al-Mansur, who were now fighting one another for the Moroccan throne. As Pallache had made this offer privately, rather than as an official envoy of the sultan, it seems reasonable to deduce that Pallache had decided to settle in the Peninsula and secure himself a job by making himself useful to the Spanish authorities. He did this by developing a plan to capture the garrison town of Larache, and his proposal was presented to the Council of State by the count of Puñonrrostro. Council members engaged in a lengthy discussion about the possible timing of the mission. Although they all agreed on the importance of Larache, they decided, however, that the time was not right to undertake such an expedition. As for Pallache himself, the council decided that "the Jew can be given something to get rid of him," inasmuch as other spies were already available to help them in their dealings with Morocco, notably Juanetín Mortara and Juan de Marchena.[15] Moreover, they noted, "it would be good to stop the Jew [Pallache] from deluding himself" about his participation in such affairs.[16]

A month later, Medina Sidonia wrote to the president of the Council of Finance to inform him of the king's order that an allowance of 150 ducats be paid to the Pallache brothers.[17] The council fulfilled its promise, and over the next four months the Pallaches received payments totaling 450 ducats in recognition of services rendered and in order to help them make the journey home. The king personally approved these payments, but although the money was delivered, the Pallaches did not go back to Morocco. In June, the council informed Philip III that it had decided to award a further 300 ducats to each of the two Jews with information on Larache, stating that it had taken into account the eight months that the men had been living in Spain. Philip wrote in the margin: "Agreed, and Prada to see to it that they now go back to their land."[18] However, the two still did not return, hoping instead to enter the king's service on a more permanent basis. Thus in August, Joseph and Samuel Pallache supplied the Council of State with another memorandum containing information on the state of the kingdom of Barbary, which was still embroiled in civil war. In this report, they described a kingdom in crisis: as well as armed struggle, there was widespread starvation, and the price of gold had fallen. The memorandum also mentioned the extent to which heavy taxes were oppressing the people, all of these details apparently provided in the hope of persuading the council to order the immediate capture of Larache. The brothers also requested permission for one of them to make another journey to Ceuta in order to collect his wife and children and, while there, to gather further information on the situation in Morocco. The council granted its license.[19]

At about the same time, the count of Puñonrrostro wrote to the duke of Medina Sidonia asking him to "grant him the favor of assisting" Samuel Pallache, who was now working for the count. The Pallaches had evidently continued their search for an influential Spanish patron by approaching Puñonrrostro, whose letter is full of enthusiastic support for Samuel's plan to capture Larache. Puñonrrostro wrote a thorough description of a detailed plan for besieging Larache with the aid of light, movable defenses. Puñonrrostro's letter also reveals his profound disagreement with recent decisions reached by the Council of State, which the veteran soldier describes as being made up of "gentlemen who know nothing."[20] This letter seems to have been carried to Medina Sidonia's home in San Lúcar de Barrameda by Pallache on his way to Ceuta. Medina Sidonia wrote to Philip III informing him of Samuel's visit, and of his offer to negotiate with Muley al-Shaykh for the surrender of Larache. Nevertheless, Medina Sidonia was not convinced by the arguments deployed either by Puñonrrostro or by Pallache, and his letter to the king expresses all too clearly the feelings of mistrust Pallache inspired in him: "His business is all trickery, for he has neither patrimony nor credit."[21]

In October 1605, Medina Sidonia also received a *consulta* from the king asking him whether he thought Samuel Pallache should be entrusted with the task of "finding things out about Barbary."[22] In reply, Medina Sidonia informed Philip for a second time that Samuel had visited him at San Lúcar to discuss talks he claimed to have held with Muley al-Shaykh and the alcayde (governor) of Larache, described as a certain "Hamete Betauri, an *andalouz* from Granada." Medina Sidonia remained unimpressed by Pallache's qualifications for such work, largely because he seemed to be "completely unendorsed [*desvalido*], poor and unaccredited [*desacreditado*]." The words *desvalido* and *desacreditado* should be taken literally here: that is to say, the duke believed that Pallache had no high-ranking supporters and had come to Spain without the proper official credentials. Medina Sidonia did not consider Pallache suitable for the Larache affair: "The said Jew did not seem at all adequate for this business, and thus he had been told for the time being to deal only with the affairs of his house [i.e., that of Medina Sidonia], and to leave for Ceuta." In reply, Philip III was pleased to hear that "the Jew Pallache is on his way and reduced to following the orders of Your Excellency."[23]

Samuel Pallache's name appears in another context at this time, and the reference allows us to form a more detailed idea of his tactics as he maneuvered for a position of influence. It also shows that Pallache was only one of a series of minor court figures who swarmed about the influential in an attempt to sell their merits as informers or go-betweens. One man who came into conflict with Pallache at this time was Martín Domínguez, the *alfaqueque*—an official in charge of arranging ransom payments for captives—of Tangier and author of a "Relación sobre Berbería y Muley Xeque" (Account of Barbary and Muley al-Shaykh). Pallache went to some lengths to denigrate Domínguez's *Relación*, and Philip III wrote to Medina Sidonia with a certain degree of irony: "I am not surprised that the Jew Pallache is jealous of the *alfaqueque*, for he must know full well how much each of them has invested in all this in order to gain some reward from the determination of my royal pleasure."[24] Philip's letter paints a sorry picture of a group of poor characters intriguing and scrambling for crumbs of a royal "pleasure" upon which they depended for their survival.

The nobles played a similar game. A letter Pallache wrote to Medina Sidonia from Ceuta toward the end of November 1605 suggests that the duke was, independently of the king, relying upon the Jew for purposes of his own.[25] An earlier document says that the duke had entrusted Pallache with certain business relating to the "affairs of his [Medina Sidonia's] house." Pallache's letter of November suggests that these "affairs" must have involved the sale in Morocco of jewelry belonging to the Medina Sidonia estate. Such transactions were not uncommon: Ana de Silva, the duchess, had sent Baltasar Polo on a similar mission in Morocco only a few years before.[26] Moreover, we know that Muley al-Shaykh, like his deceased father al-Mansur, was a great lover of jewelry and considered himself something of a connoisseur.[27] Samuel's letter illustrates the methods by which he was attempting to make himself useful and ingratiate himself with those in power—namely, through a mixture of business, information, and personal favors. The letter also notes that Pallache had met with two of his nephews in Ceuta and was now awaiting the arrival of his son and another nephew. (This was characteristic of the Pallaches, who always functioned as a family.)[28] Pallache further suggested to Medina Sidonia that the time had come for the Spaniards to take Larache, because of the turbulent political situation in Morocco. The Jew thus urged the duke to lead this enterprise himself. Although Medina Sidonia continued to be wary of entrusting Pallache with the Larache business, it was in the same year, 1605, that he arranged for Samuel to be sent to speak with Muley al-Shaykh.[29] Moreover, we know that Medina Sidonia gave safe-conducts to two Jewish brothers traveling into Spain with messages from al-Shaykh a few months later—presumably Samuel and Joseph Pallache again.[30]

In 1606, the Pallaches were back in Madrid, trying yet again to sell themselves to Philip III as mediators in the Larache affair, and they were still there at the beginning of 1607.[31] The count of Puñonrrostro, in a letter to the king dated August 15, 1607, repeated that Samuel and Joseph Pallache were serving him as informers, and said, not for the first time, that he believed the duke of Medina Sidonia should be encouraged to use them as intermediaries in the Larache negotiations.[32]

Despite such recommendations, there was no immediate improvement in the Pallaches' situation. Samuel, anxious to prove his usefulness to the Spanish king, thus chose to pursue a different line of approach. Perhaps frustrated by the excruciating sluggishness of the negotiations, or simply in search of a more generous employer, Samuel decided to offer information to the French king Henri IV, via his ambassador in Madrid, Émery de Jaubert, count de Barrault, who wrote to Henri informing him that Samuel had requested an interview with His Majesty. Pallache, he noted, intended to present Henri with documents containing details of past dealings with Philip II, among them certain letters written by the former royal secretary Antonio Pérez. The ambassador further informed his king that Pallache was in the process of handing these papers over to the Spaniards, but that his need for money was so great he had said he could wait no longer. De Jaubert added that Pallache wanted nothing from Henri except a hearing and, failing that, a passport to go to Florence. De Jaubert's opinion was that Pallache should be received, since information would at least be obtained that might be of some use in dealings with the Turks.[33] Several months later, in November 1606, Pallache was mentioned in another of de Jaubert's dispatches. On this occasion, the ambassador wrote that he had not seen Pallache for some time, but had been informed that Samuel had left Madrid for the kingdom of Aragon. This is interesting, largely because the moriscos of Aragon had recently revolted against the Spanish monarchy and were negotiating with Henri IV for military aid. As we shall see, Pallache was to work with moriscos at later stages of his career, and it is tempting to date his contacts with them from this early voyage to Aragon.[34]

Despite the ambassador's apparent endorsement of Pallache, nothing came of the Jew's efforts to solicit French aid. Pallache was resourceful, however, and in yet another effort to pressure the Spanish king, he attempted to sell his idea of an attack on Larache to the grand duke of Tuscany. Ferdinand I was an ambitious king, but an expedition to Morocco was clearly beyond his means, and he did not follow up Pallache's proposal, presented to one of the duke's envoys. It seems likely that Philip III was paying scant attention to the Pallaches' favorite scheme by this stage, and it is hardly surprising that the brothers should have lost patience and started touting for patrons from other countries. Anyone familiar with the Spanish archives in Simancas and the files pertaining to the reign of Philip III is soon assailed by the feeling that all kinds of business were forever being prolonged or postponed indefinitely. Reports were written and passed on to various assessors, then on to the council, and back again in an endless bureaucratic circle.

As noted earlier, the Pallaches were also short of funds at this point, and this must have contributed to their anxiety and their decision to offer information to other rulers. On several occasions, they referred to the fact that they had spent all their money in serving the king and complained that they had not been rewarded for their services to the crown. As a result, in April 1607, Medina Sidonia arranged for 150 ducats to be sent to each of the brothers as *ayuda de costa*—literally "cost aid," or expenses—in payment for their services and other "just causes."[35] Such payments, and the promise of further amounts, may explain why the Pallaches sought to bring the rest of their family from Morocco to Madrid, ostensibly to foster their conversion to the Christian faith and ease their subsequent settlement in Spain. A letter of March 27, 1607, indicates that the brothers had requested a royal *cédula*, or license, permitting them to fetch their families, on the pretext that Joseph Pallache's three sons were soon to be baptized.[36] The king granted his permission in April 1607. It is difficult to know how to interpret this letter, or how to estimate the sincerity of the Pallaches' intentions. It seems unlikely that they might have thought they would deceive the Spanish authorities by offering to convert in this way. They would have known, from their time in Madrid and their familiarity with the country, that to convert and settle in Spain required strict observance of Catholic norms, since they would be watched very carefully by the Inquisition. It is also inconceivable that professing a desire to convert to Christianity in a written statement to the king was something they thought could be done lightly. The letter explicitly states that the entire family are willing to serve "Our Lord and Your Majesty."

Yet whatever the degree of the Pallaches' sincerity, the Inquisition, apparently acting quite independently of the monarch, intervened in their attempt to settle in Spain. In August 1607, the French ambassador reported that Pallache had recently spent five months in El Escorial, where he had presented *memoriales* to the king,[37] and de Jaubert then went on to reveal that he had been hiding Pallache from Inquisition officials at the official French residence in Madrid.[38] This clash with the Inquisition is a key episode in Pallache's career,[39] and the story is partly covered by Samuel himself in a letter written in September 1607 from Saint-Jean-de-Luz, just across the border from Spain on France's Atlantic coast, where he fled with the rest of his family. However, little or nothing is known about the reasons for the Inquisition's sudden interest in the Pallaches, although their recent talk of religious conversion may have given the Inquisition cause for concern.[40] In principle, the Inquisition had no jurisdiction over Jews as such, merely over conversos who had judaized; nonetheless, in practice, it kept a strict eye on both groups.

The Pallaches were later to claim that they had unwittingly become involved in the Inquisition affairs of another Jew with connections at the French embassy. They said that the Inquisition had ordered their immediate departure from Spain without considering the fact that Joseph's sons were about to be baptized, or that the Pallaches had been granted a royal *cédula* and had proved useful to the Spanish crown. Nothing else is known of this affair. Inquisition archives contain no record of proceedings against either of the Pallache brothers; neither is reference made to the Pallaches in proceedings against any other person.[41]

　　　　　　　　　　　　　　　A MAN OF THREE WORLDS

The fact is that Samuel and Joseph were forced to leave Spain unexpectedly and in a hurry. A letter they wrote Philip III from Saint-Jean-de-Luz oozes frustration and grievance.[42] In it, they remind him of their years of loyal service, of how they had sacrificed their homes and wealth in order to attend him but had now lost all honor on being expelled from the country. They take their leave saying that "as for our souls, God is present in all the world and if we are not welcome in Spain, there are many other places to go and wherever we may happen to be, we are and shall be servants of Your Majesty, may God increase your life and estate."

In the months that followed the Pallaches' sudden departure from Spain, occasional references to them continue to crop up in official reports. On November 2, 1607, a letter was written to the *correo mayor* Juan de Arbeláez asking for information about the proposed baptism of Joseph Pallache's sons and instructing the viceroy of Navarre and the bishop of Pamplona to take up the affair.[43] On this evidence, it seems that the Spanish monarchy still believed that the Pallaches might one day return to Spain.

Before this, on October 11, the duke of Medina Sidonia had also made mention of Samuel and Joseph's children in a letter to Philip III about morisco families who, in advance of the official decree of expulsion promulgated in 1609, were fleeing from Spain to France and sailing from there for the Moroccan port of Safi. "It would be highly convenient to block this route, which must also have been known to the Palaches [*sic*] and their Hebrew children, for they took it and still remain in Saint-Jean-de-Luz, according to what I have been told from that town," he noted.[44] Medina Sidonia was clearly receiving information on the Pallaches' movements and seems to have thought that they were planning to take their families to Safi (whereas, in fact, they were about to travel on to the Dutch Republic).

Despite these references in the records to Samuel and Joseph's children, we know little about the makeup of their families at this time. In April 1607, the brothers had requested that Joseph's children, who, as we have seen, had traveled to Spain with the intention of converting, be given "*ayuda de costa* for their upkeep . . . and some other maintenance to help them live honorably in conformity with the quality of their persons and the service given by their fathers." In the same letter, the brothers had asked for permission to go and fetch their wives and "other children" from Barbary.[45] From later records, we know that Joseph's wife was called Benvenida, and that the couple had a total of five children: the first three were called Isaac, Moses, and Joshua, and these were the three who were willing to convert in 1607. Moses would have been about nineteen at this time; Joseph and Benvenida's other two sons, Abraham and David, must have been much younger. As for Samuel Pallache, we know that he was married to Malca/Reina (equivalent names in Hebrew and Spanish), and that his son Isaac would have been a small child in 1607, given that he was still a minor when his father died in 1616.[46]

THE PALLACHES' FAMILY BACKGROUND

A few more deductions can be made about Samuel and the Pallache family from the records kept at this time. On the one hand, it seems fairly clear that the family descended from Iberian Jews who had been expelled from Spain. Their original name would almost certainly have been Palacio: Samuel actually signs himself Samuel Palacio and Palatio in Dutch documents of 1614,[47] and the forms Palatio, Palachio, and Palazzo are all used in Amsterdam notarial records. We know nothing of the family's history after its presumed expulsion, however, nor of the date or circumstances of their settlement in Morocco.[48] The first family member for whom we have documentary evidence is Isaac Pallache, rabbi of Fez, who is mentioned in the Taqqanot, or Jewish community statutes, of the city for 1588; Isaac was Samuel and Joseph's father and the father-in-law of the grand rabbi, Judah 'Uziel. At the turn of the seventeenth century, one Isaac 'Uziel of Fez became one of the leading rabbis in the Neve Salom community of Amsterdam.[49] This second Isaac was Samuel and Joseph's brother-in-law, and thus a useful connection for them when they arrived in the Dutch Republic. When Hector Mendes Bravo, a Dutch Jew brought to trial by the Lisbon Inquisition, named 119 members of the Amsterdam community, he mentioned "Rabbi Isaac Iziel of Fez, who has been in Spain,"[50] making it likely that Uziel followed the same path as Samuel (i.e., from Fez to Amsterdam via Spain).

There is much that we do not know about Samuel Pallache, leaving aside the Spanish origin of his family. We would certainly know far more if Inquisition records had ever been kept on him. His age, style of dress, and physical appearance would automatically have been noted in any trial proceedings. Are we to imagine him as bearded, for example, as was common among Jews from Morocco and the Levant, or did he follow the example of the portugueses, who shaved and thus stood out from other Jewish groups? All we can say is that his nephew Isaac is known to have worn a beard when he lived in the Netherlands.[51]

The question of Samuel's clothing is particularly interesting. What style did he adopt: did he dress as a *judío amoriscado* (Moorish Jew) or did he wear an *hábito de cristiano* (Christian dress)? In principle, all Jews in Spain were legally required to distinguish themselves by the way they dressed, but there was a certain amount of variation. Since the Expulsion, the only Jews who could enter Spain were the so-called *judíos de permiso*—that is, those whose masters or themselves had requested and obtained permission to carry out a particular task, as was the case with the Pallaches when they went to buy jewelry for their sultan. *Judíos de permiso* were required to wear signs on their clothing that would allow for their immediate identification as Jews. In 1583, after the union of the crowns of Spain and Portugal, Philip II had ratified Portuguese laws that required Jews entering Portugal to wear "a cap, biretta or yellow hat on the head." North African Jews generally wore a special garment, called a *ganephe*, that distinguished them from Jews from elsewhere. The Sasportas, Jews from Oran, were asked by the Inquisition in 1671 "for what reasons they have changed out of their proper Jewish clothing"—why, that is to say, they did not dress as Jews. By contrast, the Cansinos, another family of important Jewish citizens of Oran, made certain that they stood out on their visit to Madrid: "Jacob Cansino arrived, a Jew by birth and dressed as one, with his worsted cassock and turban, and he was from Oran."

Further variants are mentioned in Inquisition records. At the trial of Isaac Almosnino, who will reappear later in this book, evidence was given by a Christian renegade who came before the tribunal "in Turkish apparel, with a blue cloak and what seemed a Moorish cloth on his head." This man was Sebastião Paes, who had returned to the Christian faith after living for many years as a Muslim in Morocco. Other renegades followed Paes: of Simón Méndez, we are told that "he came dressed as a Moor, with a colored cloak and a turban, dressed in the Moorish fashion." Gaspar Ramos also appeared before the tribunal "wearing a Moor's habit, with an *alquizel* [Moorish cape] and Moorish headdress," as did Luis Barreto.[52] By contrast, Andalusian moriscos who made naval incursions on Spanish coasts came in "Spanish clothing" and could not be told apart from Spaniards.[53] At all events, we should not allow our curiosity concerning the question of clothing to reach the extreme of regretting that Samuel was never interrogated by the Holy Office.

Another topic of interest is the extent of Samuel Pallache's command of Spanish. The manuscripts that have been preserved in his hand are generally indistinguishable from those of any contemporary Spaniard, and he wrote with the fluency and steadiness of a man who was obviously accustomed to the act of writing. (The same can be said of his letters in Arabic.) In the early letters, he appears to have some difficulty with sibilant sounds, writing *rasion*, *sierto*, Seuta, and *serteça* for *ración* (ration), *cierto* (certain), Ceuta, and *certeza* (certainty). Some of his vowels are also uncertain: he writes *matiria* for *materia* (matter), *hollo* for *huyó* (he fled), *imbió* for *envió* (he sent), *ynpidimento* for *impedimento* (impediment), and *sirvidor* for *servidor* (servant)—all fairly typical features in the speech of Arabic-speaking Moroccans using the Spanish language. However, it is noticeable that these features disappear from Pallache's later manuscripts.

The abundant paper trail left by Pallache during his time in the Netherlands reveals that Spanish was probably his first language. When he testifies to the fidelity of translations, whether from Dutch into French or from Arabic to Dutch, he always does so in Spanish, with phrases like the following: "I state that it is true that I wrote all that it says above to King Muley Zidan, and since it is true, I sign on this day."[54] It is very striking to find such formulae written in Spanish at the foot of Arabic or Dutch documents destined for the States General of the Dutch Republic. By contrast, Pallache's French is poor and scarcely intelligible, full of calques and loans from Spanish, including the Spanish *ñ* in his written French, as can be seen in his letters from Holland and France and the lengthy editorial annotations required to make some sense of them.[55] It is also quite clear that when he arrived in Holland, he knew no Dutch.

All of these points raise further questions about Pallache's background and the kind of education he may have received in his early years in Fez. In order to know more about such details as his possible physical appearance, his languages, and the kind of life he may have led before arriving in Madrid, let us examine the Inquisition trial records of some other Jews from Fez.

JEWS FROM FEZ AND THE INQUISITION

The archives of the Spanish Inquisition do not appear to contain a single reference to Samuel and Joseph Pallache or to the conflict that forced them to flee from Spain to France in 1607. However, records do exist of several other trials of Jews from Fez who were living in Madrid in the

A MAN OF THREE WORLDS

same period. Some of these trial reports shed light on the general situation of Moroccan Jews at this time. They reveal a great deal about the conflicts within Moroccan territory that drove Jews from their country and that would almost certainly have had a similar effect on Samuel Pallache's career. Moreover, they also hint at the reasons why Pallache may have become the target of scrutiny by the Inquisition.

The best example is provided by the case of Francisco de San Antonio, who in 1625 was arrested and tried by the Inquisition tribunal of Toledo, which accused him of being "a dogmatizer, and a creator and harborer of heretics." From their investigations into the "story of his life," the inquisitors were able to ascertain that San Antonio had been born in Fez in 1579 and had originally been known as Abraham Ruben. In 1603 (the year of the death of Sultan Ahmad al-Mansur), he had left Fez, living first in Livorno (Leghorn) in Italy and then in Istanbul, where he worked as a trader for three years. After that, San Antonio emigrated to Amsterdam, where he lived as a rabbi, teaching the Torah for a salary of 500 *cruzados*. From Amsterdam, he moved on to Antwerp, where he converted to the Catholic faith in 1616, only to return to Amsterdam and reconvert to Judaism some time later. He then went to Lisbon, where he taught Hebrew and was an instructor in Jewish rites and ceremonies to "people of his nation" until he was detained in January 1618 by the Lisbon Inquisition and sentenced to imprisonment as a result of his activities. San Antonio was released on April 5, 1620, on condition that he "abjure *de levi*" (i.e., swear to avoid sin in the future), and in 1621 he was expelled from Portugal for life.

However, San Antonio was clearly undeterred by his first brush with the Inquisition. From Portugal, he traveled to Madrid, where he made contact with other Fez Jews, among them Pedro de Santa María, an assistant to the count of Benavente, and Francisco Enríquez, who worked for the Trinitarian friar Father Hortensio, to whom Enríquez gave Hebrew lessons. Enríquez was saving up money to return to Fez, and he urged his countryman San Antonio to imitate his example.

Far from heeding this advice, San Antonio reconverted to Christianity in the royal chapel in June 1621, in the presence of Queen Isabella. According to testimony he presented at his trial by the Inquisition in 1625, San Antonio claimed to have done this in order "to enjoy the alms which their Majesties provide for those who baptize" and because he needed the money to travel back to the Netherlands. It is quite obvious that San Antonio was an insincere Christian convert: other New Christians testifying at his trial declared that they had heard him say that for all the humiliations the Jews had endured in Fez, life there was far better for them than in Christian lands.[56]

In Madrid, San Antonio lived a "missionary" life: he sought out "Portuguese" merchants (i.e., New Christians) and devoted himself to "judaizing" among them. He possessed a printed Hebrew primer, with the Hebrew characters in very large print and the corresponding Spanish letters printed alongside them. He also had a folio-sized notebook with Hebrew printed in it, which provided instructions about certain rites and ceremonies. He gave instruction on how to slaughter chickens and cows and was said to have "insulted those who were not people of his nation." In addition, San Antonio taught Hebrew prayers to those who requested tuition and wrote them out for them; he also rented out his dictionary and notebook for 30 *reales* a month. As a result of all this evidence against him, San Antonio eventually received a sentence of life imprisonment.[57]

Another Fez Jew mentioned at San Antonio's trial was the man now known by his Christian name of Pedro de Castro, who is described as a "translator and interpreter" working in Lisbon. In March 1625, de Castro sent a statement from Lisbon providing information to be used against San Antonio, a former acquaintance. De Castro had once lived in Madrid, where he had converted, and then moved to Lisbon where he worked for Jerónimo de Gobea, the bishop of Ceuta, who paid him a salary of two *reales* a day. De Castro is known to have provided the Inquisition with information about other North African conversos.[58]

Another case that helps to piece together some notion of the common experience of Fez Jews is that of Francisco del Espíritu Santo, prosecuted by the Inquisition between 1615 and 1618.[59] Francisco was initially accused of casting spells and enchantments, and of having the ability to locate hidden treasure. However, the Inquisition was not interested in trying him for witchcraft per se. It was rather more concerned about his use of amulets, or talismans, written in Hebrew. During his trial, Francisco declared that he was a thirty-three-year-old shoemaker, a "Jew by birth," who had been born in the city of Marrakech in Morocco to a Jewish mother and father. At the age of twenty, he had moved to Fez, converted to Islam, and served the sultan of Fez for ten years. In 1611, he had traveled to Spain, where he converted to Christianity, and was now living in Madrid at the house of the *corregidor* Pedro de Guzmán, for whom he worked. Despite these successive "conversions," Francisco informed the Inquisition that he lived his life by the law of Moses and wished to continue to live by it and die in it, because he was the son of Jewish parents, descended from "Aaron Acoén," and had been brought up in that "law." When the Inquisitors asked him why in that case he had converted to Islam when living in Fez, he first replied that it was because he had had an argument with his parents and then said that it was "because Jews are not respected by the Moors and cannot do anything," and that he wanted to be respected and to live and eat well. But, he clarified, he had only converted in speech and not in his heart. In Spain, it had seemed to him at first that Christianity was not very different from the law of Moses, but he soon saw that he had been mistaken and found himself deeply disturbed by the images Christians used and by the fact that they believed they ate the body of Christ. Francisco's talisman was presented at the trial, together with a manuscript page in Hebrew that he always carried with him. Juan Bautista Ramírez, an Inquisition prisoner sentenced for judaizing, was called upon to certify that this manuscript was a text from the Psalms and was subsequently instructed to translate it into Spanish. (Juan Bautista's own Inquisition trial is discussed immediately below.)

At his trial, Francisco signed all of his statements in Hebrew. When asked why he signed in that way and did not use the name Francisco del Espíritu Santo, he answered that he did not want to be called by that name but by his old Jewish one. When the Inquisitors insisted that he use his Christian name, he refused and said that if he was Jewish, how could he sign with a Christian name? The name he wrote in Hebrew appears to be Isacar (?) ben Isaac Alqasim.

Francisco/Isacar was eventually sentenced in 1618 to five years as a galley slave, a relatively lenient punishment considering that he met every requirement for being handed over to the Inquisition's secular arm, especially in the matter of the *pertinacia*, or obstination, of his apostasy. When taken prisoner, he began to scream and to insult the inquisitors, completely beside himself and out of control, crying out that he should be burned as soon as possible. A gag was placed in his mouth to silence him. The inquisitors may have decided that Francisco was mentally ill: there is a certain insistence in their reports on the fact that he was *descompuesto* (literally, "not composed," i.e., lacking in self-restraint and serenity). It is particularly disturbing to read the records of this trial, in which poor Francisco comes across as a clear example of a man who lacked the strategies for defending himself employed by most other prisoners of the Inquisition.

Juan Bautista Ramírez, mentioned above, was a rabbinical student from Fez who in 1608 traveled to Seville via Melilla, another Spanish outpost on Morocco's Mediterranean coast. After being baptized in Seville, "he sold cloth in the streets" until he had gathered together enough money to go to the Italian port of Livorno, where he married a Jewish Portuguese woman. He then returned to Spain, where he was denounced by another converted North African Jew.[60]

A number of preliminary conclusions can be drawn from the information contained in these records. From the sheer number of Moroccan Jewish prisoners and witnesses involved in the trials, to say nothing of references to other Jews known to have attended religious meetings, it can be seen that Madrid was home to several Jews from Fez who had converted to Christianity and were now serving noblemen or courtiers there. These Jews actively sought the patronage of the influential, a strategy they had used successfully in Morocco and that, as we have seen, Samuel Pallache also applied during his time in Madrid. Jews are known to have pursued a similar strategy in Lisbon: in his *Jornada de África del rey Don Sebastián* (King Sebastian's African Expedition), written in that city in the early seventeenth century, Jerónimo de Mendoça speaks of several Jews living in Lisbon who had converted to Christianity after having been "brought up in that land [Morocco]."[61] During the seventeenth century, the Lisbon Inquisition prosecuted numbers of Moroccan Jews in Portugal who had traveled there with Portuguese masters for whom they had been working in one of the Portuguese garrison towns in Morocco. Forced to convert in order to live in Portugal, several of these Moroccan Jews were later placed on trial as judaizing apostates accused of acting as *maestros dogmatizadores*—"dogmatizing tutors," or proselytizers—of Portuguese conversos.[62]

These converted Moroccan Jews, or at least those of them who were brought to trial by the Spanish Inquisition, often had contacts in Portuguese converso circles, and it is clear that they were watched very closely by the Inquisition. They were seen to possess solid Jewish culture and deep religious knowledge, and it was this that caused them to be suspected of revitalizing the weakened Jewish faith of the conversos. Trials of North African Jews accused of working as "dogmatizing tutors" can be found in the records of several different tribunals. The dogmatizing tutor was seen, or perhaps imagined, as an individual who came from overseas, especially from North Africa or other areas where Jewish religion could be freely practiced. Possessed of canonical Jewish culture, his perceived mission was to induce conversos to return to heresy. It should not be forgotten that one of the main factors that had led to the decision to expel Jews in 1492 was the wish to prevent contact between the conversos and those of their old religion. The argument obviously continued to carry much weight in the early seventeenth century.

Evidence of the perceived importance of the dogmatizing tutor can be seen in the situation in the city of Málaga in the 1660s. Málaga had a large colony of Portuguese conversos, and by this time much of the city's trade was under their control, as was the management of numerous royal rents. Some of these conversos occupied prominent posts in the city. It seems that within this converso community, there must have been many crypto-Jews, judging by the fact that in 1669, the city's jails had become home to 162 convicted Judaizers. Despite the tenacity of their faith, these Málaga Judaizers were all too aware of the impoverishment of their religious rituals, and they yearned for knowledge and information about Jewish religion. One way of gathering such information, or of buying relevant books, was to travel to Jewish quarters in North Africa. Another was to make contact with newly arrived North African Jews in Málaga, who were greatly revered by the converso community. Málaga conversos are also known to have sent donations to Jewish communities "as a sacrifice offered by the Jews to their rabbis so that they will forgive them for not observing the law of Moses." The trials of North African Jews in Málaga give some idea of the kind of contacts that were made between such Jews and the conversos. One example is the case of Baltasar de Orán, who was said to have "told them the dates of their Passover, holy days, fasts and other things of the law of Moses and their observance." Baltasar enjoyed great prestige among the Judaizers of Málaga, and he reaped the benefit of this prestige in his many business dealings.[63]

As we have said, the Pallaches are not mentioned in any of the Inquisition trials we have located, and it is therefore impossible to state with certainty what they might have done to arouse the Inquisition's curiosity about their lives in 1607. But from the trials of Fez Jews summarized above, and from other trials in previous years, it can be seen that two actions in particular tended to attract the attention of the inquisitors.[64] Firstly, the mere possession of Hebrew papers, or papers containing Hebrew characters, was enough by itself to justify detention and imprisonment. Secondly, as we have seen, any Fez Jew who made contact with portugueses was immediately suspected of working as a "dogmatizer," and was liable to be questioned about his activities. Samuel Pallache may easily have been implicated in either, or both, of these two "crimes" during the time he lived in Madrid.

Further questions are raised by the evidence given at these trials. Above all, perhaps, we need to know more about the reasons that lay behind Fez Jews' decisions to leave Morocco for the Iberian Peninsula.[65] The next chapter deals with the country they left behind.

CHAPTER 2

JEWS IN MOROCCO

All that we know for certain of Samuel Pallache's background and early years is that the Pallache family was of Spanish origin and that Samuel lived in the city of Fez during the late sixteenth century.[1] It therefore seems logical to start this chapter with an outline of the history of Fez, placing particular emphasis on the fluctuating fortunes of its Jewish community after 1492.

FEZ AND MARRAKECH: HISTORICAL BACKGROUND

Fez was one of the most important cities in the Islamic west during the medieval period, and it seems to have had a large number of Jewish inhabitants from the moment of its first foundation. Both the city and its Jewish minority flourished from the thirteenth century on with the rise to power of the Marinid dynasty, which made Fez the capital of its kingdom and employed Jewish servants and administrators at court. However, problems frequently occurred. As in medieval Christian Spain, public animosity toward Jews tended to vary in proportion to the degree of protection and favorable treatment they received from the monarchy. For this reason, in the mid fifteenth century, the Marinid sultan Abd al-Haqq ibn Abu Sa'id took the step of removing the entire Jewish population of Fez to the new palatine city the dynasty had built for itself on the outskirts of the capital, where the Jews could be protected from the constant danger of popular revolts against them. In this new city, known as Fas al-Jadid (New Fez), the sultan established what was the first Jewish quarter in

North Africa, in an area known as the Mellah. The Mellah of Fez remained a densely populated and renowned center of Jewish life for the next 150 years, the word "Mellah" becoming a synonym for a Jewish quarter throughout the whole of Morocco. According to the traveler Luis del Mármol, who visited Fez in the middle of the sixteenth century, the Mellah then had some ten thousand householders, or a total population of between forty and fifty thousand individuals. Most of these inhabitants were of Spanish origin.

Spanish Jews had been taking refuge in Fez ever since the persecutions of the late fourteenth century. Large numbers of them went there immediately after the Expulsion of 1492, but they are also known to have fled to Fez even before that date. Andrés Bernáldez, a late fifteenth-century Spanish chronicler, specifically states that Jews left Spain in droves prior to 1492, and that "many of them passed to the lands of the Moors, either here or there [i.e., either in the Nasrid kingdom of Granada or Moroccan territory in North Africa], to be the Jews that they were: and others went to Portugal and others to Rome."[2] Similar routes were taken in 1492. Options were limited: there were very few places in Europe where Jews were allowed to live as such—in practice, only Portugal and certain Italian cities, such as Venice—and this was the main reason why most Jews preferred to move to Islamic areas.

But Jews had other reasons for resettling in Islamic rather than Christian territories. For one thing, their integration into Islamic society was made much easier by the general application of the so-called *dhimma* pact. This was a protective statute that allowed non-Muslims to keep their own religions and customs and to uphold their own community leaders. Under the terms of the pact, Jewish communities were granted a certain degree of independence, though always within a general framework of submission and subjection. The *dhimma* statute resembled laws that had governed Jewish and Mudejar rights in the Christian kingdoms of the Iberian Peninsula during the medieval period. As we shall see, the term *dhimmi* is consistently used in Moroccan Arabic records to describe Samuel and Joseph Pallache.

There was also another factor underlying the decision of so many Jews to migrate to North Africa rather than to a European country that might have tolerated them. It was not just that Islamic lands offered opportunities for the free practice of Jewish religion; in addition, Jews tended to be influenced by the notions they harbored about Islam's role as the triumphant enemy of Christianity. The persecutions endured by Jews in the

Iberian Peninsula, especially after 1391, had fueled them with messianic and apocalyptic hopes of wreaking some sort of historical revenge on Christians. For many Jews, Islam came to assume a providential role in a common struggle that appeared to swing decisively in their favor when Constantinople fell to the Ottomans in 1453. In the ongoing conflict between the Christian West and the Turkish East, many Jews saw signs of their own possible liberation and the dawning of a new messianic era.[3] (This vague, all-pervading messianism is perhaps most clearly seen in the writings of the exegete, preacher and cabbalist Abraham ben Jacob Saba, who after his expulsion from Spain lived in Portugal, Fez, and then Venice, where his commentary on the Torah, *Tseror ha-mor*, was published.)[4] Jewish identification with the Islamic cause was still to be seen in Morocco as late as 1578, after the defeat by Moroccan forces of the Portuguese army led by King Sebastian at the famous battle of Al-Qasr al-Kabir ("Alcázarquivir" to the Spaniards and "Alcáçer Quibir" to the Portuguese themselves). The Jewish communities of Fez and Tétouan publicly celebrated this crushing defeat for the Christian army and established a *purim*, or ritual expression of gratitude at the dispersal of a destructive threat, a ceremony still observed to this day.[5]

After the Expulsion, a limited number of Jews arrived in Morocco, occasionally through the ports of Tangier, Larache, Azemmour, and Safi, although most of them went either to Arzila or Salé. Once there, they are known to have suffered tremendous hardship in a country already devastated by famine and drought. One of the best accounts of their troubles is the chronicle *Sefer ha-Qabala*, written in 1510 by Abraham ben Salomón de Torrutiel, who was only ten years old when his family joined the southward exodus. According to Torrutiel, the Jewish exiles were roughly handled by the Portuguese governors of the ports where they came ashore, and their possessions were often confiscated on arrival. Their treatment by the local Moroccan peoples was little better, but the sultan of Fez showed public goodwill toward them by sending mules, provisions, and guides out to Arzila to help them make the journey to the capital. In Fez, the sultan ordered temporary homes to be built for the Jews on the city's outskirts, close to the Mellah. These "homes" were actually tents and wooden or straw shacks, which only eight months later all burned to the ground in a fire. Some Jews lost their lives, and almost all lost personal belongings, in this fire, and contemporary Jewish sources particularly lamented the loss of Hebrew books that they had brought with them from Spain. Torrutiel claims that it was at this point that many Jews tried to return to Spain.[6] However, the situation later improved, and by 1508, Rabbi Abner Hassarfaty, a Jewish chronicler residing in Fez, was able to write that the Spanish Jews, known as *megorashim*, or immigrants, to distinguish them from the autochthonous Jews, called *toshavim*, were living in brand-new houses of several storeys embellished with paintings and arabesques. By this time, the *megorashim* also had a number of synagogues in the Mellah and thriving schools, which were said to be full of young students.[7] In the years that followed, Iberian Jews continued to arrive in the city, many of them coming from the Portuguese garrison towns on the Moroccan coast.[8]

Several European travelers visited Fez throughout the sixteenth century, and some wrote descriptions of its Mellah, the neighborhood that was almost certainly home to the young Samuel Pallache in the years before he left to seek his fortune in Spain.[9] The following account was written by the Spaniard Luis del Mármol, who visited Fez in the 1540s, and it is worth quoting at length for the wealth of detail it contains:

> [In the third district of New Fez . . .] is now to be found the Jewish quarter, which was previously located in Old Fez; and because whenever a king died, the Moors then ran to loot the houses of the Jews, King Busaid [Abd al-Haqq ibn Abu Sa'id] moved them on condition that they paid him a double tribute. In this quarter there is a great square with many shops and synagogues and very well built houses, and the Jews live there as if in a separate town; and there are 10,000 householders, and four or five dwellers in each house, and most of them were turned out of Spain at the time of the Catholic monarchs Don Fernando and Doña Ysabel. Among them there are some who are rich, and they have a *shaykh* who, as a sort of governor, administers justice for them and delivers the tributes that they pay to the king. And in order that the Jews be left undisturbed, the *shaykh* has leased from the king all punishments, fines, and calumnies, and takes per head the taxes paid on what they sell and on the public works carried out by officials, because they pay taxes on everything.
>
> The Jews in Africa are greatly despised by the Moors, and wherever they go the Moors spit in their faces and beat them, and they do not allow them to wear shoes unless they happen to be favorites of the king or of the alcaydes; all the others wear espadrilles, and they must pass barefoot at the door of the king, and on their heads they have to wear black cloths, and on their heads or on their hats a little piece of colored cloth sewn on as a signal, and the same on their clothing, so that they may be distinguished and known to the Moors. If any of them becomes wealthy and the king manages to find out about it, he

A MAN OF THREE WORLDS

takes their riches away and often even has them killed for it. But they are so hard-working, and they know so much about business, that they commonly administer the estates of the king and of the alcaydes; because Moorish gentlemen, as I have said, do not hold the custom of trading in much esteem, nor do they understand so well as the Jews the little details and subtleties, and each one endeavors to have a Jew for his majordomo to govern his estate, and in this way the Jews enrich themselves greatly.

Next to the king's palace is the house they call that of the Çeca, where the coins are minted, and within which the alcayde lives, together with all the officials who understand the making of them, and close by is the silversmiths' district and the house that has the seal and the hallmark for coins and decides the carat for gold and silver, since nothing can be made in Fez from those metals without them first being stamped with their hallmark, and being stamped they can use them as coinage by weight.

Most of the Jews are silversmiths who have their shops and who work in New Fez, and they go to sell what they make in Old Fez, in a square put aside for this purpose next to the spice district, for in Old Fez, gold and silver may not be beaten, nor do the Moors much stoop to carry out this task, since although they do have some silversmiths, they perform only simple jobs such as the making of rings, earrings, and silver beads for the Arab women and other mountain peoples.[10]

The Jewish quarter Mármol described was surrounded by a wall, and because of a lack of space, its buildings had several storeys, and the streets were narrow and tortuous. The gate to the Jewish quarter, still known today as Bab al-Mellah, opened onto a main street that crossed the district from northeast to southwest, as it does to this day. This was the main trading avenue where the Jews had their stalls. To the north were the luxurious houses of the richest Mellah citizens, which adjoined the garden of the royal palace. Beside this garden, on a steep slope, was the Jewish cemetery, described by the Portuguese writer Jerónimo de Mendoça as "a very peaceful place," which remains one of the most beautiful and moving parts of the city of Fez. In the lower part of the quarter was the poorest and most densely populated district, that of the artisans.

The Jewish quarter was also home to all non-Muslim visitors to the city, who were legally required to lodge within its bounds. Such visitors included Christian travelers, ambassadors, commercial agents, and, above all, captives awaiting the fulfillment of their ransom payments. Thus, after 1578, the Mellah housed a large number of Portuguese soldiers taken prisoner at the battle of Al-Qasr al-kabir, and these soldiers lived in the Mellah for the often lengthy time it took to negotiate their ransoms. Jerónimo de Mendoça, himself a captive, describes the number of Portuguese prisoners taken at Al-Qasr al-kabir who were conducted to the Mellah, and he claims that they were the luckiest of all the hostages, because they were so well treated by the Jews, "who mourned a thousand times their banishment from Spain." He also explains that the Jews had neither the power nor the means to mistreat their prisoners, and that for the latter it was a great relief to be able to speak with the Jews "because in general they speak Castilian."[11] The count of Vimioso, an apparently privileged Mellah captive, was allowed to share his house with one Fray Vicente de Fonseca, a preaching friar, and the pair of them engaged in religious polemic with leading Jewish figures. According to Mendoça, the meetings were attended by twenty or thirty rabbis, who argued and listened "with much moderation and good reasons." Mendoça claims that some of the Jews became Christians as a result of these debates.[12] Another writer who described life in the Mellah for the captive Portuguese was Fray Bernardo da Cruz, who wrote that the noblemen "lived with as much opulence and splendor in the treatment of their persons as if they were the lords of the land, and as well as having their own rooms in some very splendid Jewish homes, with expensive beds and tapestries, they spent very generously on rich silks and on food, making greater expenditures than if they had been living at home in Portugal." In order to meet these great expenditures, the Portuguese were forced to borrow money from the Jews or give them letters of credit for money to be paid in Portugal.[13]

Fez reached the peak of its political and economic development not long after Mármol's visit in the 1540s. By then, the city was a powerful magnet for Jews hoping to work in trade or finance. Fez Jews specialized in professions that were either forbidden to the Muslim population, such as money lending, or disdained by them, like metalwork. They also became arms manufacturers, jewelers, gold- and silversmiths, minters of coins, blacksmiths, and makers of special varieties of braid and cord. As we shall see, a number of Iberian Jews had even come to occupy key posts in Moroccan government and diplomacy by the end of the century.

Intellectual standards in the Mellah seem to have been high. Nicolas Clénard, a humanist and scholar who visited Fez with the aim of evangelizing among the Muslims, was impressed by the scholarship of the Jewish population there. He forged close friendships with a Jewish doctor and an astrologer and was able to find work for himself as a teacher of Latin,

A MAN OF THREE WORLDS

Greek, and classical Arabic to Jewish students.[14] A printer named Samuel Isaac even briefly produced Hebrew books in Fez between 1516 and 1524, using a press imported from Lisbon, until he was apparently stopped from doing so by a Spanish embargo on paper.[15]

All in all, sixteenth-century Fez became an important cultural and intellectual focus point for both Muslims and Jews. It was a place of return to Jewish religion for crypto-Jews, or conversos, from Spain and Portugal, and a place where they could acquire or regain Jewish culture.[16] Spanish and Portuguese Inquisition archives contain many references to Jews who traveled to Fez for broadly educational purposes.[17] One well-known example is that of Rui López, a converso from the Canary Islands, who in 1530 sent two of his brothers to study in Fez, where they lived in one of the synagogues and learnt the Torah of Moses.[18] Another is the case of Juan Robles, prosecuted in absentia by the Inquisition of Toledo between 1532 and 1535. Robles, a glazier's apprentice from the village of Cadalso de los Vidrios, traveled to Fez in the company of his master, Francisco Ydobro. Once there, Robles abandoned Ydobro, however, and converted to Judaism. He was circumcised and set about learning Hebrew in order to improve his knowledge of Jewish law. He later adopted the name Abraham Aguer and married a Jewish woman.[19] Similar cases can be found in Portuguese archives.[20]

FEZ'S FORTUNES CHANGED DRAMATICALLY after 1578, the year in which the new Sa'adian sultan Ahmad al-Mansur came to the throne in the wake of the battle of Al-Qasr al-Kabir. One of the sultan's first steps was to make Marrakech the new capital of his kingdom, to the detriment of Fez, and this signaled the beginning of a period of decline for the older city. Al-Mansur poured huge sums of money into the development of his new capital, and his reign (1578–1603) came to be known as one of the most brilliant periods of the Sa'adian dynasty, but little of this new wealth found its way to Fez.

António de Saldanha, a Portuguese nobleman who was taken captive at the battle of Al-Qasr al-Kabir and who lived in Marrakech until the payment of his ransom nearly thirty years later, wrote a detailed account of how Ahmad al-Mansur worked to improve his new capital and invest it with economic importance.[21] Al-Mansur's aim was to create a new political and economic center for Morocco that would be lavishly furnished with all the visible trappings of regal power. He urged his alcaydes to build fine houses and adorn them with beautiful orchards and walled gardens, "the like of which will not be found in the whole of Europe." To make the creation of such gardens possible, al-Mansur put in place a program of canal-building operations and large-scale waterworks. In his desire to emulate the capitals of Europe, he embarked on ambitious building projects like that of the famous Badi' Palace. According to Saldanha, al-Mansur was particularly anxious to match the achievements of Philip II in Spain: "The Sharif did not cease to ennoble Marrakech, and as it had reached a degree of grandeur never before reached by any, and receiving news of Philip II's near-perfect completion of El Escorial, he wished to begin the construction of a mosque that might compete with all the heroic works that had been known before his time." He thus laid the first stone of the great Riyad al-Zaytun Mosque, which, like the Badi' Palace, no longer stands today.[22]

Saldanha, whose admiration for al-Mansur is obvious, also praised the economic and financial policies adopted by the new sultan. Knowing that the prosperity of a realm depended on its capacity to manufacture and export its own products, al-Mansur oversaw the creation of various workshops and factories in Marrakech, which were soon producing gunpowder, artillery pieces, swords, weaponry, and armor, as well as tiles and glazed pottery. Saldanha commented that "all these workshops were directed by excellent English, Flemish, and French masters, and their workmen were boys who had been captured at the time of Alcazarquivir and assigned to his own house by the Sharif." It was part of al-Mansur's general strategy to attract foreign merchants to Marrakech by offering them economic facilities, as well as free housing and physical protection. They were given "walled houses for the safety of the merchants, very capacious and fortified, and the walls dotted with sentry boxes where Moorish guards slept." Saldanha noted that "in the streets set aside for their shops, all the goods of France, Italy, England, and Spain were sold at lower prices than in the lands where they were produced. . . . The town of Marrakech then attained such greatness as it had never attained before nor ever would again."[23]

Al-Mansur's initiatives were not entirely limited to the city of Marrakech. When it was discovered that sugarcane could be grown in the southern Sous region of the country, he financed the construction of a number of sugar refineries in the area, and by the time of his death in 1603, some eighteen refineries were in operation in the Sous, each of them employing two thousand men.[24] Interestingly, several Jews of Portuguese origin are known to have been employed in the management of these refineries,[25] and Samuel Pallache himself spent much of his life trading in the sugar that they produced.

The Jewish quarter of Marrakech came into its own during the period of al-Mansur's reign, and the number of its inhabitants increased substantially. In addition, more than two thousand captives were transferred from Fez to Marrakech soon after the accession of the new sultan. Most of these captives were Portuguese prisoners from Al-Qasr al-Kabir, and new houses and a hospital had to be built especially for them. According to Saldanha, "there is no doubt that many of them [the Portuguese prisoners] forgot all about their Christian lands, and that if they could ever be certain that the life of the Sharif were to be a long one, none of them would ever want to go back home, because they would not be able to live there with such largesse nor at such discretion [as here] . . . because they all live as they wish without anyone coming to bother them."[26] Foreign travelers and envoys were housed in the thriving Mellah of Marrakech, and many of them were recorded to be enjoying lives of extraordinary luxury and extravagance.[27]

IT IS NOT HARD TO IMAGINE the effect of Marrakech's sudden rise to prominence on its rival Fez, or on life for Fez's Jewish population. Many Jewish families abandoned Fez for the turmoil of the populous new capital, which teemed with fresh commercial opportunities. Marrakech, as the new site of the sultan's court, became the diplomatic center of Morocco, and Jews also found positions for themselves at court there. Fez gradually declined in both economic and political importance. However, if Fez and its Mellah deteriorated sharply during the years of al-Mansur's reign, far worse disruption was to come to the city in the years immediately after the sultan's death.

Ahmad al-Mansur died suddenly in 1603, victim of a plague epidemic that swept the country, and Morocco entered upon a disastrous period of civil war between followers of the old sultan's sons, who disputed their right to the throne. The kingdom was plunged into a decade of bloody conflict, and we must try to appreciate the nature of the confused situation that ensued if we are to make sense of Samuel Pallache's career. His arrival in Spain, and his subsequent life in the Dutch Republic, can only be understood if we have some idea of the chaos and general sense of crisis that followed al-Mansur's death in Morocco.

After al-Mansur died, one of his sons, Muley Zaydan, was proclaimed the new sultan in Fez. Another son, Abu Faris, was made sultan in Marrakech. Abu Faris immediately sent his own son, accompanied by his brother Muley al-Shaykh al-Ma'mun, to attack Zaydan's Fez. Zaydan was defeated and forced to retreat to bordering Ottoman territory, where he started to negotiate for military aid. However, the war in Morocco was given a further twist when Muley al-Shaykh, preempting his brother Abu Faris, decided to proclaim himself the new sultan of Fez.

Al-Shaykh sent his son Abdallah to attack Marrakech, who succeeded in conquering the city and subjected it to a bloody round of looting and pillage. However, Muley Zaydan, assisted by Ottoman troops, now returned to Morocco and successfully reconquered both Fez and Marrakech. Al-Shaykh fled to Carmona in southern Spain, where, playing on Spanish fears of Ottoman expansion in North Africa, he attempted to solicit military assistance from Philip III. There is no doubt that the Spaniards were considerably alarmed by developments in Morocco. The victorious Muley Zaydan was allied with the Ottomans, who had already pushed the borders of their empire as far west as Algeria, and this caused Spain to fear a possible annexation of the Moroccan kingdom by the Ottomans, who would then be separated from Spanish territory only by the narrow waters of the Strait of Gibraltar. Spanish council minutes from this period are full of provisional defense measures to be taken against the imminent danger, as are the reports sent by Spanish agents working in North Africa at this time. In 1609, one such agent advised that Muley al-Shaykh be given help in defeating his rival as soon as possible, and suggested that the task force might consist of about ten to twelve thousand Spanish moriscos. The agent assumed that the moriscos would be only too willing to assist in this mission, which he predicted would simultaneously eliminate two dangers to Spanish national interests, namely, Muley Zaydan and Spain's own resident moriscos.[28]

In Carmona, al-Shaykh offered the Spaniards the port of Larache in exchange for arms and men. Larache was one of the few Moroccan ports still in Moroccan hands and had been a constant source of worry to the Spaniards for decades. During the reign of Philip II, Spanish officials repeatedly looked for a means of gaining control of Larache, hoping to use it as a bulwark against Morocco, which was vital in blocking the advance of the Ottoman empire. Larache assumed even greater significance for the Spaniards when it became a haven initially for Moroccan and morisco corsairs and later for corsairs from England and the Netherlands, who posed a serious threat to the southern coasts of Spain and Spanish routes to the Indies. The turmoil in Morocco thus provided an opportunity for

A MAN OF THREE WORLDS

Spain to neutralize Larache, and al-Shaykh agreed with Philip III on the transfer of the town in exchange for 200,000 ducats, plus the loan of 6,000 soldiers to help him regain his kingdom.

The deal was swiftly carried out. Spanish troops led by the marquis of San Germán entered Larache in 1610, took control of the town, and removed the local populace. Al-Shaykh subsequently used the Spanish soldiers to recapture Fez and the entire northern region of Morocco. However, Muley Zaydan continued to govern the southern half of the country from his base in Marrakech—as we shall see, Marrakech was the city to which Samuel Pallache always traveled when returning from Holland to report to his master Zaydan. Even so, neither of the competing sultans ever gained complete control over what was nominally his own territory, and in 1613, al-Shaykh was forced to leave Fez in order to fight his rebellious governor of Tétouan, Ahmad al-Naqsis. A few months later, in October 1613, al-Shaykh was killed by Abu l-Lif, a nephew and supporter of the now-forgotten Abu Faris. Muley Zaydan, though never able to bring about complete reunification of the territory, was finally recognized by European powers as the legitimate Moroccan sovereign.

The decade of civil war was a time of tremendous suffering for the entire Moroccan population, but particularly horrific for the Jews of Fez whose city was subjected to successive waves of attack and looting throughout this period. As if this suffering were not enough, Mellah residents were also forced by both of the rival pretenders to pay special taxes to cover the costs of their military campaigns. It was during the civil war that Samuel Pallache chose to leave Fez, and in the circumstances, his decision to gamble on an uncertain and risky adventure in an openly hostile Spanish environment is not surprising. Some idea of the effects of the early years of the war on the Jews of Fez can be gained from this passage by Saul ben David Serero, a contemporary Jewish chronicler:

> For three-and-a-half years [1603–6] we have been victims of starvation and many other calamities . . . some 800 souls have starved to death in Fez. The beautiful children of Fez are bloated like wineskins and dying of hunger. They have fallen to the lowest abjection, searching in the rubbish dumps for scraps, like hens. More than 600 [Jews] have apostatized. The roads are no longer safe, lines of communication have been cut off, whoever remains in the city starves, and whoever leaves it becomes a victim of the knife. Each man swallows the next alive. Israel has reached the extremest possible state of poverty.[29]

As Serero suggested, this was a period in which many Jews abandoned their faith and converted to Islam in a desperate attempt to improve their chances of survival. We should bear in mind that such conversions are an important part of the story of the Jewish community of Fez, although this book focuses mainly on Jews who clung to their faith in spite of all adversities and on those who, like Pallache, for various reasons converted to Christianity rather than Islam.[30]

JEWISH MERCHANTS, COURTIERS, AND FAVORITES

The names of several Moroccan Jews can be found in historical accounts and in diplomatic and commercial records from the sixteenth century on, and these references help us form a more detailed picture of the kinds of work that Jews did in Morocco during this period. As we shall see, many of these cases also provide us with further information on the difficulties experienced by Moroccan Jews during and after the civil wars. Specifically, it will be seen that those Jews who had been employed by one or other of the rivals competing for the Moroccan throne were often forced to opt for exile when their master failed or died.

Jews played important roles in both Moroccan diplomacy and Moroccan trade.[31] Often they found ways of combining their work in the two fields. Their contacts with fellow Jews in the Iberian Peninsula, the Netherlands, or the Ottoman empire gave them access to trade networks that were closed to other Moroccans. Typically, they dealt in sugar or supplied wheat to Spain and Portugal. They also purchased weapons from northern European Protestant nations, which were unaffected by the papal ban on the sale of arms to Muslim countries, and their familiarity with the arms trade made them especially valuable to Moroccan governments.

In diplomacy, Jewish exiles in Morocco were able to draw on the knowledge and skills acquired by families whose members had traditionally worked as functionaries and servants at the Castilian and Aragonese courts. In Spain, they had been employed as secretaries, commercial agents, and treasury officials, and in the process, they had become intimately familiar with European court usage. They had proven experience in government, accountancy, and diplomatic relations, and their continuing command of the Castilian language was a useful asset to them. In fact, it was partly through their influence that Castilian became the required language of diplomatic communication with Morocco throughout the sixteenth and seventeenth centuries.[32] What is more, Morocco's diplomatic rela-

A MAN OF THREE WORLDS

tions with Europe intensified after the victory at Al-Qasr al-Kabir in 1578. European nations came to realize the potential importance of Morocco as an ally against Spain and the Ottoman Empire, great powers that had now begun to decline, and some of these nations began to send unprecedented numbers of political and commercial emissaries to Sultan al-Mansur. As agents, translators, and interpreters, Moroccan Jews were essential participants in dealings with these European representatives.[33]

The Sa'adian dynasty employed Jews in key court posts, just as the Marinids and Wattasids had done before them. Ahmad al-Mansur had a financial adviser by the name of Ya'aqob Ruti,[34] known as Jeque or Jaco Rute in Spanish records, where his name occurs in almost all the documents concerning Morocco to be found in the Archivo General of Simancas.[35] Ruti was the latest in a line of influential members of his family, many of whom had worked in previous generations as government agents and interpreters for the Wattasids. Ruti's grandfather, also known to Spaniards and the Portuguese as Jaco Rute, had been employed as an interpreter by Sultan Abu Hassan al-Wattasi and had often been mentioned in Portuguese correspondence because of his close relationship with Bastião de Vargas, João III's Moroccan agent.[36] The assiduous Vargas had provided the Portuguese court with detailed information on his dealings with Ruti, who was said to speak good Portuguese.[37] Ruti had also worked in the lucrative business of the ransoming of captives, from which he derived substantial profits,[38] and he is known to have had commercial interests in the ports of Azemmour, Larache, Mamora, and Arzila, where he had employed delegates to negotiate with the Portuguese governors. Ruti's agent in both Tangier and Arzila had been his own brother Moses, who seems to have provided the Portuguese with court news from Fez.[39] Ruti possessed his own fleet of ships, and in 1539–40, he had arranged for a shipment of Moroccan wheat to Portugal, where he made contact with judaizing New Christians.[40] Vargas thought highly of Ruti and often claimed that his good offices were absolutely vital to Portuguese interests in the region.

Other Jewish families with a history of involvement in trading and diplomatic activities included the Ben Zamirro/Zamerro family of Safi. Abraham ben Zamirro, grand rabbi of Safi, had mediated in the peace process that followed the Moroccan siege of Safi, then held by the Portuguese, in 1526. His nephew Salomón, who had also acted as a mediator between the Portuguese and the Moroccans, was arrested and imprisoned in Cádiz in 1556 when traveling from Lisbon to Morocco with letters from

João III to the Moroccan sultan.[41] Another nephew, Yehuda ben Zamerro, became a rabbi in Fez; Isaac ben Zamerro was a rabbi in Tétouan in the early seventeenth century; and David ben Zamerro was also a *naguid* (Jewish community head or chief) in the Fez community.[42] Moysen ben Zamerro went to Spain and converted to Catholicism in El Escorial in 1589.[43] These cases are interesting, because they show members of a leading Jewish family, with important religious and leadership roles in their community, working as peace brokers in dealings with the Portuguese or Spaniards. Some of them went so far as to seek employment from Christian masters and were prepared to make formal conversions to the Christian faith in order to secure such posts.

Jews had sometimes been employed in negotiations of peace agreements in Luso-Moroccan conflicts over garrison towns. In Azemmour, a Jew known simply as "Abraham" is known to have mediated in peace dealings with Portugal,[44] and when Azemmour was later attacked by the duke of Braganza and the Muslims evacuated the local population, it was the Iberian Jew Jacob Adibe who communicated this news to the duke, at the same time pleading for protection for himself and the town's Jewish community.[45]

Another important Jewish family was that of the Senanes, many of whom enjoyed careers that paralleled those of the Rutis. Menaham Senanes, treasurer to the community of Fez, was an informer and confidant of Sultan Abu Hassun al-Wattasi in the 1540s, as well as being his secretary and personal emissary.[46] He is known to have had dealings with the Portuguese via Alfonso de Noronha, the governor of Tangier.[47] Many of these Fez families had branches in Tétouan, where a number of them later resettled, and Abraham Senanes became the grand rabbi of Tétouan in the early seventeenth century.[48]

Salomón Pariente acted as an intermediary in dealings with the Spaniards over Larache, and once the town was occupied by the Spaniards, the entire Pariente family settled there, though refusing to live in the Jewish quarter.[49] Pariente was close to Alfonso de Noronha, and he worked in Tangier and Tétouan, mainly in the jewel trade. Pariente served the Spanish crown, which paid him a salary of eleven *reales* a day and three *fanegas* (approximately 375 pounds) of wheat a month. He was also renowned for his ability to "counterfeit Muley al-Shaykh's signature as well as the man himself."[50] Pariente made frequent journeys to Madrid, and also to San-lúcar de Barrameda, where he carried messages for the duke of Medina

Sidonia. In 1619, he took part in negotiations over the surrender to Spain of the morisco-occupied town of Salé.[51]

Another important Jewish intermediary between Morocco and Spain was Jacob Cansino, whose family, originally from Seville, had settled in Oran in 1512. Cansino was sent by the Spaniards to the Moroccan court and played an important role in Hispano-Moroccan relations in the 1550s.[52] His son Isaac, a royal interpreter of Arabic in Oran, was called to Madrid in 1580, and spent several months there at a time when Philip II, after Spain's union with Portugal, had assumed control over Ceuta and Tangier. Isaac's own son, Hayim, also an Arabic interpreter, spent seven months by royal command in Sanlúcar de Barrameda in 1608, where he assisted the duke of Medina Sidonia in negotiations over Larache and La Mamora.[53]

THE BROTHERS AND RIVAL SULTANS Muley al-Shaykh and Muley Zaydan also employed Jews at court. At the start of his reign, Muley Zaydan had two Jewish treasury officials in his retinue, by the names of Abraham ben Waish and Juda Levi. Waish and Levi were merchants who played a important role in Moroccan relations with the Dutch Republic, and in 1617, Muley Zaydan entrusted them with a large cargo of merchandise, which included sugar and animal hides, to be sold in Middelburg.[54] (Two other Jewish factors, Moses Levi and Benjamin Cohen, traveled with them on this occasion, and were described by Zaydan in a letter to Maurice of Nassau as "our Jewish servants.")[55] From about 1608, Waish was generally thought to exert great influence over Muley al-Shaykh: Coy, a Dutch agent in Morocco, complained in a letter to the States General that Waish had turned the sultan against him because Waish feared having to compete with Coy for business. Other Christian merchants also lodged complaints about Waish, alleging that he sought to monopolize trade with Morocco for his own benefit and that of his family. Waish had serious clashes with Paul van Lippeloo, a representative of the Amsterdam merchants, who also had disagreements with Samuel Pallache himself, as we shall see later. As a matter of interest, Abraham ben Waish seems not only to have served Muley Zaydan but previously to have worked for Abu Faris, one of Zaydan's rivals during the wars.[56]

Yamin ben Remmokh was another Jew employed by Muley Zaydan in negotiations with the Dutch Republic and in commercial trading with both England and the Dutch Republic. Remmokh was sent to sell sugar in Holland in 1615 and traveled to Holland again between 1624 and 1628.[57] On these journeys, one of his duties seems to have been to warn the Dutch against selling arms to Muley Zaydan's opponents in Morocco.[58]

Like his brother, Muley al-Shaykh also employed Jews in his entourage. In records of the earliest negotiations that al-Shaykh held with the Spaniards over Larache, mention is made of a Jew called Gibre, said to be a member of an important family from Tétouan.[59] These negotiations were later set back at a crucial stage by the intervention of a powerful enemy of Gibre's, one Juda Sinafé, who made too many concessions for his sultan's liking. Al-Shaykh was greatly displeased by Sinafé's conduct and had him imprisoned in 1606.[60]

Al-Shaykh's main Jewish favorite was Nathan Benterny, described in various chronicles and written records as "the king's Jew." These records make constant reference to the affection and friendship between the sultan and Benterny, who had been brought up in the royal household. Nathan Benterny was considered a indispensable factor in all dealings with al-Shaykh. He made many journeys to Spain in connection with the Larache negotiations and accompanied al-Shaykh during the latter's exile in Carmona.[61] (Spanish records refer to him either as "Ulet Natán" or "Natán Benterni.") Benterny was sometimes described as being from Livorno, but more usually as "a Jew of Fez," and he seems to have been a very careful and zealous servant of his sultan. The writer Juan Luis de Rojas described him as follows:

Regarding this Natán, it is worth knowing that he is the shaykh of all the Jews: he was brought up as a child in the household of Muley al-Shaykh together with the other children, and he grew up among them serving in those tasks for which kings use Jews: in tongues, as a go-between, and for other purposes in which the Moors themselves are not trusted. He gained the favour of Muley al-Shaykh through secret and suspicious services, and he accompanied and followed him, always receiving many favors from the king and advancing more rapidly than others who were older than he. He came to Spain in his service, and there he was his secret interpreter, through whom all business was performed, and although Juanetín Mortara was perfectly informed of all things, he was not so trusted by them as Natán Ulet. The ministers of His Majesty [the Spanish king] rewarded him in kind, favoring him with gifts of money in the form of *ayuda de costa* and promises of fifty escudos per month, which even rose to one hundred, and they allowed him to live for two years in his law and granted him many other facilities that, since he is a true Jew, he was able to extract from them in his own interest, and as he came and went to Spain so often, he brought those cloths that were entrusted to him in Barbary, selling his merchandise well.[62]

This paragraph is interesting for what it reveals about the kind of relationships that both renegades and Jews were able to enjoy with their Muslim masters, creating an ambit of personal and emotional relations that tend to be expressed in highly familiar or even sexual terms. Note: We do not suggest that there was a sexual relationship![63]

Nathan Benterny sometimes took advantage of his diplomatic travels to promote his business interests. On more than one occasion, he transported merchandise that he had purchased with money given him by the Spaniards. The marquis of San Germán is known to have been particularly generous to him, and he seems to have had little difficulty keeping his side of bargains with the Spaniards without ever losing the trust of his Moroccan master. In this sense, Benterny's was a case of perfectly achieved double loyalty, given that the two sides he served never came into conflict. After the death of al-Shaykh, Benterny made an official application to live in Spain, stating firstly that he had "made many voyages at great risk for the negotiations with Muley Xeque [al-Shaykh] and that he had not been paid" and then, in February 1611, requesting a royal *cédula* "so that he can come here and be reduced to the faith."[64] As explained by Rojas above, Benterny was not only granted the *cédula* he sought but was also awarded one hundred escudos a month and the right to a two-year adaptation period during which he was permitted to continue practicing his Jewish religion. It seems likely that the cautious Benterny would have insisted on this two-year margin as a safeguard against Inquisition curiosity.

Nathan Benterny's case shows that many Jews clearly found themselves in awkward positions after the death or defeat of the candidate for whom they had worked. Although apparently powerful, such Jews occupied posts that made them entirely dependent upon their personal relationship with a sultan or governor. As Jews, they were not allowed a retinue and not entitled to honors or the highest-ranking posts. This was a convenient way of neutralizing the dangerous power conferred upon them by their positions at court, and it made them particularly valuable as employees during power struggles or at times of internal rivalry. However, it also made them vulnerable in the event of the disappearance or fall from power of the master whom they served. In such circumstances, many Jews tried, often successfully, to resettle in Spain.

IT SHOULD BE NOTED THAT JEWS were not only employed by members of the Moroccan royal family. There are also references to them working for shaykhs who were leaders of religious brotherhoods, and some of these shaykhs, known as *morabitos* or *morabutos* in Spain, headed their own military factions during the wars. One of the most influential of these leaders was Muhammad al-Ayyashi, who, in the 1630s, became the effective ruler of the entire northern half of Morocco. Muhammad al-Ayyashi employed several Jews, including Benjamin Cohen, a "Portuguese" Jew who lived in Salé and had a brother called Joseph in the Netherlands. Cohen and Aaron Querido, another Jewish servant, were given responsibility for al-Ayyashi's relations with the Dutch Republic, and at one stage Cohen managed to persuade the States General to supply his master with gunpowder.[65]

Military captains on the Hispano-Portuguese borders and Spanish agents working in Morocco also made frequent use of Jews as messengers and informers. Such men are mentioned in their *avisos de Berbería* (Reports on Barbary), sometimes in terms such as "a Jew known to me" or "a trustworthy Jew," or occasionally giving the names of the Jews concerned. It was relatively common for such Jews to request permission to settle in Spain and convert to the Christian faith—further evidence of the wretchedness of the situation in Morocco throughout the first quarter of the seventeenth century, with its plagues and continually devastating wars. Employment as a messenger, an informer, or a spy was often a first step toward moving to Spain or Portugal. Others took the more direct route of converting first and making a direct request for royal favor. In May 1609, Francisco de Robles Lorenzo and Juan Bautista de Zayas ("by nation Jews from the city of Fez") entered Spain in the company of Francisco de Guelba, a native of Al-Qasr al-kabir described as a Moor by birth with a Christian mother. All three requested baptism from the bishop of Málaga, and as soon as they were converted, they wrote to Philip III asking for "some sort of favor in Lisbon or wherever Your Majesty may desire, to serve you in whatever we are instructed to do, for we shall serve as good, loyal Christians."[66] The three may well have been "Portuguese" Jews who had settled in Fez and returned to Judaism, but now wished to go back to Lisbon. There were also cases of Muslims who voluntarily presented themselves in Spanish garrison towns requesting conversion and the opportunity to live in Spain.[67]

Many other individuals are less easy to identify. A number of what might be termed "anonymous" Jews, that is, those who did not belong to traditionally important families, also left Morocco for Spain, as did many moriscos recently expelled from the Peninsula who were desperate to return to their homeland.[68] One example might be Juan Ludovico Rodríguez, a Jew from Tétouan who in 1614 presented plans to the Spaniards for the capture of the towns of Salé and La Mamora. Rodríguez asked for permission to travel to Spain with his family, settle there, and convert to Christianity,[69] thus replicating the strategy pursued by Samuel Pallache in the early stages of his career.

In fact, archive records show a very considerable number of individuals crossing the borders, and this was not merely a consequence of the dire conditions in Morocco during this period. In the seventeenth century, borders, though clearly defined, were flexible and permeable, especially for those who possessed what might be termed multiple identities. This included Jews, moriscos, and renegades with cultural backgrounds that gave them at least something in common with inhabitants of the Iberian Peninsula.

These kinds of cases are more frequent than might be thought or has until now been shown. They prove how changeable loyalties could be. Or rather, they show that religious conversion was often used as a way of adapting to social reality, a way of surviving in awkward circumstances. Conversion to another religion became a sort of passport for those who were forced to live, quite literally, on the margins of society.

JEWS IN PORTUGAL AND SPAIN

Having established the circumstances in Morocco that help to explain why Samuel Pallache may have been tempted to leave Fez in 1603, we need to turn our attention briefly to those developments in the Iberian Peninsula that made it possible for him to attempt to settle there. What had happened in Spain and, in particular, Portugal, in the years after the Expulsion of 1492, and how did these events affect the situation for Fez Jews entering the Iberian Peninsula at the beginning of the seventeenth century?

In order to answer this question, we must first remember that many of the Jews who had settled in Fez during the late fifteenth and sixteenth centuries went there from Portugal as well as from Spain. In 1497, King Manoel I of Portugal had decreed the compulsory conversion of all his Jewish subjects, making it almost impossible for them to take the alternative of exile from the country. New Christians were similarly forbidden from leaving the territories of the Portuguese crown. However, this particular restriction was lifted in 1507. For the next three decades, they were permitted to take part in the commercial activities of the Portuguese empire and to travel within its territories, and as a result, the expansion of the Portuguese empire and the diaspora of Portuguese conversos became simultaneous, synchronized movements.[70] Many of the New Christians took advantage of their trading interests to move to Brazil or the East Indies. Some settled in Egypt and played an important role in Portuguese trade with India.[71] Others went to the Portuguese coastal garrisons in Morocco (Tangier, Ceuta, Mazagan [Al Jadida], Arzila, and Azemmour) so that they could then pass over into Muslim territory and return to Judaism. The number of New Christians leaving Portugal increased even more sharply after 1536, when the Inquisition was established under João III, who revoked the concessions on freedom of movement promulgated by King Manoel in 1507. For the next sixty years, the Portuguese Inquisition proved to be even more zealous in its hounding of conversos than its counterpart in Spain, which in turn prompted conversos to leave the country by whatever routes they could find.[72]

A favored destination for many of those escaping was Fez. To get there, conversos first had to pass through the Portuguese garrison towns in Morocco. Except in Arzila, where Manoel I had succeeded in enforcing his policy of compulsory baptism for Jews, most of these enclaves harbored significant Jewish communities, which the Portuguese had been forced to leave virtually undisturbed when they realized how vital they were in trade with the surrounding Moroccans. The existence of Jewish quarters had therefore continued to be allowed in these ports, their inhabitants being required to wear a sign on their clothing.[73] (A similar situation arose in Spanish garrison towns, where Jewish quarters also survived.) These Jewish quarters were used by Jews and New Christians as staging areas on their way to Fez, where they were able to make a untrammeled return to their faith. Bastião de Vargas, a Portuguese factor in Morocco, informed João III of these developments in a famous letter written from Fez in June 1542.[74] He told his king that New Christians were traveling from the garrisons to trade in Fez, where they settled permanently and returned to Judaism. Vargas called for certain measures to be taken, such as a prohi-

A MAN OF THREE WORLDS

bition on their venturing outside the garrisons, and the insistence that they trade only from within the towns themselves. He also recommended that these traders be prevented from traveling from one garrison town to another by land, and that they only be granted permission to travel by sea, in order to make it more difficult for them to flee to Fez or Tétouan.[75] None of Vargas's ideas were ever put into practice, and it seems likely that Fez continued to receive large numbers of Portuguese Jews and New Christians from the garrison towns throughout the whole of the sixteenth century.

By the start of Philip III's reign in 1598, Portugal and Spain were still united under one crown, so that when Philip initiated a policy of improving conditions for Jews living within his kingdoms, the policy automatically applied to Portugal as well. Unlike his father, Philip II, the new king proved himself open to persuasion by economic means, and in 1601, the New Christians of Portugal paid out a huge sum of money in order to recover their legal right to travel freely. (They also insisted that restrictions on their movements would never be renewed.) Enticed by the promise of further payments, Philip brushed aside complaints from the Church and even placed pressure on the Vatican to make life easier for the conversos. As a result of these urgings, the papacy issued its Brief Indulgence of 1603, whereby it pardoned New Christians for crimes pending with the Inquisition. Inquisitorial archives in Portugal and Spain dating from this era show a marked reduction in the number of trials of crypto-Jews. Meanwhile, Philip turned his attention away from Jews in order to focus on Spain's morisco population in the years ahead of the Expulsion of 1609–14. Official policy toward Jewish conversos in both Spain and Portugal showed signs, therefore, of becoming more tolerant and inclusive.[76]

Under Philip IV (1621–65), the situation of the conversos improved further when the king's chief minister, Gaspar de Guzmán Olivares, decided to replace the Genoese, the monarchy's traditional bankers, with Portuguese merchants of New Christian origin. There were even times during Philip's reign when it was rumored that Jews were about to be allowed to make an official return to Spain—that is, that their existence would be legalized, as was to occur in some other European countries. Some Jews are even thought to have started to return from the Middle East, and a contemporary witness reported the following scene in 1634: "It has become a valid custom for Jews to enter Spain; they certainly come and go to speak with the king and give him *memoriales*, and today I saw one with a white headdress at the door to the king's room. It saddened me to see it."[77] Matías de Novoa, the court chronicler and *ayuda de cámara* to Philip IV, wrote at about this time:

> I have heard it said that the Jews of Oran and those who live inland in Africa have here their advocates who would admit them to Madrid circles and give them land to live on freely and within their law, together with all those who would come and live with them, and that they would register themselves, and that the Jews would be prepared to give many millions for permission to do this. Who can doubt that there is not one of them in the kingdom of Portugal or anywhere else who would not take up residence here?[78]

It seems obvious to us now, with the hindsight of several centuries, that the situation of the conversos (to say nothing of the Jews who were planning their return) had in fact reached an impasse by this stage. However, we must remember that this would still have been far from clear at the beginning of the new century. With Portuguese conversos flooding into Spain, and inquisitorial repression of the portugueses easing considerably, the early 1600s can be seen as a period of relative calm. Pallache's decision to settle in Madrid becomes easier to understand in the light of these developments.

MELCHOR VAZ DE AZEVEDO AND ISAAC ALMOSNINO

Our understanding of the events of Samuel Pallache's life is further enhanced by the records of Inquisition trials, which provide precious information on Moroccan Jews who came into contact with Spain and Portugal. The files of two men whose lives were poles apart are highly illuminating for what they tell us about the general situation of Jews in Morocco.

The first trial, chronologically, is that of a Portuguese converso named Melchor or Belchior Vaz de Azevedo, who was brought before the Lisbon Inquisition in 1561.[79] From references to him in various other sources, plus the evidence given at his trial, it is possible to piece together an outline of Azevedo's life story. He had originally been a tailor in Arzila and had also worked as a tax official both in Arzila and in Tangier until 1546, when he started to serve the kings of France, working first for François I and then for Henri II. In 1556, Azevedo shared a cell in Cádiz with Salomón Ben Zamerro, a member of a leading Jewish Moroccan family, mentioned above. Azevedo had been detained in Cádiz as one of a group of suspicious Frenchmen traveling in Spanish territory. At the time of this arrest, Ben Zamerro informed João III that Azevedo had been heading for an interview with the sultan of Morocco with instructions from the king of France "to act against the interests of the emperor Charles V and to bring [French] galleys and ships to his ports [i.e., those of Morocco]." When arrested, Azevedo was found to be in possession of accredited letters to take him through the ports of Portugal and Castile, and he claimed to be on a mission to capture a corsair ship. According to Ben Zamerro, this was simply a cover for his real intentions. Ben Zamerro said that the sultan "would be very pleased to have an alliance with the king of France for the benefits it would bring to his kingdoms on being supplied with goods and defensive weapons." Azevedo seems to have remained in prison in Cádiz for about two years.

Around 1560, Azevedo was also involved in the attempt by the king of Navarre, Antoine de Bourbon, to gain control of trans-Pyrenean Navarre. In exchange for it, Antoine offered Philip II an unspecified African garrison town, which he was still in the process of acquiring. The Navarran king sent Azevedo to interview the sultan of Morocco and negotiate for the town of Alcazarseguer, which had previously belonged to the Portuguese. Azevedo was instructed to offer the sultan five hundred armed men and a garrison of thirty harquebusiers and ten knights, plus enough munitions and war equipment for the sultan to defend himself from possible attacks by the Turks.[80] Philip II was warned about this mission by the Spanish ambassador in France, and because of Philip's unwillingness to enter into negotiations, no deal was ever made.

Azevedo's name also occurs in other contexts. In 1561, the English ambassador to France wrote to London that a "named Capten Melchior" (i.e., Melchior Vaz de Azevedo), had expressed his desire to work for the English. The ambassador described Azevedo as a sixty-year-old man with great experience in Barbary affairs who had lived in North Africa for twelve years and was an outstanding seaman. Azevedo had previously worked for the kings of France and the king of Navarre, but was now unhappy with his pension payments, which he had said were not generous enough to support his family. He claimed to be an expert in the secrets of trading with Morocco, where, he said, gold, copper, gum arabic, wax, leather, hides, sugar, horses, and many other things were to be had. Azevedo was familiar with market prices, and he knew the right goods to offer the Moroccans in exchange: namely, tin, sword blades, lances, and oars. (Military equipment, in other words, which Catholics were forbidden by papal bull from supplying to Muslim countries.) Later that year, Azevedo traveled to London and was apparently unable to convince either merchants or authorities of the general feasibility of his projects, but in September, he is known to have traveled to Larache on an English ship carrying weapons to be sold in Morocco. The Portuguese ambassador to Morocco claimed that Azevedo also on this occasion took with him a chest full of Hebrew books for the Jews of North Africa.[81]

Azevedo, who had never completely severed his links with Portugal, traveled to Lisbon after this voyage and offered his services to the Portuguese. It was at this point that the Inquisition intervened.

The first denunciation of Azevedo to the Holy Office branded him a Protestant. His denouncer, Domingo Paes, said that he had known "Belchior Vaz" from the time that Paes was held captive in the Jewish quarter of Fez. He said that Azevedo had worked for the king of Navarre and was a well-known supplier of arms to the Moroccan sultan. According to Paes, Azevedo was generally considered to be a "Lutheran" and had told other captives that "he confessed in his heart." Nevertheless, other witnesses traveled from Tangier to testify that Azevedo had in fact always been a practicing Jew, whereas Bernardo Rodrigues, a chronicler from Arzila, declared that he had been on very good terms with the defendant and knew him to be a good Catholic. A picture thus gradually emerges from the contrasting evidence of a man who was a Jew in Tangier and Fez, a Catholic in Portugal, and a "Lutheran" in France and England.

Despite the gravity of his sins and their undeniability, Azevedo received an amazingly benign punishment: he was told to abjure *de levi*, to promise to rid himself of all heresy, and to allow himself to be indoctrinated in all that was necessary for the salvation of his soul. Azevedo was clearly too important, and his practical knowledge too great, for the Portuguese to allow him to rot in an Inquisition cell. That his skills and knowledge should be so useful as to release him from the grip of the Holy Office tells us a great deal about the general value of experience in Moroccan trading. Other factors were probably important too. Azevedo had been involved in negotiations for garrison towns, he had direct access to the sultan's court, and as an experienced seaman, he could assist in the fight against Mediterranean corsairs. Azevedo's arrest and subsequent release show that his talents were double-edged weapons that could sometimes be used against him and sometimes in his favor. Samuel Pallache was to learn a similar lesson when he was himself arrested and imprisoned toward the end of his life.

ISAAC ALMOSNINO'S CASE provides a complete contrast to that of Vaz de Azevedo and others described more briefly above. So far we have focused on Jewish individuals or families whose identity was "borderline" almost by definition, and whose attachment and commitment to their communities were demonstrably vague and variable. The Almosnino family was different: it represented the very nucleus of the Jewish community as it survived outside the Iberian Peninsula. No member of it ever made a living by mediating between two worlds, and the trial record of Isaac Almosnino certainly does not reveal an individual of flexible beliefs capable of adapting to different roles in different lands. However, his case is richly illustrative of what life was like for an Iberian Jew in Fez in the last third of the sixteenth century.

Everything we know about Isaac Almosnino comes from two thick folders of documents preserved in the Torre do Tombo Inquisition archive in Lisbon.[82] Isaac and his brother Abraham were originally arrested in 1617 at the home of the flamboyant English adventurer Sir Robert Shirley (or Sherley) in Portuguese-held Goa on the west coast of India. Shirley was then employed as the shah of Persia's ambassador to the Moghul empire. Almosnino had first met Shirley in Persia, where he had decided to accompany the Englishman on his journey to India via Hormuz.[83] Almosnino's presence in Goa had been reported to the authorities by two Old Christians from Oporto, who mistook him for one Manuel López, a doctor and New Christian from Spain who had practiced medicine in Oporto for several years. López had fled Oporto because of problems with the Inquisition, and there had been reports of him traveling with his younger brother to Flanders, and then moving on to Istanbul. To some extent, these facts explain the confusion between López and Isaac Almosnino: Almosnino had also worked as a merchant in Istanbul, and he had been seen to arrive in Goa in the company of his younger brother, Abraham. Almosnino resembled López in other ways too: they were both of medium height with fair beards and large noses, and like López, Almosnino was a doctor who spoke good Portuguese and perfect Castilian.

When first mistakenly arrested in Goa, Isaac Almosnino declared that he was forty-five years old and described himself as a *judío de nación y de profesión*, the son and grandson of Jews who had never converted to any other faith (a Jew "from Abraham until now"). He said that he was a descendant of Jews expelled from Spain in 1492 and was a native, like his parents and grandparents, of the city of Fez in Morocco. In Fez he had learnt "the art of physic" and had practiced medicine for many years in Fez and Marrakech, but he had never worked as a doctor outside Morocco. He had been forced to leave Morocco by the awkwardness of his situation after the civil wars (the Almosninos had been close to the defeated Muley Zaydan), and decided to become a merchant like his father. Isaac said that he had traded with associates in Marseilles, Italy, and the Levant, especially Istanbul.

In his first declaration, Isaac Almosnino angrily denounced his accusers and said that they bore grudges against him because he was protected by the Persian ambassador and because they were his business competitors. He insisted on being taken to Lisbon, claiming that he would otherwise have no chance of defending himself or of demonstrating who he was. Both of the Almosnino brothers were therefore taken to the Portuguese capital, where they arrived in February 1618, one year after their arrest in Goa. The records kept of their trial tell the story of a process that went on until 1621. These records constitute a truly exceptional document, given that the Almosninos were neither conversos nor Judaizers, but Jews who had never pretended to be anything else. This was the first time that either of them had ever entered the Iberian Peninsula, the original home of their ancestors before expulsion in 1492.

In all this extraordinary case, we are most interested in precisely the same points that were emphasised by the inquisitors themselves. Throughout the trial, the Almosnino brothers were interrogated about the makeup of their family and the professions of its different members. They were asked about the languages they knew and how they had learnt them, and also about their studies as children in Fez, when they went to the synagogal school with their cousins and close neighbors. They were even required to describe the street on which they had lived in Fez, and all the other Jews who had lived on it, as well as their dealings with non-Jews in the city, especially Portuguese captives.

The inquisitors called upon a large number of witnesses to give evidence, most of whom were Fez Jews who had converted to Christianity and now lived in Portugal. The Almosninos also cited a number of Jews from Fez and Tétouan, including members of their own family, who could testify that they were who they said they were. In order to be able to hear this evidence, the Inquisition requested assistance from the bishopric of Ceuta, and relatives were allowed to travel to Ceuta to make their statements. These statements were made in Castilian, and signed in both Castilian and Hebrew, except those made by the women of the family, who signed in Arabic. The Almosnino file also contains three letters written in *aljamía*, that is, in Castilian but using the Hebrew alphabet: these were written by Isaac Almosnino's father-in-law and brother-in-law and sent on to his prison cell in Lisbon.

The inquisitors were particularly interested in specific aspects of Isaac Almosnino's way of life. Above all, they wanted to know as much as possible about his studies. They asked him at which of the schools he had studied medicine, whether at Coimbra or Salamanca, and Isaac replied that it had been at Fez. The inquisitors asked him how he could be a doctor if he had not studied at either Coimbra or Salamanca, and also whether he knew any Latin. In his reply, Isaac gave precious information on the standard education in Fez of a child from an elite Jewish family. He said that he had learnt to read and write at the Jewish school in the city, together with other boys. He declared that he knew Hebrew, Arabic, Castilian, and Chaldean (Aramaic), some Italian, and a few words of the French spoken in Marseilles, because of his time there as a merchant, but no Latin. He spoke Portuguese very well because of the large number of Portuguese in Morocco and because of his contacts with captives from the battle with King Sebastian (he had known the son of the count of Vimioso), and also because of his dealings at the Portuguese borders in Africa. Isaac was clearly proud to belong to an important and distinguished family and claimed, it was recorded, that "all men who are from Fez and rabbis know him and know his father and his lineage."

The inquisitors were extremely curious about the languages Isaac spoke and read, and he explained that at home he had been brought up in Castilian and Arabic like all Jews of Spanish descent, and that he had studied Hebrew and Chaldean at school, just as Latin was studied in Spain. The inquisitors pressed him for more details about his schooldays in Fez, asking him about his teachers and classmates. It is not entirely clear whether these questions were asked out of mere curiosity, "anthropological" interest, or in the hope that he might mention the name of some other Jew of Portuguese origin. If it was for the last of these reasons, the inquisitors asked in vain, for Almosnino provided them with no such names, and indeed did not make the slightest effort to ingratiate himself with them in any other way. Isaac Almosnino seems to have perplexed the inquisitors by being so close to them and at the same time so alien, so different, and so "exotic." This perplexity fueled their interest. They seem to have wanted to know what it was like to be a man like Isaac Almosnino, how it felt to lead a life like his.

The inquisitors asked Almosnino if he knew of any Portuguese in Fez who had ever returned to Judaism, to which his answer was no. They also asked him if he knew any Jews who had converted to Christianity, and he gave the names of several converts in Tangier from the times of Alfonso de Noronha, such as the brothers Camondo, Abraham Gibre, and Moysen Ben Zamerro, adding that all of these people knew him very well and could vouch for who he was. Later in the trial, Salomón Ben Zamerro was called upon to make a statement. This member of the Zamerro family had converted in Lisbon and taken the name of Manoel de Noronha. Moysen Ben Zamerro's name does not resurface in the trial, and yet we know something about him from other sources: in 1589, he had converted to Christianity in El Escorial under the name of Pablo de Santa María.[84] Almosnino said that the Camodos or Camondos, known as Jacob and Salomón when Jews, lived in the same street of the Jewish quarter as Isaac's own family, and the Gibres just a little further along. In addition, Isaac said he was related to the Parientes and had married one of his daughters to a member of the Pariente family.

THE ANSWERS GIVEN BY ISAAC at his trial reveal some of the strategies employed by the Jewish community in Fez, of which they represented the nucleus, in its struggle to maintain itself during the years of exile. One such strategy was intermarriage between cousins at a very early age, and another, seen very clearly in the history of the Almosninos, was the transmission of knowledge and professional skills within the same family. Religious faith and cultural symbols were quite rigidly preserved. All of this coincides with what is known of other Mediterranean Jewish communities in the same century.[85]

Isaac Almosnino was a direct contemporary of Samuel Pallache, and his trial provides fascinating evidence of the kind of standard education received by a young male Fez Jew at this time, which is complemented, and supported, by other sources. The Hebrew chronicles of the Jewish community show that a child's formal education began at about the age of four. Learning took the form of memorizing texts, first the Bible, with the commentaries of Rashi, explained in Arabic, which students also learned to read and write.[86] The Jews spoke Castilian, but we do not know whether they were taught to write it, a task that would have involved learning another alphabet.

The Almosninos were eventually declared innocent and allowed to return to Morocco, where the family survives to this day. Throughout their trial, mention had been made of many of the main Jewish families of Fez: the surnames Ruti, Zamerro, Camondo, Gibre, Pariente, and Senanes are all to be found there. The Pallaches are never mentioned, however, which seems to support the impression given by the Spanish documents that they were not among the city's leading Jewish families. Alternatively, it is possible that the Pallaches had moved on to Tétouan by this time— Spanish records consistently described them as Jews of Fez, but it should be remembered that the term could be used to refer, not just to the city itself, but to the entire Moroccan "kingdom"—that is, the northern part of today's Morocco. However, it is our belief that the Pallaches were probably not among the Jewish elite of Fez. A relatively inferior social status would explain many of their later actions: initially removed from the inner circles of power, they were forced to take dangerous risks in order to improve their standing.

TO SUMMARIZE, we have seen that there were two broad movements of Iberian Jews in the period with which we are concerned. The first, which took place between the late fifteenth century and the start of the seventeenth, was a movement away from the Iberian Peninsula and toward Morocco, which thereby gained a reputation as a focus of opposition to Spain and Portugal. As we have seen, Jewish identification with the Islamic cause was still discernible in the late sixteenth century, as is shown by the Jewish celebrations after the defeat of King Sebastian at Al-Qasr al-kabir. At the same time, Jews in Morocco clearly held on to certain cultural symbols of their identity as inhabitants of the Iberian Peninsula. This was especially true of the languages that they spoke. Most of the early exiles spoke Castilian, and increasing numbers of them were Portuguese-speaking as the sixteenth century went on, owing to the rise in emigration of Portuguese New Christians to Morocco, and because of an increased presence of the Portuguese in the Maghreb more generally. Language seems to have been an important element in the cultural identity of Moroccan Jews, and it is noticeable that written communication within the community was carried out in Hebraic-Spanish *aljamía* and not in Hebraic-Arabic *aljamía* as in all other Jewish communities throughout the Arab Muslim world.

The second movement started in the first decade of the seventeenth century, and it went in the opposite direction, as increasing numbers of Moroccan Jews converted to Christianity and emigrated to Spain and Portugal. These new emigrants had a far greater knowledge of Arabic and

Hebrew than the crypto-Jews who had opted to stay behind in Iberia; they had had the opportunity to study at Jewish schools in Morocco, where they acquired a more solid foundation in Jewish culture. A curious situation had thus arisen: the descendants of precisely those Jews who had been firmest in their faith, that is, those who had preferred exile abroad to forced conversion at home, were those who opted three or four generations later for strategic conversion to Christianity in order to "return" to a country they had never known.

In these two broad movements, the Jews were not alone, since they were joined by the other main Iberian minority group, the moriscos. Many morisco families had fled to Morocco after the war of the Alpujarras (1568–72), and these families are known to have been welcomed by Sultan Ahmad al-Mansur in Marrakech and given land to build homes for themselves in the meadows outside the city.[87] Al-Mansur and his successors employed a number of them, mainly as interpreters and foreign agents.[88]

Perhaps the most striking example of these moriscos was Ahmad ben Qasim al-Andalusi, known as al-Hajari, who was born in Spain in 1569 or 1570, probably in Extremadura, although he also lived in Seville and Madrid. Al-Hajari was involved in the two strange affairs of the "discoveries" in Granada of the Torre Turpiana Parchment and the Sacromonte Lead Books. These "ancient" documents were probably forgeries perpetrated by educated moriscos. The documents purported to record the presence of Arabs in Granada at the time of the Apostles and revealed that these Arabs had been converted to Christianity by none other than Saint James and his disciples. The authors of these texts sought to preempt the moriscos' imminent expulsion from Spain by invalidating the very concept of the "New Christian": had they been genuine, the versions of history they contained would have made moriscos "older" and more indigenous Christians than anyone else in Spain.[89]

Disguised as an Old Christian, al-Hajari later sailed from the port of Santa María in Cádiz to the Portuguese garrison of Mazagan. From there he made his way to Marrakech, where he was received by al-Mansur in 1599. Al-Hajari settled in Morocco, where he married and founded a family. In 1608, when Muley Zaydan made Marrakech his capital, al-Hajari was appointed to be his secretary and translator and played an important role in the intellectual life of the city. Zaydan later sent al-Hajari on a diplomatic mission to France and Holland, where he made contact with the first Arabists of Leiden. Al-Hajari also met Prince Maurice, and Jews from the Iberian community, who shared his native language, and with whom he apparently engaged in religious debate. Samuel Pallache was in Holland at the time of al-Hajari's visit, but nothing is known of a meeting between the two men, which al-Hajari would probably have recorded in his fascinating account of his European travels.[90]

Other moriscos in Morocco were used for specific missions, especially as translators and interpreters. One such was Side Abdallah Dodar, a morisco "andalouz being borne in Granada," who spoke good Spanish and some Italian and who traveled to England in 1600 as interpreter to the Moroccan ambassador.[91] In addition, al-Mansur employed another Andalusian morisco interpreter, Abd al-Rahman al-Kattani, who also worked as a translator for Muley Zaydan in Marrakech in 1609.[92] Several Moroccan ambassadors to England and the Dutch Republic were also moriscos, such as Ahmad ben Abdallah al-Maruni and Yussef Biscaino.

Morisco exiles to Morocco played important roles in the armies of sultans, or in government-encouraged corsair activity, both before and after the period of their expulsion from Spain. One good example is provided by the career of Said ben Foraj al-Dugali. Born in the kingdom of Granada, al-Dugali emigrated to Morocco at some time before the war of the Alpujarras. He settled in Tétouan, where he worked as a corsair, and in about 1563, he was given the task of recruiting an artillery corps for the Moroccan army to be made up entirely of Spanish moriscos. This unit eventually consisted of about 2,000 men and came to constitute an elite corps at the orders of al-Dugali, playing an outstanding role in several military campaigns.

Al-Dugali also continued to work as a corsair at sea. In 1571, he led a force that attacked the Spanish Canary Islands with seven specially equipped corsair galleys and carried out a famous two-month occupation of the island of Lanzarote, during which the town of Arrecife was completely sacked and looted. In 1573, he supervised the sacking of the town of Las Cuevas de Almanzora in the province of Granada, and carried off the entire population to Morocco as hostages. Al-Dugali and his morisco harquebusiers (described by Arab records as "Andalusians") also fought for Sultan Abd al-Malik in actions against rebellious tribes that refused to pay taxes, and took part in actions leading up to the battle of Al-Qasr al-kabir. Al-Dugali's last ambitious adventure was to attempt a military coup against Abd al-Malik's successor, Ahmad al-Mansur, for which he was executed in 1579.[93] As we shall see later, Samuel Pallache came into close contact with moriscos whose careers bore some resemblance to that of the corsair al-Dugali.

It is in many ways surprising to see the extent of the links between the Maghreb and the Iberian Peninsula at a time when Spain and Portugal had begun to turn their backs on the Mediterranean and on their long confrontation with the Islamic world. The border between Iberia and the Maghreb was so porous that it hardly existed as such. In fact, it might be more appropriate to liken it to a wide stretch of seashore over which the tides rose and fell in slow, repeated movements. The sand was never under water for long, yet never totally dry either.

CHAPTER 3

BETWEEN THE DUTCH
REPUBLIC AND MOROCCO

AMSTERDAM

After the Expulsion of 1492, Saint-Jean-de-Luz on France's Côte Basque became a common staging post for Jews fleeing Iberia, who traveled on from there to Venice, Tunis, Istanbul, and other places.[1] At some time in the spring of 1608, Samuel and Joseph Pallache followed the well-established route from Saint-Jean-de-Luz to Amsterdam, a powerful magnet for exiles, where the first Jewish congregations were then starting to take shape.[2] Journeys to the Netherlands were facilitated by the contacts of the great converso trading families of Saint-Jean-de-Luz with Jews in Amsterdam.[3] These conversos had done much to create the Dutch commercial network of which Saint-Jean-de-Luz was a part: they transported high-quality Castilian wool to French Atlantic ports, where it was traded for merchandise unloaded from Dutch ships, the boom in this trade allowing for a rapid growth in Portuguese Jewish communities in southwestern France and guaranteeing the presence of conversos with Dutch connections.[4]

As well as conversos, French towns like Saint-Jean-de-Luz also contained significant numbers of moriscos after their expulsion from Spain in 1609. Indeed, the expulsion of the moriscos created further trading opportunities for the conversos and provided them with openings for more illicit kinds of trafficking. Legal regulations prevented moriscos from taking precious metals, jewels, or letters of credit out of Spain, and some moriscos sought to subvert these restrictions by smuggling wealth over the border. The converso traders, with their wide experience of fraudulent transactions, became the ideal agents to assist the moriscos in these clandestine undertakings, and archives at Simancas show that Jews and moriscos often helped one another obtain papers or export money from Spain.[5] Further evidence of such dealings is provided by a series of letters sent to Philip III from Saint-Jean-de-Luz between February and June 1612 by an agent named Lorenzo Suárez. Suárez informed the king about the movements of moriscos in the south of France, telling him that many of them had used false passes to reenter Spain and transfer wealth out of the country, often with the assistance of Jewish financiers in cities like Tunis and Istanbul.[6]

On April 8, 1608, shortly after arriving in Amsterdam, Samuel applied for Dutch passports for himself and his brother Joseph. His application to the States General makes mention neither of the years the Pallaches had previously spent in Spain nor of their attempts to find permanent posts for themselves there. It simply describes the brothers as two Jews "from Fez in Barbary" who wished to leave Morocco and settle in Holland because of the wars and domestic uncertainty.[7] The passports were granted, but were then withdrawn two weeks later for reasons that are unknown, but that may have had something to do with their recent Spanish past. The Pallaches were forced to return to Morocco at this stage. In the event, however, this proved to be only a minor setback for Samuel, who had already accumulated enough contacts and experience during his brief time in Amsterdam to be able to return the following year as an official envoy of Sultan Muley Zaydan.[8]

It is possible to add some detail to what is known of Samuel's first months in Amsterdam thanks, firstly, to a declaration made before the Dutch notary Willem Benninck on June 21, 1617, more than a year after Samuel's death. The statement was signed by a group of Portuguese merchants led by Duarte Fernandes, a prominent member of the Jewish community, who is thought to have assisted Samuel in the months after his arrival in the city. Fernandes and the other merchants declared, at Joseph Pallache's request, that the Pallache brothers had arrived in Amsterdam about ten years earlier and that they had possessed a considerable amount of money at that time. The merchants stated that the Pallaches had chartered a ship a few months after their arrival, which was loaded with goods to be sold in Morocco, and that they had intended to use the same ship to bring their wives, children, and personal effects back to Amsterdam.

Samuel Pallache commanded the ship, which sailed to Tétouan and then on to Safi, where it was seized by pirates, who stole all his personal possessions, including gold, amber, and many household items. Samuel had thus returned to Amsterdam without any personal property whatsoever and had then devoted himself exclusively to the loyal and disinterested service of his master the sultan, without ever indulging in personal business of any kind.[9] (This statement was made at a time when serious accusations of corruption were being leveled at the Pallache family.)

This version of events is at least partly confirmed by other sources. Coy, a Dutch agent in Morocco, stated in a letter to the States General in 1608 that Samuel Pallache had arrived in Safi from Holland a few days earlier and had then sailed for Tétouan with the intention of collecting his wife and children and sailing back with them to Amsterdam. From this and other clues, it is possible to deduce that Tétouan must have been the Pallaches' habitual place of residence in Morocco at this time, but Pallache had other business there too. In Tétouan, he spoke to the governor of the city, the *muqaddam* Ahmad al-Naqsis, who had declared himself independent of Muley al-Shaykh and was now seeking an alliance with al-Shaykh's brother, and Pallache's master, Muley Zaydan.[10] Samuel was given the task of carrying a message from al-Naqsis to Zaydan in Marrakech, and he took advantage of this interview with Zaydan to impress the sultan with his supposed expertise in Dutch affairs.[11] In fact, Pallache managed to give such an idea of the importance and prosperity of the Dutch Republic, and of his own contacts and reputation there, that Zaydan decided to send him to Amsterdam as his agent.[12] Pallache traveled back to Amsterdam armed with a letter from Zaydan to Maurice of Nassau, the prince of Orange. "It is well known that embassies bring greatness to empires, in spite of the difference in the matter of religion. . . . The servant of our illustrious house, who is zealously managing its interests, . . . the *dhimmi* Samuel Pallache, will soon reach you if God is willing," Zaydan wrote to the prince.[13] Samuel's attempts at self-advancement, unsuccessful for so long in Spain, had finally been rewarded with an official post in the service of the Moroccan sultan.

The Pallaches must have returned to Amsterdam a short time later. By February 1609, Samuel was already at work as Zaydan's agent, requesting three warships from the States General with which he could transport troops and weapons to the Moroccan sultan. The States General responded by sending two ships under the command of Wolfert Hermansz, and Samuel himself traveled on one of these ships with merchandise supplied by a consortium of Amsterdam merchants.[14] The arrangement was that Samuel would return from Morocco with payment for the goods, but when he went back to Holland in August, accompanied by the Moroccan ambassador Hammu ben Bashir, it seems that he failed to pay the businessmen the amounts originally promised. As a result, Pallache found himself involved in the first of his many lawsuits and was officially declared bankrupt, although this seems to have had little effect on the subsequent development of his vertiginous business career.

BY TRAVELING TO AMSTERDAM, Samuel Pallache had gone to one of an increasing number of European cities that had recently started to guarantee freedom of religious worship for Jews and even to encourage the establishment of Jewish communities.[15] These developments were directly related to the radical transformation in European culture that had followed the great religious and political upheavals of the late sixteenth century. The realization by both Catholics and Protestants that their struggles had ended in deadlock without a clear-cut victory for either side had given rise to a radically new political and intellectual climate from about 1570 on. A long spiritual and intellectual crisis created an atmosphere of profound skepticism, verging on atheism, and it was this crisis and the new modes of political and economic behavior that accompanied it that, in the view of scholars like Jonathan Israel, permitted the reappearance of Jews in Europe and allowed them to develop a new role for themselves in European society.[16]

In 1579, Holland had adhered to the Union of Utrecht, which forbade persecution for religious reasons, and freedom of conscience was guaranteed within the territories of the United Provinces so long as religious worship was conducted privately. In public, however, the only permissible form of worship remained that of the dominant church. Very few cities in the United Provinces extended official tolerance to cover Jewish religious practice, and the first members of the so-called "Portuguese nation" to settle in Amsterdam were forced to do so as nominal Christians.[17]

But where had most of the so-called "Portuguese" of Amsterdam come from, and why? To answer this question, we must look briefly at the history of the city of Antwerp.

Antwerp had emerged and developed as a prosperous port in the late fifteenth century as a consequence of the establishment of new trade routes to the New World and the East. Its geographical position and political circumstances allowed it to become the commercial capital of northern Europe. The Spanish Habsburg emperor Charles V upheld the city's ancient privileges, and its burgomasters were able to guarantee investment security, low taxes, and civil rights for foreign merchants, who soon came to form veritable colonies within the city. One such colony consisted of Portuguese Jewish conversos, also known as *gente de la nación* or *la nación portuguesa* in contemporary Spanish documents. These conversos enjoyed freedom from inquisitorial vigilance so long as they were outwardly Christians.

Things changed in the years after the Dutch revolt. First, the sack of Antwerp in 1576 caused many Portuguese merchants to flee for Cologne and other cities, although most of them eventually returned. Then Antwerp adhered to the Republic of the Seven United Provinces in 1577, but it was captured by the Spaniards in 1585, and this provoked a spectacular migratory wave of Protestants of various denominations toward the northern provinces. This exodus had a debilitating effect on the economic life of the city. Initially, most members of the "Portuguese nation" stayed behind in Antwerp, regarding themselves as less of a target for the Inquisition than Protestants. However, the naval blockade imposed on Antwerp by the Dutch Republic in 1595 placed a stranglehold on the economic life of the port and led to the eventual emigration of most of its Portuguese Jewish businessmen. The majority of them moved on to other ports, such as Hamburg, Emden, and Rouen, and continued to operate from there.

However, the city of Amsterdam was now starting to exert a powerful influence on international commerce, especially after the signing of a twelve-year truce between Spain and the Dutch Republic in 1609, and the converso merchants increasingly adopted that city as their main center of operations. From Amsterdam, they set about trading with the Iberian Peninsula and Brazil, and they soon established themselves in several important branches of foreign and industrial trade, such as the cutting of precious stones. The truce paved the way for an extraordinary boom in Dutch commerce, and the maintenance of the Antwerp blockade allowed merchants in the northern provinces to assume the role of commercial intermediaries and to benefit from the trade in silver from the Americas. Fraud and smuggling on a massive scale were also practiced assiduously, and Portuguese merchants were often associated with these, especially with the entry of false coinage and the movement of silver through France.[18] The Amsterdam community was further boosted by the emigration of Jewish merchants directly from Portugal, and they were joined by Jews from as far afield as France, Italy, the Levant, and North Africa. Overseas immigration to the city started in the 1590s and increased particularly after 1605, when the Portuguese Inquisition renewed its persecution of "New Christians."[19] Many of these New Christians were able to return to the faith of their ancestors in Amsterdam, thus becoming "New Jews."[20]

As a religious community, Amsterdam Jews were forced to proceed very cautiously, and some time had to pass before they were to gain legal recognition. However, the Jews' commercial activities assumed great importance for Amsterdam, and it was largely for this reason that their legal existence gradually ceased to be called into question. In about 1603, the municipal authorities of Amsterdam seem to have granted the small nucleus of Hispano-Portuguese businessmen the possibility of practicing their Jewish faith, but only on condition that religious ceremonies be conducted in private. The first congregation, Beth Jacob (House of Jacob), began to meet in 1603 at the home of a Portuguese Jew called Jacob Tirado. The second, the Neve Salom community, dated from somewhere between 1608 and 1610.[21] Some of the most committed members of this community seem to have sought permission in about 1612 to build a public synagogue, but the request led to strenuous Calvinist protests, and the city authorities decreed a halt to the building works. Nonetheless, it seems likely that the building, situated close to where the church of Moses and Aaron stands today, was used as a synagogue by the Neve Salom community after 1612.[22]

The Jewish community flourished between 1612 and 1675, as can be seen from the number of different congregations formed then. These were established by "New Jews" who had been prevented from practicing their religion publicly for generations, and they were often unclear about rites and procedures. As a result of this, they found themselves faced with the need to attract qualified rabbis and learned advisers from other parts of the world. Their main point of reference was Venice, but to a lesser extent, they also drew on Fez and the Ottoman domains.[23] The first rabbi of Neve Salom seems to have been Juda Vega, who was brought to Amsterdam from somewhere in the Ottoman empire, and between 1616 and 1622, the Neve Salom rabbi was Isaac Uziel of Fez.[24] Another difficulty the Jews faced was that of finding a place to bury their dead. Initially, the Jewish communities were obliged to carry out burials in Groet, near Alkmaar. They made two unsuccessful requests for a more suitable site, and permission was eventually granted in 1614, when they were allowed to purchase land in the village called Ouderkerk aan de Amstel, just outside the city. The Ouderkerk cemetery was to be Samuel Pallache's final resting place when he died in 1616.

After the early seventeenth century, the Jewish community started to define its ethnic limits more clearly and forged an increasingly Portuguese identity for itself. But it is worth bearing in mind that before 1614, the Amsterdam community was not an exclusively Portuguese one. The most important manifestation of the gradual move toward the definition of a distinctly Portuguese identity was the establishment of the Santa Companhia de dotar orphas e donzelas pobres (Holy Society for Endowing Orphans and Poor Young Ladies), known as the Dotar. This society, which still exists today, was founded with the aim of assisting poor orphans and brides from all those places in Europe where peoples of the "Portuguese nation" were to be found.[25] As the seventeenth century went on, relations within the Portuguese Jewish community became closer and more tightly knit, as can be seen from records of their marriages and the makeup of their commercial networks.[26] In Bodian's view, however, the Amsterdam community would have had little difficulty in integrating older Sephardic Jews, that is, members of communities of Spanish or Portuguese origin that had been settled for over a century in various parts of the Mediterranean basin. This, obviously, was the world to which the Pallaches belonged.[27]

It is interesting to note that numbers of morisco exiles from Spain were also arriving in Amsterdam at the time of Samuel Pallache's early settlement there. The *Annales* of Frans van Dusseldorp (1566–1615), a Dutch historian with broadly pro-Spanish sympathies, contain a very interesting passage on the moriscos' arrival after their expulsion in 1609–10: "Some of them [the moriscos] made their way immediately to Amsterdam, a city in which they were conceded a meeting place [in Latin, *synagoga*]. The most outstanding heretics of that community presented themselves there, after being circumcised. To such an extent were Calvinism and Islam seen to be agreeable to one another."[28] Van Dusseldorp is not currently regarded as a credible historian, but there is other evidence to support what he says about the arrival of moriscos in Amsterdam.[29] The duke of Medina Sidonia warned Philip III in 1609 about the warm welcome that moriscos were receiving from the Dutch and informed him that great numbers of them were fleeing for Holland.[30] Once there, some moriscos are even known to have tried to convert to Judaism. Lorenzo Escudero, a morisco musician and comedian from Andalusia, traveled to Amsterdam in the mid seventeenth century and made it known that he wished to convert to the Jewish faith, but community leaders refused to admit him as a member.[31]

JOSHUA AND MOSES PALLACHE

Before continuing with Samuel Pallache's return journey to Amsterdam in 1609, we should not lose sight of other members of the Pallache family at this time. Samuel's nephews Joshua and Moses were involved in events that reveal a great deal about the family's general aims and shed light on the interesting question of Samuel's relations with Jewish communities in the Dutch Republic.

In July 1609, Joseph Pallache's son Joshua presented himself at the Brussels home of the marquis of Guadaleste, the Spanish ambassador to Flanders, saying that he possessed information that he wished to pass on to the Spanish king. By way of introducing himself, Joshua Pallache said that he had traveled to Madrid in 1607 with the intention of converting to Christianity, but that his father and uncle (Samuel) had prevented him from doing so. Joshua said that the pair of them had forced him to leave Spain with them via Bayonne, a port from which the Pallaches had sailed on to Amsterdam. He also claimed that both his father and uncle had been so pleased with life in Amsterdam that they had decided to leave Fez and settle there permanently. He informed the Spaniards that the Pallaches had returned to Tétouan in Morocco to collect their belongings, and that Samuel had obtained an interview with the *muqaddam*, Ahmad al-Naqsis. Joshua offered the Spanish ambassador details, provided by his uncle Samuel, of al-Naqsis's plans to capture Ceuta and ally himself with Muley Zaydan in order to make a joint attack on the town of Larache. In a further effort to ingratiate himself and prove the sincerity of his intentions, Joshua also provided the names of some converted Jews he knew to be living in Spain, Portugal, and Holland, who he claimed were practicing Judaizers. Joshua said that he would be able to name many more such Jews if the Spaniards decided to employ him on a regular basis.[32]

Joshua's behavior on this occasion was not unprecedented. It was relatively common for conversos or others wishing to be reconciled to the Catholic Church to inform on former friends and colleagues as proof of their sincerity. The most striking case is perhaps that of Hector Mendes Bravo, who at around this time provided the Lisbon Inquisition with the names of 119 Portuguese Judaizers living in Holland.[33] What is perhaps more surprising about Joshua's offer is that he placed particular stress in his report on the name of Duarte Fernandes, the merchant who had been instrumental in assisting the Pallache family in Amsterdam. Duarte Fernandes was a known acquaintance of Samuel Pallache throughout his years in the Dutch Republic, and, as we have seen, he testified in favor of the Pallaches at Joseph's request after Samuel's death.[34]

Joshua did not mention in his statement the reason for his departure from Spain (i.e., the Pallaches' problems with the Inquisition), and he was at pains to portray his brother Isaac and himself as innocent victims of their father and uncle, whom he accused of forcing them out of Spain to prevent them from converting to the Christian faith. The truth of the matter, as we have already seen, is that Samuel and Joseph had been trying to use Isaac's conversion as a means of staying in Spain. This is not the only surviving document in which Pallache family members appear to distance themselves from one another in their written statements, but it seems probable that the Pallaches were in fact working as a team on this and other similar occasions. The most likely explanation for Joshua's approach to a Spanish diplomat is that the family wanted to establish a bridgehead in Spain by placing one or two of its members there. They were apparently unconcerned that this required Joshua to pretend that he had been rejected by his own father and uncle. A careful reading of Guadaleste's report on Joshua's offer, sent to Philip III, allows us to conclude that Joshua was almost certainly following his uncle Samuel's instructions. Joshua had insisted that "it would be very worthwhile to take measures to bring his uncle to Spain and reveal great secret deals," by which he referred to a treaty of cooperation that the Dutch had started to negotiate with Muley Zaydan. Joshua said that "his uncle had negotiated with the states of Holland, that whenever the Moorish king needed armed assistance against Spain, he would be given warships with all that was necessary [for their use]." He also said "that to be able better to negotiate the coming to Spain of his uncle Samuel Pallache, it would be convenient to have it published that he is going to La Rochelle, where he conducts business with merchants known to him since he was in Fez." These do not sound like the words of a man no longer on speaking terms with his uncle. In fact, Joshua's overtures to Guadaleste make it easier to understand a comment made by the French ambassador in Madrid, Monsieur Descartes, when he reported on the Pallache brothers' journey to Amsterdam that "after traveling to the Netherlands, one of them has gone from there to the king of Marrakech with the terms they have agreed on and the other has gone to the archduke, from where he sent one of his sons to report on what has been negotiated with the lords of the States General," adding that the Pallaches were "cheating one side and the other for their own benefit."[35]

Furthermore, it should perhaps be mentioned that Joshua does not appear ever to have become a Christian convert, despite his alleged enthusiasm at the time of his approach to the marquis of Guadaleste. He is never spoken of as a Christian throughout his entire career, and by 1640, he had become a tax official of the sultan of Morocco in Safi, where he lived until his death in 1656. Of Joseph Pallache's other sons, the same can be said of Moses, who worked alongside his uncle Samuel for several years, and then as an interpreter to Muley Zaydan. Joseph's oldest son, Isaac, did later become a Protestant, but in the circumstances explained in the final chapter of this book. As in so many Fez Jewish families, there was variation of religious observance among the Pallaches. It seems likely that offers of religious conversion, whether followed up or not, were simply part of a wider strategy of positioning family members in various national territories. Joshua's sudden offer of secret information to the Spaniards was almost certainly another element in this strategy.

In the very same autumn of 1609 in which Joshua was sounding out the marquis of Guadaleste, Moses Pallache had traveled to Paris, where he obtained an interview with the French king on the pretext that he had served the French in Flanders and had come to request his pay. Descartes wrote from Madrid that he had been told of Moses' visit by someone who had spoken with Moses in Paris. The French ambassador had also been informed that, as we have seen, Moses' father and uncle had traveled to Holland to negotiate with the States General, and then returned to Muley Zaydan in Morocco. According to Descartes, Moses Pallache had traveled from Paris back to Amsterdam and then made a secret journey to Madrid in order to give the Spaniards details of the deal being negotiated between the Dutch and the Moroccans. (This was exactly what Joshua had offered to do for the marquis of Guadaleste.) Descartes claimed that Moses had reported that the deal committed Holland to assisting the sultan of Morocco with a hundred warships for an attack on Spain, where a great uprising was soon to take place.[36] We now know that the Dutch had not in fact committed themselves to any such deal, but if Moses Pallache said in Madrid what Descartes claims he did, the impact of his words would have been considerable: it was in this year, 1609, that the moriscos began to be expelled from Spain, and the moriscos of Valencia had already risen in arms as a result. According to Descartes, Moses claimed to have traveled to Madrid without the knowledge of his father and uncle in Amsterdam, but the Frenchman was unsure whether to believe him: "I do not know if the other two [Pallaches] who he says have stayed there [in Holland] are ignorant of his journey as he claims, or if they are party to it and are trying to take advantage of all sides as is common with them."

Like Descartes, we find it hard to believe that Moses was acting behind the backs of his father and uncle. It is not hard to detect Samuel's influence on Moses' actions as well as Joshua's. Both nephews claimed to be acting without their uncle's knowledge, but both volunteered to provide information on dealings between the Dutch Republic and Morocco that could only have been provided by Samuel himself, and Joshua had even gone so far as to offer his uncle's services openly to the Spaniards. It is difficult to avoid the conclusion that the Pallaches were working together. Dissimulation was clearly an important part of a family strategy that also involved the deliberate diversification of its members on all sides of religious and political frontiers.

This brings us on to the interesting question of the true extent of Samuel Pallache's involvement and integration in the Jewish community of Amsterdam. It has generally been assumed that Samuel was a leading member of the Amsterdam community, and that he was known as an extremely pious man, touching whose faith there was never any doubt. Claims have often been made that the Pallaches helped to create the Neve Salom community, although their participation in the start of this new congregation has never been firmly established. But how active a Jew was Pallache, and how close was he to other Jews in Amsterdam?

On the one hand, it is certainly true that the oldest death register of the Jewish communities of Amsterdam, the *Livro de Beth Haim do Kahal Kados de Bet Yahacob*, mentions Samuel Pallache on several occasions and speaks of the siting of his grave. He is also mentioned in relation to funeral vows (*promesas no emterro*) of community members, a context in which he is always described as *haham*, or "reverend," showing that he almost certainly belonged to the Neve Salom community and that it recognized his level of religious instruction.[37] The fact that the community acquired his *seffarim*, or scrolls of the Law, after his death also seems to point to a degree of religious affinity between Pallache and the congregation.[38] In addition, we know of the relationship between Pallache and the active Duarte Fernandes, and of his links with Rabbi Isaac Uziel from Fez, although Uziel did not arrive in Amsterdam until 1615.[39]

On the other hand, there are important reasons for believing that

Samuel Pallache was never fully integrated into the predominantly Portuguese Jewish community. Throughout his business career, Pallache does not ever seem to have worked with the Portuguese, but only with non-Jewish businessmen and sailors. When he needed money, he would obtain loans from Dutchmen and not from members of "the Portuguese nation." When forced to send for a doctor for one of his children, he is known to have turned to Dutch rather than Jewish practitioners.[40] In addition, it seems significant that no male member of the Pallache family ever married a woman from the Amsterdam Jewish community.[41] (Isaac Pallache was at one time engaged to be married to Catirina or Catalina Lopes, the daughter of Jerónimo Lopes, but the engagement was later broken off and Catirina married another man, at which point Isaac Pallache sought compensation for the loss of the bridal dowry.)[42] One factor that was the cause of a purely physical rift between Pallache and the Portuguese of Amsterdam was the fact that from 1611 on, he was obliged, as a foreign agent, to live in The Hague, site of the States General.[43] There was no Jewish community in The Hague, and Pallache's place of residence and the frequency of his travels to Morocco and elsewhere would have made it difficult for him to participate fully in the life of the Amsterdam community after that date.

One intriguing story that seems to provide clues to an understanding of this issue of the relations between the Pallaches and the Jews of Amsterdam is that of the denunciation made by Isaac Pallache, another of Samuel's nephews, to the authorities in Brussels of Henrique Garces, an Antwerp merchant of Portuguese origin, in 1610. Isaac informed the authorities that Garces, though baptized, was in fact a practicing Jew, and went on to extend his denunciation to include a number of other Portuguese merchants based in Amsterdam. He declared, for example, that he had seen Simao de Mercado, a leading member of the Portuguese community, in the synagogue that met at the home of Guines Lopes, alias Jacob Tirado, the eponymous founder of the first Amsterdam synagogue. As a result of Isaac Pallache's information, Mercado was brought to trial in Antwerp, where Isaac himself gave evidence to support his claims.[44] The story is worth considering in detail.

ISAAC PALLACHE'S LAWSUIT

Isaac Pallache's denunciation had its origin in an unsuccessful legal action that he brought against Henrique Garces/Garcez in Brussels in July 1610.[45]

Records of the case, which occupy a thick file in Castilian and Portuguese, describe Isaac as a *judío de Fez* and Garces as a forty-three-year-old Portuguese merchant from Oporto, then living in the city of Antwerp. Henrique Garces was a nephew and brother-in-law of Duarte Fernandes and one of the grandparents of the philosopher Baruch Spinoza. He had settled in Amsterdam in about 1605, but is known to have stayed aloof from Jewish community life, to such an extent that after his death in 1619, he had to be circumcised in order to meet the requirements for burial in the Ouderkerk cemetery.[46] Isaac accused Garces of taking illegal possession of some jewels that Garces had been given to sell in Antwerp by Isaac's father Joseph. Though he was later forced to change his story, Garces initially denied all knowledge of these jewels, which were listed as: ambergris in stones of between forty and sixty ounces; a batch of balas rubies,[47] the biggest of up to forty and the smallest of up to twenty ounces; a large amount of gold; some rings; diamond jewelry with crests, and a number of loose, unmounted diamonds of up to three or four carats. Antwerp was then one of the main centers of the European jewel trade, and Jewish merchants were frequently involved in the sale of jewels and diamonds at European and Muslim courts. As we have already seen in Chapter 1, Joseph and Samuel Pallache's first mission to Spain involved the purchase of precious stones, and it seems likely that they continued to trade in them when living in the Netherlands. In fact, we happen to know from a report written by the merchant Jorge de Henin, a secret Spanish agent at the court of Muley Zaydan, that Pallache took diamonds and rubies with him for trading purposes when he made his second journey to the Dutch Republic with the new Moroccan ambassador in 1610.

Garces's legal representative was his brother-in-law and cousin Juan Mendes Henriques. Relations between Isaac Pallache and Mendes became strained to breaking point as the case went on. At one point, Isaac accused Mendes of repeated slander against him and said that when they had met in Brussels, in "an open and public street," "he spoke and threatened me in this way, taking the ends of my beard in his hand, calling me a traitor, a foul Jewish dog, saying I will have to kill you and stab you sixty times with my own hands, for you are a traitor."[48] Isaac demanded that justice be done, saying that amends should be made for Mendes's attack on his person. Isaac had other complaints too. He said that, according to what he had been told by another Portuguese merchant, Cristóbal Pinto, Henrique Garces had been forewarned of the case about to be brought against him. Knowing that his house was due to be searched, Garces had thus had time to remove all incriminating objects from it, "and he left none of these things in his house, and that is the truth, and [he took away] books and papers too." Isaac also took advantage of the case to accuse Garces of being a traitor to his God and to his king: he said Garces had worked for the king of Barbary, who was a great enemy of Spain, and against the interests of the Catholic Church, despite calling himself a Christian. Portuguese conversos, Isaac said, "should not be regarded as neighbors and Catholics, since they are not in these states for any reason other than their own interest and the profit they gain from being here, and then they go to Holland where they all profess another religious law with all those of their nation . . . or they go to the ghetto of Venice, and those who do this blaspheme more in the Faith than those of us who are Jews by birth because we know nothing of any religion that is not our own . . . whereas they, who were born in the Christian religion, are those who speak evil of it as much as they want or worse . . . I beg Your Highness to take note of the Christianity that these Portuguese do so publicly proclaim." He further claimed that Garces was married to a woman (the daughter of Duarte Fernandes) who had been born in Lisbon, baptized eight days later, and then taken by her parents to Venice, where the whole family adopted Jewish professions and names. As further proof of his animosity toward the Portuguese, Isaac launched accusations against another enemy he alleged to have slandered him, a friar by the name of Fray Martín del Spiritu Santo.[49] He said that he possessed letters written to this friar from an uncle of his that proved that Fray Martín had been prior of the Misericordia in Lisbon for thirty years "and now is a declared Jew who openly shows himself to be one in Amsterdam, and only God knows what each one prays." Juan Mendes, defending his cousin Garces, said that he was no traitor nor enemy to His Catholic Majesty the king of Spain, "for they [the Portuguese merchants] were enemies of those from Barbary and the infidels [i.e., Muslims], and all the more so for having lost and for losing every day their merchandise to those people's pirates," and that "the said Jews and infidels of Barbary would never have wanted to trust for such important business a Catholic and a Christian man like the said Henrique Garces."

Faced with these contradictory accounts, the Brussels authorities requested the testimony of several Portuguese merchants, all of whom said that they knew nothing of Garces ever having sold jewelry, nor of his having played any part in the dealings of which he was accused. They knew

Isaac by sight as "a son of one of the Barbarians [i.e., North Africans] in Amsterdam called Pallaches." If the evidence of these merchants is anything to go by, there was little love lost between these Barbary Jews, or *judíos de nación*, and the Portuguese conversos. One such converso, an inhabitant of Antwerp by the name of Emanuel Lopez Perrera, stated that he had been told by several people that Isaac was disobedient and rebellious toward his father Joseph, and that due to his bad behavior, he had at one time been locked up by Joseph in a cell in the castle of Purmerend near Amsterdam.[50]

Nevertheless, Garces was forced to modify his story when Isaac threatened to produce letters Garces had written to his uncle Samuel. Garces had addressed these letters to "Manuel Díaz," a false name, instead of Samuel Pallache,[51] and Isaac insinuated that the letters contained names and facts in cipher that were relevant to the case. He also referred to other letters written to Duarte Fernandes in which the rubies were mentioned, and his threats had their desired effect. Garces was compelled to acknowledge that he did indeed know Samuel Pallache, and he gave his version of the story behind the letters written in cipher. He said that while in Amsterdam, he had gone to see the newly arrived ambassador of Barbary [i.e., Morocco], along with many other people who were moved by curiosity (the Moroccan ambassador and his retinue would certainly have constituted an exotic spectacle), and that while there, he had been introduced to the Pallache brothers and invited by them to dine at the ambassador's table. He had spent the night in the same inn as the Pallaches, and the following day, he had made the journey from Amsterdam to The Hague in Samuel Pallache's company. On separating from Samuel and continuing his journey homeward to Antwerp, Garces had promised that he would write to Pallache and inform him of his safe arrival. This he had duly done, as an act of courtesy, and did not therefore regard it as an offense, although he had been writing to a known Jew and Barbarian. When asked why he had addressed Samuel Pallache as Manuel Díaz, and why he had used words in cipher, Garces found himself at loss for an answer. He eventually explained that as a converted Jew, he had not wanted to be seen having dealings with professing Jews. He also admitted that he had once possessed a number of rubies, but claimed he had been given them by Duarte Fernandes to sell in Antwerp and had returned them when he had not managed to get the price Fernandes wanted for them. Garces further admitted that it was true that his wife, out of fright, had removed all his accounts books from their home just before his case was heard. The books were presented at the trial, although the entries for June and July had yet to be drawn up.

The case seems to have been resolved with the rejection of all of Isaac Pallache's accusations.[52] It is difficult to arrive at a clear understanding of this complex affair and the personal motives behind it. On the one hand, there can be no doubt that Henrique Garces knew Samuel Pallache, and it seems quite likely that Garces might have taken it upon himself to sell jewelry for Samuel in Antwerp. At the same time, it is not easy to understand Isaac Pallache's reasons for bringing his lawsuit. Were his denunciations made at his uncle Samuel's instigation, or did he make them, as the converso merchants claimed, because he had fallen out with Garces and his own father Joseph and wanted to ruin their business dealings? Isaac made a point of declaring: "I have left my parents and I have no one to turn to other than Your Most Holy Highness," but this is the same kind of rhetoric that had been used by Joshua and Moses when touting for patrons. Such statements may have been no more than another element in the Pallache strategy, designed by Samuel and Joseph to obtain the assistance of the Spanish authorities in defense of their interests against Henrique Garces, who may well have held on to some merchandise. Against this interpretation, which seems to be the most plausible one, stands the simple if surprising fact that Henrique Garces was one of the merchants who declared in favor of Samuel Pallache in 1617 in the notarial document mentioned above. Isaac certainly went to great lengths in this case and when he failed to win it, he proceeded to denounce as practicing Jews a number of other Portuguese merchants he had known in Amsterdam.

Although it seems likely that the complete truth of this affair will always be hard to come by, it is in fact possible to pick holes in some of Herique Garces's testimony as a result of evidence given at the Lisbon inquisitorial trial of Henrique's brother Paulo several years later. Statements made at this trial enable us to say that when Henrique Garces traveled to The Hague to see the Moroccan ambassador in 1610, he was not making the trip out of mere curiosity, as he later claimed. Neither had his meeting with the Pallaches on that occasion been purely accidental. As nephews of Duarte Fernandes, the Garces brothers had in fact been in contact with Samuel Pallache from the very moment of his first arrival in the Netherlands.

Paulo Garces appeared voluntarily before the Lisbon Inquisition in

April 1620 with the aim of being reconciled to the Catholic Church and readmitted to its bosom.[53] He stated that he was twenty-two years of age and a native of Oporto. He explained his decision to come before the Holy Office by saying that while living in Flanders, he had been illuminated by God and had decided to convert and return to Portugal. He had subsequently sailed to Cádiz, from there to Seville, and then on to Lisbon to present himself before the tribunal. He related the story of his life and willingly submitted himself to interrogation by the Inquisitors: he had been born in Oporto and at the age of six had been sent by his mother to Amsterdam to be brought up as a Jew at the home of his mother's brother, Duarte Fernandes. Shortly after arriving, he had been circumcised by the "Levantine" rabbi Joseph Pardo at the House of Jacob synagogue and given the new name Abraham Garces. He then studied at the school of the rabbi Joseph Coén (*sic*), of Ottoman origin, who gave him instruction in Spanish on the law of Moses and also taught him Hebrew. He had learnt the Psalms in both Hebrew and Spanish. He also learnt to read and write Portuguese and Dutch, a tongue that he mastered rapidly. Paulo Garces told the inquisitors that when "the ambassador" Pallache had arrived from Barbary, his uncle Duarte Fernandes had placed Paulo with Pallache to help him with the Flemish language. Moreover, "nine or ten years ago," that is, in about 1610, when Paulo was a young boy of about twelve years of age, his uncle Duarte Fernandes had sent him to Barbary with the sultan's ambassador. This man's name was given as "Joseph Pallache" by Paulo Garces, but from the dates and Paulo's account of the mission can only have been Joseph's brother Samuel. Paulo accompanied "the ambassador" for two or three months in Mogador, Safi, and Santa Cruz [Agadir] and then returned to Holland on the same ship as Pallache: "He went with the said ambassador to read the letters in Flemish into Spanish or Portuguese, as in effect he had done in the presence of Muley Zidan, and the said letters were mostly about peace and business that the states of Flanders had with the sultan." Paulo said that the ship on which they traveled carried great quantities of muskets, munitions, and gunpowder and that they brought back with them money in the form of gold. Muley Zaydan, noticing that Paulo was a bright and very useful boy, had offered him the chance to remain at his court in Morocco, but Paulo rejected the proposition. It is pleasant to imagine Samuel Pallache accompanied by this clever boy, almost a child, acting as his personal interpreter. What is also interesting is that these events must have occurred at about the same time that Isaac Pallache was denouncing Paulo's brother Henrique in Brussels, and that the latter was claiming never to have had any contact whatsoever with the Pallache family.

The inquisitors asked Paulo if he knew any Latin, always a subject of great interest to them. Garces told them again "that he knows no Latin, but speaks Flemish very well and Portuguese better, and he can also read and write Portuguese, which he learnt to do in Flanders at the office of his uncle Duarte Fernandes, and that he can also speak French and English." He spoke of journeys he had made to London and Hamburg on business. He described in great detail how and when he had prayed in the synagogue as a child, and how he had been dressed for this, what fasts he kept, what he ate, what feasts he observed, and so on. But above all, Paulo Garces supplied the inquisitors with information about some ninety Portuguese Jews in Amsterdam, giving their names and those of their wives and children, as well as their professions and the family relationships between them. There are some very well-known surnames on Paulo Garces's list, such as Osorio, Alvares Mello, Esteves, Gomes de Acosta, and Montalto, and it occupies page after page of inquisitorial records. Paulo also spoke of his older brother "Luis Garces," who he said was married to Gracia Henriques. It is impossible to be sure if this brother is the same person as Henrique Garces, who was certainly married to a woman from the Henriques family, or whether we are dealing with two different brothers.

Paulo's freely volunteered gift of information is in many ways reminiscent of Joshua Pallache's approach to the marquis of Guadaleste. As in that case, and in Isaac Pallache's lawsuit, here, too, it is impossible to distinguish dissembling and strategy from honest intent. Even if Paulo Garces's case was designed for strategic personal benefit or that of his family (which is the hypothesis we are inclined to believe), it is not easy to see how his denunciations could have seriously threatened anyone in the Amsterdam community. After all, what harm could come to an Amsterdam Jew as a result of his name being known to the Portuguese Inquisition? Paulo's denunciation may have been a less "treacherous," or less portentous, act than it now seems. It may simply have been that Duarte Fernandes needed an agent in Lisbon and had decided to install the polyglot Paulo in that city. Whatever the explanation, we can be sure that all these decisions will have been weighed up and mulled over at great length. They were maneuvers too complex and devious, too wrapped up in baroque spirals of deliberation, for us ever to be fully confident of grasping their true meaning.

However, one conclusion can be confidently drawn from these documents. Despite the known Pallache connections with Duarte Fernandes and his Garces nephews, the "Barbary Jewish" Pallaches seem to have had rather less in common with the Portuguese conversos and New Jews than we might at first expect. Neither kinship nor business ties appear to have brought them very close together, and it seems that there was a great deal of mistrust and disagreement between them. As we have already suggested, it is surely significant that neither Samuel nor any of his heirs were ever to marry into any of the great trading families of "the Portuguese nation."

BUSINESS AND DIPLOMACY, 1609–1614

Once he had gained the confidence of Muley Zaydan, Samuel Pallache became deeply involved in Moroccan diplomatic activity. As we have seen, he accompanied the Moroccan ambassador Hammu ben Bashir to the Dutch Republic in 1609, and a letter from Zaydan to the States General early that year refers to Pallache as "our servant and agent."[54] The letter makes it clear that Bashir was Zaydan's *safîr*,[55] or ambassador, and Pallache his interpreter. These roles are confirmed by a letter written by Ralph Winwood, an English agent in Holland, dated October 7, 1609, which gives notice of the arrival of Bashir, accompanied by "a trucheman [interpreter], a Jew, who treates in Spanish."[56] Bashir and Pallache had been given the task of negotiating a treaty of commercial and military cooperation with the Dutch[57] that would guarantee freedom of trade between the two countries and promote military collaboration against Spain, with the moriscos included as an interested party under the second of these headings.[58]

The terms of the treaty were negotiated by Bashir and the man who replaced him as ambassador in June 1610, Ahmad ben Abdallah al-Hayti al-Maruni. Al-Maruni is referred to as "Ahmed Elhaitia Biscaino" in Spanish records and is thought to have been a converso or renegade of Spanish origin of Marrón, in Cantabria.[59] Samuel Pallache was also a member of the al-Maruni embassy, which lasted until the treaty was signed in January 1611.[60] Indeed, he is thought to have played a more important role in the second embassy than in the first, although records continue to make it clear that al-Maruni was the ambassador and Pallache simply the sultan's agent and interpreter.[61] Pallache's signature appears on the treaty alongside that of al-Maruni, and after it had been signed, the States General resolved to award Pallache a gold chain, a gold medal, and the sum of 600 florins. Joseph's son Moses, another official interpreter in this embassy, also received a gold medal. Some idea of the relative importance of those making up the Moroccan embassy can perhaps be gauged from the size of the gifts they received: the medal awarded to Samuel weighed 17.5 ounces, whereas the ambassador's weighed 41.5.[62] As soon as negotiations had been finalized, Samuel obtained permission to depart for Morocco with al-Maruni so that the treaty could be ratified by Muley Zaydan. During his absence, which lasted a year, Samuel's brother Joseph acted as his representative, as would become standard family procedure whenever Samuel was forced to leave Holland on business.

We also know interesting details about the agreements reached between the Dutch and the Moroccans thanks to the diligence of Jorge de Henin, the Spanish agent at the court of Muley Zaydan. Henin wrote a series of fascinating reports on Samuel Pallache, described by him as "a servant of the States and of Muley Sidan," and also as "the one who handled the correspondence between the States and Muley Sidan."[63] As we have mentioned above, Henin claimed that when Pallache returned to Holland on the second Moroccan embassy, he took with him diamonds and rubies to exchange for Dutch money and arms on the sultan's behalf. Henin also wrote that Pallache, "in company with some of those moriscos banished from Spain, proposed with eight ships and two thousand harquebusiers whom they would collect on their coasts" to organize "attacks on the coast of Málaga where they are bound to make off with many captives and much wealth."[64] The plan was that Muley Zaydan would procure ships from the Dutch that Pallache and the moriscos could use for raiding missions, after promising to give the sultan a quarter of any booty they managed to obtain. Zaydan himself was in favor of the plan, but Henin had access to Zaydan's mother and managed to get her to dissuade her son from undertaking so risky an enterprise.[65] Nonetheless, this is the first hint in the records that Samuel Pallache had decided to add piracy to his considerable range of activities, which already included diplomatic correspondence, trading in jewels, and espionage. Henin's reports are also remarkable for what they tell us about planned alliances between Jews and moriscos, given that such alliances had occurred only very rarely when these two groups were living in Spain. United by mutual interests, by their knowledge of Iberia, and, no doubt, by a shared feeling of embittered resentment of it, the Jews and the moriscos found themselves in a position where they could try to take advantage of their common backgrounds.[66]

A MAN OF THREE WORLDS

Neither is this the only report of contacts between the moriscos and Muley Zaydan. In April 1611, the Spanish chronicler Cabrera de Córdoba recorded "that certain moriscos had passed over to Africa with an embassy from the rest to the King Muley Cidan offering him 60,000 armed men in Spain and much money, and also to be found there were other ambassadors from the Isles who offered him all the ships he might need to bridge the Strait of Gibraltar." However, Muley Zaydan did not take these morisco representatives seriously and was reported to have "laughed at the morisco embassy."[67]

IN THE YEARS THAT FOLLOWED the signing of the treaty, Samuel continued to be involved in a flurry of commercial, diplomatic, and military activity. The thick volumes of collected documents from which we have already quoted so often, the *Sources inédites de l'histoire du Maroc* (*SIHM*) on the Netherlands, collected and edited by Count Henry de Castries, are full of papers containing references to the Pallaches, who displayed tireless energy throughout this period. Samuel made at least five journeys to Morocco between 1609 and 1614, and in 1611, he also made a business trip to Plymouth in southwestern England.[68] Joseph acted as Samuel's deputy when he was away, but Joseph and Moses both found time to make their own journeys to England. They also traveled widely within the Netherlands, going to Rotterdam, Flushing, and The Hague, where Samuel was based. Joseph and Moses traveled even more frequently to Middelburg, where they sought to take advantage of their alleged status as foreign "ambassadors" to gain exemption from customs dues on imported merchandise.[69]

In business, Samuel Pallache traded with Morocco in collaboration with his Dutch partners, who included leading merchants such as Jan Janz de Jonge and Symon Willemsz Nooms. We know from a letter of protest from the States General that Samuel was thought to enjoy a virtual monopoly on all Moroccan trade with the Netherlands.[70] This trade consisted mainly in the transportation of Moroccan sugar to Europe, and of Dutch arms and other war material to Morocco. Samuel and Joseph both requested, and were granted, permission to export military equipment to their master Muley Zaydan.[71] They also made incessant requests for loans and advances of money from both the States General and the admiralty of Rotterdam for the chartering and fitting out of ships and the recruitment of crews. In 1614, the admiralty went so far as to lend Samuel and Joseph 20,000 florins. In this decision, it was backed by Prince Maurice, who openly protected Pallache throughout his time in The Hague and served as a mediator, when necessary, between him and the States General.[72]

Between 1609 and 1614, the Pallaches were involved in frequent litigation with the Dutch crews of the ships whose operations they directed. Some of these lawsuits were brought by the sailors themselves, who accused the Pallaches of not paying their wages and sued them for compensation.[73] Sometimes, however, it was the Pallaches who brought legal actions against their own crews, accusing them of rebellion and, on one occasion, of having stolen part of a sugar cargo.[74] The Pallaches turned continually to the States General in attempts to obtain tax exemptions, to release cargoes that had been detained in Middelburg,[75] or to protest at the mistreatment of one member or another of the family, as on the occasion when Moses traveled to recover a sugar cargo in Flushing and was very badly received.[76] On such occasions, Samuel did not hesitate to declare himself "a public personage and ambassador of his Imperial Majesty in the Netherlands." In addition, Samuel was required to defend himself against various other claims and summonses,[77] and litigation sometimes arose from overseas sources: Pallache's longest and costliest case seems to have been that involving a Frenchman, Jean Le Comte, who intercepted one of Samuel's ships and retained the merchandise it carried on the pretext that it was war material.[78] (Muley Zaydan was forced to pay for the recovery of these items, and he later applied to the States General for reimbursement.) In another case, in 1612, a ship placed at Pallache's disposal by the States General was captured at sea by a Spanish vessel. The captain of the ship, Jacob Jansz, embarked on a long legal action against Pallache, which was continued after Jansz's death by his widow—as always, what was at stake was the question of responsibility for losses and compensation.

In all of this documentation, Samuel is presented as the head of the Pallache family, chiefly supported by his brother Joseph and his nephew Moses. He engaged in mercantile activity that was extraordinary both for its intensity and its danger, as is shown by the constant flows of litigation and the adventurous nature of his decisions. These decisions were economically and personally hazardous, given that Samuel himself often traveled on ships undertaking extremely risky though lucrative missions. These journeys must have been far from straightforward or relaxing. Voyages were tough and dangerous, and the route from Amsterdam to Morocco, which could not be covered in less than fifty days, was threatened by pirate and corsair ships of various nationalities, as well as the navy vessels of several warring nations. In all the records, Samuel comes across as a typical representative of the mercantile age: a man who missed no opportunity and was prepared to take huge gambles even when he had nothing with which to back them, as well as being a man who was willing to bend or break the law if necessary and who did not retreat when faced with the threat of litigation. Reading the descriptions of Pallache's activities, it becomes increasingly difficult to distinguish between legitimate commerce, smuggling, and privateering. Perhaps the most astounding aspect of all his frenzied activity is that Pallache was able to carry it out at the same time that he was working as a diplomatic agent of Muley Zaydan.

As well as acting as a representative of the sultan in the Dutch Republic, Samuel also assumed control of diplomatic relations with the English court. In 1611, he traveled to England with the Moroccan ambassador and the English agent John Harrison to deliver a letter from Muley Zaydan to James I.[79] Harrison proved to be an important contact for Samuel, who succeeded in gaining the Englishman's trust and friendship on this voyage. Harrison was a key figure in English relations with Morocco, and he traveled there some eight times between 1610 and 1632, twice in the company of Pallache. It was through Pallache that he met members of the Moroccan Jewish community (he studied Hebrew in Safi with one "Rabbi Shimeon"), and while in Morocco, in 1610, he wrote a polemical treatise against Judaism, which was published in Amsterdam in 1612.[80] Harrison also had close links with the moriscos of both Tétouan and Salé, for whom he felt great sympathy, later becoming an agent and spokesman on their behalf. Like the Jews, the moriscos may have aroused Harrison's missionary zeal: in Tétouan, he devoted himself to explaining the superiority of Protestantism over Catholicism to them. Harrison also tried to persuade Charles I of England to sign a treaty with the morisco republic of Salé, but Charles did not accept that it constituted an independent government rather than a group of pirates in rebellion against their king. However, when war broke out between England and Spain in 1625 and the English were preparing an expedition against Cádiz, Harrison offered to recruit a morisco army in Morocco that might collaborate with English forces, and on this occasion, Charles I agreed to the idea. Harrison traveled to Tétouan, where the proposal was so well received that the moriscos even offered to fight the Spaniards at their own expense. The defeat of the English in November of that year brought an end to the planned collaboration, but Harrison left a detailed account of his relations with the moriscos of Tétouan and Salé.[81]

THE DUTCH-MOROCCAN TREATY of 1611 had contemplated the possibility of military collaboration between the two countries, and Samuel Pallache also made decisive interventions in this area. As we have already seen, one of his very first acts in The Hague had been to request three warships from the States General that could be used to transport Muley Zaydan's troops to Tétouan. These troops were needed to assist Tétouan's governor, al-Naqsis, then an ally of Zaydan, in the continuing struggle with Zaydan's brother, Muley al-Shaykh.[82]

In July 1610, al-Maruni and Samuel Pallache again requested the loan of Dutch warships on Muley Zaydan's behalf.[83] The States General gave its authorization on December 27, 1610, and three ships, under the command of captains Rijsbergen, Roest, and Coppendraaijer, were sent to Morocco and placed at the sultan's disposal.[84] According to the ever-watchful Henin, these ships arrived in Safi on May 23, 1611, and both al-Maruni and Samuel Pallache were on board one of them:

> During these days there arrived at the port of Açafy [Safi] the alcayde Hamete Biscaino [i.e., al-Maruni], whom Muley Sidan had sent to Holland as his ambassador, and he came with three warships that had been purchased in Holland for the service of Muley Sidan. There came in his company Martin Raisberguen as ambassador of the States and admiral of the ships, and also with them was Samuel Pallache, who handled the correspondence between Muley Sidan and the States. They brought one thousand lances and one thousand *alfanjas* [short, curved sabers] and six hundred guns and a gift of weapons from Count Maurice, and after Martin de Raisberguen had handed over his cargo, Muley Sidan ordered him to go with his ships to the coast of Spain to make a fine capture of Spanish ships and then he sent him off and in his company went Samuel Pallache. Muley Sidan fancied that in a short time he would be the lord and master of many ships and that the world would become too small for his conquests, for they had filled his head with airy notions. Later he ordered war to be declared on the Spaniards.[85]

Henin also describes what happened next:

> Martin de Raisberguen arrived at the port of Safi with Muley Sidan's ships, and they brought with them two French ships, a prize of small importance, and they went from Safi to Mogador to tar the ships, but the galleons of Spain came and sank them, and only Martin de Raisberguen escaped, fleeing to Santa Cruz

and from there on to Holland. Those from the ships who were lost were saved on land and came back to Morocco. Muley Sidan made captives of the Frenchmen and sent the Dutch to Salé on a ship that he had there, and so they went back to their lands.[86]

Henin's report is confirmed by records at Simancas. Amongst items captured in this battle, the Spaniards found documents in Arabic and Dutch signed by al-Maruni and Pallache in which it was specified that the main aim of the convoy was to attack Spanish shipping.[87] The Spaniards were able to use these papers as proof that the Dutch had ignored the clause in the Twelve Year Truce, in effect since 1609, stipulating that the Dutch would refrain from attacking Spanish vessels. Although it might be more accurate to say that the Dutch had in fact found a way around this clause by placing their ships in the formal service of the Moroccans, the Spanish crown made it clear that it had no intention of looking on while the Dutch built a navy for Morocco. A letter to this effect was sent from T. Rodenburch to the States General on April 29, 1611.[88]

IBN ABU MAHALLI

The Pallaches were also implicated in an affair taking place on Moroccan soil at this time that provides further illustration of the difficulty of delimiting the family's commercial, diplomatic and military activities. This was the uprising of the religious and military leader Ibn Abu Mahalli, who placed Muley Zaydan's reign in grave danger between 1610 and November 1613, when Ibn Abu Mahalli was killed in battle. Ibn Abu Mahalli was one of many warlords thrown up by a broad messianic movement originating in the lands bordering the Sahara desert in southeastern Morocco. This movement is best interpreted as a response to the appalling general situation of a country devastated by famine and prolonged civil wars.

Ibn Abu Mahalli was an ascetic and puritan reformer who led a military rebellion supported by thousands of enthusiastic followers, who were convinced that Ibn Abu Mahalli was the Mahdi, or Messiah, who would come at the end of time to restore the pristine purity of Islam and the rule of justice on earth.[89] Ibn Abu Mahalli and his soldiers began by conquering the city of Sijilmassa and expelling the governor appointed by Muley Zaydan. Then, accompanied by a ever-increasing band of supporters, Ibn Abu Mahalli began a march on Marrakech, Muley Zaydan's capital. The situation was so precarious for Zaydan that he was forced to abandon Marrakech and take refuge in the port of Safi, and he is believed to have had plans to flee to Holland from there.[90] In February 1612, Zaydan wrote a despairing letter to Samuel Pallache in which he begged him to come to his assistance as soon as possible with two ships and a thousand men.[91] On May 20, the rebel Ibn Abu Mahalli entered Marrakech and proclaimed himself the new sultan. He was immediately recognized as such throughout the entire southern half of Morocco.

Zaydan's situation was desperate. His allies, and especially the Dutch, began to harbor serious doubts about his chances of triumphing over Ibn Abu Mahalli and making a return to power. They began to show some reticence in their dealings with Zaydan, and to express reservations about their previous offers of aid.[92] Their doubts were fed by Paul van Lippeloo, a Dutch agent who represented the interests of Amsterdam merchants in Morocco and wrote reports highly favorable to Ibn Abu Mahalli.[93] It seems likely that van Lippeloo's judgment was prejudiced by a series of disagreements with employees of Muley Zaydan. Van Lippeloo had clashed with Abraham ben Waish and Juda Levi, Jewish agents and traders of the sultan,[94] and these clashes had brought van Lippeloo into conflict with Samuel Pallache and Hammu ben Bashir, who had been instrumental in bringing about the Dutchman's arrest on charges of commercial misconduct in Amsterdam.[95] As a consequence, van Lippeloo always regarded Pallache as his enemy.

In July 1612, van Lippeloo and other Christian merchants attended an interview with the self-proclaimed "new king" Ibn Abu Mahalli. The merchants came away from this interview clearly impressed by the force of Ibn Abu Mahalli's personality, as well as by his promises never to employ Jews in high positions, and even to take certain measures against them. Van Lippeloo wrote to the States General recommending that official diplomatic relations be established with Ibn Abu Mahalli and making the confident forecast that Ibn Abu Mahalli was likely to retain a definitive hold on power. A similar line was taken in a text of September 1612 written by an English trader who was almost certainly one of the group of Christians who had been invited to the interview with Ibn Abu Mahalli.[96]

In the Netherlands, the Pallaches did not hesitate to take a very public stance on Ibn Abu Mahalli's uprising. Moses Pallache led a propagandistic countercampaign against the Mahdi by writing his "True History of What Has Occurred in the Land of Barbary," a pamphlet that was printed in Rotterdam in 1614.[97] The aim of Moses' text was to defend the legality and legitimacy of Muley Zaydan's reign and to recommend the continuation of the States General's support for the sultan. The pamphlet portrays Ibn Abu Mahalli as an unscrupulous charlatan who had taken advantage of the gullibility of the masses, and who lacked the ability to hold onto power. Moses' pamphlet is significant, because it provides proof of the Pallaches' loyalty to Muley Zaydan at a time of great difficulty. It shows how committed they were to their master, and this commitment is a factor to be taken into account when considering subsequent events in their careers.

Ibn Abu Mahalli was killed in 1613 by followers of Zaydan, who were led into battle by another holy man, Sidi Yahya ben Abdallah. Zaydan ordered the immediate imprisonment of Paul van Lippeloo, who was accused of treason and support for Ibn Abu Mahalli in his rebellion against the sultan.[98] Zaydan explained to the States General that van Lippeloo had been imprisoned for going beyond his role as a merchant and involving himself in "affairs of the service of the accursed saint."[99] The sultan was clearly aware of van Lippeloo's favorable reports on Ibn Abu Mahalli, and it seems reasonable to assume that this knowledge may have been provided by members of the Pallache family. Van Lippeloo also wrote a bitter letter to the States General blaming Samuel Pallache for his downfall and disgrace.[100]

JEAN CASTELANE AND THE SULTAN'S BOOKS

At the height of Muley Zaydan's struggle with Ibn Abu Mahalli, the sultan found himself involved in another diplomatic conflict of international proportions. This was the famous affair of Zaydan's stolen books, forever associated with the name of Samuel Pallache thanks to the misleading account of it by Miguel de Barrios that appears as an epigraph to Chapter 1. As we shall see, the Pallache family did play a limited role in this affair, but it was Samuel's nephew Moses who took part in the negotiations rather than Samuel himself.

Unable to resist the all-conquering Ibn Abu Mahalli and his forces, Muley Zaydan had been forced to abandon Marrakech and take refuge in the coastal town of Safi in 1612. However, Safi itself was soon threatened by Ibn Abu Mahalli, and Zaydan had to make plans to retreat even further from his enemy, to the remote southern region of the Sous. In June 1612, Zaydan therefore leased a ship belonging to the Provençal captain Jean Philippe de Castelane in order to transport his most valuable possessions southward. Castelane had recently arrived in Morocco with letters from

Louis XIII of France and the duke of Guise. Although his rank was only that of a consul,[101] he had already taken it upon himself to conclude a treaty of alliance with Zaydan, which also involved the Turks.[102] In doing so, Castelane had undoubtedly gone above his station, as the French authorities were later quick to point out, but he probably hoped to justify his actions to Louis XIII by virtue of their later success. (Such actions were also fairly typical of Samuel Pallache.) As a result of this treaty of alliance, Zaydan freed all the French captives within his territory and requested Castelane's assistance in guaranteeing the safety of his personal possessions.

Zaydan handed his belongings over to Castelane, who was to take them by sea to Santa Cruz de Cap de Gue (Agadir), where he had arranged to meet up with the sultan and his entourage, who were making the journey overland. However, Castelane had other intentions. After leaving Safi, he did not sail south as instructed, but immediately made off with the sultan's prize belongings in the direction of France. Unfortunately for him, he did not get very far. Just off Salé, he ran into Spanish ships under Don Pedro de Lara, lieutenant to Admiral Fajardo, who captured Castelane's vessel and carried the precious booty off to Spain.

The most significant part of Fajardo's capture was the sultan's entire private library, made up of some four thousand volumes collected by his father Ahmad al-Mansur. The library comprised books on medicine, philosophy, grammar, law, and politics, many of which contained magnificent examples of the arts of calligraphy and illustration. In March 1614, Juan de Peralta, the prior of the monastery of El Escorial, applied to have these books deposited in the convent library. After consulting with his private confessor as to whether the books could be considered an affront to the Catholic faith, Philip III decided to agree and donated them to the library, where they remain to this day. They currently constitute one of the most important European collections of Arabic volumes, despite a fire that decimated the library in 1671.[103]

As can be imagined, Castelane's behavior enraged Muley Zaydan, who held the king of France personally responsible for what had happened. The books held great personal value for Zaydan, and their theft disturbed diplomatic relations between Morocco and France for many years. In fact, Zaydan went to great lengths to try to get them back until the very end of his life. For this purpose he first turned for help to his main European ally, the Dutch, and later to the English, via Samuel Pallache's friend John Harrison.[104]

The first step was taken in August 1612, when the latest Moroccan ambassador, Ahmad al-Gazzali, appeared before the assembly of the States General, accompanied by Samuel and Moses Pallache and one of Zaydan's court eunuchs. Al-Gazzali presented a letter from Zaydan explaining recent events and requesting aid and support for the ambassador al-Gazzali against the French.[105] Zaydan wanted the States General to give al-Gazzali letters of recommendation and to place the Dutch ambassador in Paris at al-Gazzali's disposal.[106] The States General complied with this request by instructing François van Aerssen, its ambassador in France, to assist the Moroccan.[107] A letter was written to Louis XIII, and Moses Pallache was instructed to accompany al-Gazzali to Paris as his official translator.[108]

One year later, in August 1613, al-Gazzali returned to Morocco after the complete failure of the mission. To the surprise of the Moroccan delegation, the French did not have Zaydan's books, and Louis XIII was in any case unwilling to pay any form of compensation for their loss. Zaydan recalled his ambassador from Paris,[109] and the States General wrote to Marie de Medicis, Louis's mother, asking her to intercede with the king of Spain for the return of the books.[110] This opened a long period of diplomatic negotiation with the Spaniards, which was to continue throughout the seventeenth and eighteenth centuries. Zaydan's books possessed enormous symbolic significance for both Morocco and Spain, and diplomatic efforts to get them back were always doomed to failure. With time, the books came to acquire far greater importance than any other diplomatic issue between the two countries.[111] When Samuel Pallache negotiated with the Spanish government for a return to its service in the final months of his life, he made frequent mention of the value and symbolic importance to Morocco of its "captive" books.

In 1612, the issue was still delicately poised from the point of view of diplomacy and maritime law. The Spaniards decided to declare Fajardo's capture legitimate for two reasons: because Castelane's cargo was a stolen one, and because this stolen cargo belonged to a king who was at war with Spain. The French objected that Castelane had committed an abuse of trust in his dealings with the Moroccan sultan, that he was not a pirate, and that his ship belonged to a nation (Morocco) that was at peace with Spain. The situation was embarrassing for the French, who had no desire for Castelane to be identified as the consul who had signed a treaty of alliance with Muley Zaydan.[112]

After the failure of his negotiations with the French, Zaydan negotiated directly with Spain, and offered the huge sum of 100,000 ducats for the return of the books. Zaydan's offer received the backing of the Trinitarian monks of Mazagan, who argued that such a sum would allow them to redeem a substantial number of Spanish captives in Morocco. But the Council of State decided to press for the release of all Spanish captives in Morocco as a necessary precondition for the books' return, and Zaydan considered this demand excessive and unacceptable. The affair was left unresolved, and Zaydan nursed feelings of tremendous resentment toward France and Spain for the rest of his life. French and Spanish captives were singled out for special punishment, and the Franciscan Juan de Prado was executed in Marrakech, promoting him to the category of martyr in the eyes of Catholic captives. All of this served only to raise the value of the books in the Spaniards' eyes. A Turkish ambassador who had been allowed to examine the volumes at El Escorial, "when asked how much they might be worth, said: 'Infinite ducats.'"[113]

CHAPTER 4

PRIVATEERING, PRISON, AND DEATH

LA MAMORA

As we have seen, it can be difficult to distinguish clearly between commerce, smuggling, and piracy in the early seventeenth century. Samuel Pallache took full advantage of this gray area on several occasions, and there are indications that he concentrated increasingly on the least reputable of these activities as the years went by. Nevertheless, one important distinction does need to be made if we are to understand the next series of events in Pallache's life, and that is the crucial difference that existed between pirates and privateers (also known as corsairs). Essentially, a privateer sailed in his own ship, which was chartered and armed by authorization of a government that laid down the privateer's conditions and precise objectives. Privateers sailed under the flag of the state that had sponsored them and conceded them letters of marque, and they generally adhered to certain widely accepted rules of conduct. Such privateers were often employed by states, such as Morocco, that were too weak to run a regular or merchant navy because of their situation of quasi-colonial dependence on greater powers. Pirate ships, by contrast, engaged in straightforward acts of maritime banditry. They flew no national flag, and their actions were not curbed by the acceptance of rules or any criteria other than their owners' material gain. Pirates robbed any ships that came their way, whereas privateers, at least in theory, only attacked ships from countries with which their sponsoring government was at war, or with which no treaty arrangements existed.

This distinction between piracy and privateering is important to an understanding of a new chapter in the life of Samuel Pallache, which began with a resolution taken in October 1613 by the States General, at the suggestion of Pallache's loyal supporter Prince Maurice, to grant Samuel permission to prepare a ship for a voyage to Barbary.[1] Maurice recommended that the States General lend Pallache 5,000 florins, half of it in the form of weapons, and the latter ordered Pallache to provide a list of the crew members he planned to employ. (As we shall see, this precaution derived from the fear, or knowledge, that most of Pallache's crew were likely to be notorious pirates.)[2] The planned expedition was approved in October, but the onset of winter meant that the journey had to be delayed until the following spring.[3] In March, the States General again communicated, via a letter drawn up by its secretary, Cornelis Aerssens, that it would permit Pallache, as Muley Zaydan's agent in the Dutch Republic, to recruit a crew to be employed on a warship and a *jaght* (yacht) that Pallache had prepared in Rotterdam.[4] Pallache now belonged to a company of Dutch businessmen that leased its own ships for commercial and military operations,[5] and his main vessel was a warship of English origin called the *George Bonaventura*.[6] The voyage was publicly proclaimed by "strike of drume," and Pallache was designated to act as his ship's "general." Jan Jansz Slobb, or Slobbe,[7] of Hoorn was appointed captain of the *Bonaventura*, and Gerbrant Jansz became captain of the yacht.[8]

The official purpose of the voyage was to provide assistance in the struggle against pirates off the coast of Morocco, but its real aim was to prepare for Dutch occupation of the town of La Mamora,[9] a small port on the Moroccan Atlantic coast at the mouth of the river Sebu, close to where the town of al-Mahdiyya is situated today. La Mamora had become home to many of the French, Dutch, and English pirates who had been expelled from Larache when the Spaniards occupied it in 1610, and Spain was now faced with the need to remove these from their new enclave just a few miles to the south. Both Muley Zaydan and the Dutch were well aware of Spanish designs on La Mamora, and Pallache had been involved in negotiations over it with Holland from 1610 on.[10] Pallache had been given the task of negotiating a joint Dutch-Moroccan policy for protecting the town from the Spaniards, which essentially consisted of two steps: first, the pirates would be removed from La Mamora, and then the town would be fortified to enable it to withstand future assaults by the Spaniards.[11] However, negotiations over the fortification of the town had progressed very slowly. Muley Zaydan had asked the Dutch to send him, not only building materials and engineers, but also a number of warships with which to hold off possible Spanish attacks.[12] However, the Dutch had been reluctant to finance and equip an entire Moroccan navy in this way.[13] Despite the difficulties, Pallache had led the Dutch to believe that they would be allowed to occupy La Mamora once the pirates had been driven out.[14] The Dutch also assumed that by fortifying the town at their own expense, they would in future be able to use its port as they saw fit.

Pallache left Rotterdam with a written license and commission from the States General in April 1614.[15] This was the journey on which Samuel was accompanied to Morocco by the Englishman John Harrison, and the only other non-Christians onboard were Pallache and the servants who prepared his food, which according to the later declaration of the crew was kasher. According to later declarations by members of the crew, Pallache's custom when he traveled to Morocco was to sail first to Safi and remain there for three weeks. But on this occasion, standard procedure was disrupted just off the Spanish coast. Either deliberately or as a result of the bad weather, the yacht became separated from the *Bonaventura* and set off on a series of independent raiding adventures.[16] Sailing with a crew "mainly made up of former pirates, as the general [Pallache] knew full well,"[17] the yacht captured first a unnamed French ship and then a Dutch one, the *Winthont*, close to Cape Saint Vincent. These prizes were followed by the taking of the *Otter*, a vessel sailing out of Lübeck. They thereupon mounted cannon on the *Winthont* and the *Otter*, scuttled the yacht, and headed for the Strait of Gibraltar in the two ships, abandoning the captured crews aboard the French vessel.[18] In short, it was quite an expedition.

In the meantime, Pallache had arrived in Safi and then traveled on to Marrakech, where he was interviewed by Muley Zaydan. Although we do not know exactly what was discussed during this meeting with the sultan, Cornelius Cleysen, a member of Pallache's crew, later testified that Pallache had been given instructions by Zaydan to "harm the Spaniards and make war on them and on the other enemies with whom they were at war."[19] Pallache was given letters of marque by his master, in other words. Nevertheless, privateering was not the sole or even the main aim of the voyage Pallache had been due to undertake. The Dutch expected Pallache to sail to La Mamora and provide military support for Admiral Jan Evertsen, who was already sailing toward the town in command of a group of Dutch warships.[20] Evertsen's brief was to enter La Mamora, oust the pirates, and start building a fort that could be defended and provisioned by the Dutch.[21]

Evertsen arrived in Morocco in June 1614 and waited close to Salé for further instructions from Muley Zaydan. In the meantime, he took advantage of John Harrison's presence in Safi by asking Harrison to speak with the English pirates in La Mamora and persuade them to go somewhere else. Harrison obliged, appealing to the good relations between the Dutch and English.[22] The English pirates were convinced by Harrison's arguments and duly moved on, but still Evertsen had neither news nor instructions from Zaydan, who was occupied in the fight against Sidi Yahya ben Abdallah, who had fought for Zaydan against Ibn Abi Mahalli but had then launched a rebellion of his own.

Evertsen was also waiting for Pallache to join him as arranged, but for some reason Pallache now fell into sudden disgrace with Muley Zaydan. This fall from favor was to mark the rest of Pallache's career. The sultan may have discovered that Pallache had exceeded his brief in negotiations with the Dutch over La Mamora; perhaps he had made too many concessions for the sultan's liking. Pallache himself attributed his fall from grace to the interference of Paul van Lippeloo, who had spoken to the sultan shortly before Pallache's arrival.[23] In a letter of June 1614 to his brother Joseph, who submitted it to the States General, Pallache complained that van Lippeloo had been meddling in his affairs and trying to mediate between the sultan and the Dutch authorities, whom he asked for confirmation that he was their sole representative authorized to deal with Muley Zaydan.[24]

These delays proved fatal to Dutch interests. The Spaniards were mysteriously well informed about Evertsen's maneuvers and sent ships under the command of Fajardo with instructions to occupy La Mamora as soon as possible. Fajardo, who had originally been on his way to dismantle a fort built by the Dutch in La Mina, changed course and sailed into La Mamora in August 1614, taking control of the town virtually without a fight before Evertsen's very eyes.[25]

Harrison and Evertsen both accused Pallache of playing an equivocal role in the whole affair, and the Dutch certainly had their reasons for wondering how the Spaniards came to know so much about their intentions. In July, a Dutch merchant passing through Cádiz had written to the States General to warn that the Spaniards possessed detailed knowledge of the Dutch plans for La Mamora and knew everything about Muley Zaydan's dealings with Holland.[26] This is hardly surprising in view of a fact we are able to reveal for the first time, namely, that Samuel Pallache had been sending information to the Spaniards for years. At the same time that Pallache had been instructed to deal with the Dutch, Zaydan had also been using him as an intermediary in secret contacts with the duke of Medina Sidonia, who wrote as early as the summer of 1610 that he knew "from a good source" that the Dutch were planning to build a fort at La Mamora.[27] In 1614, Pallache was instructed by the Spanish to inform Zaydan of their offer to trade Mazagan for La Mamora "as a sign of friendship" and in exchange for military aid,[28] and Philip III specifically referred to Pallache as "the confidant in these intelligences" who had informed him that Zaydan had offered La Mamora to the Dutch.[29]

Zaydan had his reasons for opening secret dealings with Spain. In the midst of his conflict with Ibn Abu Mahalli, at a time when there were serious doubts about the continuation of Dutch aid to Morocco, Zaydan probably decided to turn to the Spaniards for help in recovering his throne. After the death of Muley al-Shaykh in October 1613, Spain had no allies in Morocco, and Philip III had written to Medina Sidonia underlining the need to do something for Muley Zaydan to "make him obliged to us."[30] This seems to suggest that the original impulse may have come from the Spaniards rather than Zaydan or Samuel Pallache himself. What is certain is that Samuel offered Medina Sidonia the town of La Mamora in exchange for military aid. Philip III wrote in March 1614 that "if Zidan prevailed, it would be good to admit his friendship and see what emerges from the offer to trade Mazagan for La Mamora that you mention, for that port is important, as is well known, and if fortifications had to be made there, it would be better to do so in terms of friendship. And we could also look at the offer made by the Jew Pallache."[31] This letter seems to indicate that Pallache made an additional, or different, offer to the official one made by Muley Zaydan. Everything points to the possibility that, not for the first time, Pallache was acting on his own behalf and probably going beyond the limits of his brief. He may have been encouraged to do so by the desperate situation of Muley Zaydan, who was still on the verge of losing his kingdom; Pallache's contacts with the Spanish authorities may also have continued for longer than we know. Alternatively, Pallache may simply have decided to offer La Mamora to the highest of two bidders, the Dutch Republic and Spain.

Whatever the explanation, Philip III eventually decided that Pallache was a double agent and ordered Medina Sidonia to look for other Jews who might serve as confidants and intermediaries.[32] Medina Sidonia maintained the secrecy of all his dealings with Pallache but had clearly been au fait with the negotiations in Holland, the purchase of Dutch ships by Muley Zaydan, and so on, for some time.[33] All of this may help to explain Zaydan's anger with Pallache and his rejection of him from 1614 on: after offering La Mamora to two opposing parties and negotiating for years with both of them, Zaydan had ended up losing the town and getting absolutely nothing in exchange.

THE LONDON TRIAL

The disgraced Pallache made haste to leave Morocco. According to Evertsen, he had lost the sultan's trust completely and would have run the risk of losing his head if he had remained in the country even a day longer.[34] At about the same time, John Harrison wrote that Pallache had asked him for letters of introduction to be used in England by himself and his brother Joseph. According to Harrison, Pallache was unlikely ever to return to either Morocco or Holland unless forced to do so, given his mishandling of dealings between the two countries.[35]

Pallache set out from Safi on a privateering expedition, and after three or four months, his ships had managed to capture a Portuguese caravel and a Spanish ship close to the Azores. Both ships were returning to Europe from Santo Domingo with cargoes of sugar and animal hides, and a Portuguese sailor was killed during the attack on the caravel.[36] After taking the merchandise, Pallache's men abandoned the ships' crews on the island of Santa Maria. Pallache later attacked a ship called the *Penelope*, which belonged to the London businessman Richard Hal. As a result of this attack, Dominicus Bouwens, a Dutch businessman based in London, lodged a complaint on Hal's behalf with the States General on September 23, 1614, stating that the *Penelope* had been close to the coasts of Barbary when attacked by two ships under the command of Samuel Pallache. The States General replied that Pallache's ships were in the service of "the land of Barbary," and that it could not be held responsible for Pallache's actions.[37]

The usual practice when captures had been made by a ship sailing under a Moroccan flag was to return to Morocco and sell the booty, usually in Salé.[38] Many Amsterdam Jews had commercial links with Rabat-Salé, which had been populated since 1610 by moriscos who had recently been expelled from Spain. The city also had a significant Jewish population of Iberian origin.[39] The town thus provides another interesting example of cooperation between groups of expelled Iberian Jews and moriscos. However, on this occasion, the return route to Salé was blocked by the Spanish navy,[40] and Pallache decided to take his booty to the Dutch Republic, where the two captured ships arrived safely in due course. His decision not to sail to Morocco may also have been influenced by a desire to steer clear of the irate Muley Zaydan. Unfortunately for Pallache, however, his own ship was driven off course by poor weather[41] and this, combined with illness among his crew, forced him to seek refuge in Plymouth, on the southwestern coast of England. Another of Pallache's ships was blown into the port of Veere, near Middelburg, and its captain wrote to Joseph Pallache from Veere asking him for money to repair a damaged hull and torn sails, and also to feed the crew, who had arrived in an exhausted state.[42] The crew were forced to remove their stolen booty from the ship to prevent it being ruined by leaking water, and this booty was later impounded by the Zeeland admiralty, which sold some of it off to finance the crew's needs.[43]

When the owners of the two captured ships, subjects of the Spanish crown named Hierónimo Fernandes Pretto and Antonio Bento, discovered that their vessels had been taken to Holland, they placed a formal complaint before the Spanish authorities. On November 4, the States General were informed that the marquis of Spinola had requested the retention of these ships until their owners were in a position to defend their rights.[44] The States General responded with the standard argument that Pallache had been working for Muley Zaydan and not the Dutch government. However, its reply mentioned that certain legal steps had already been taken in this case. The States General is known to have looked for a legal solution to the dilemma of the captured ships,[45] even going so far as to consult the famous jurist Grotius [Huig van Groot] in this connection.

ARREST AND TRIAL

Pallache's arrival in Plymouth was brought to the attention of the Spanish ambassador in London, Diego Sarmiento de Acuña, count of Gondomar, who persuaded the English to order Pallache's arrest. When he heard that Gondomar was making moves to have him detained, Pallache panicked and fled from Plymouth harbor before his ship could be properly repaired. He managed to sail as far as Dartmouth, where his ship ran aground and he was restrained by harbor authorities.[46]

Gondomar's official petition for Pallache's arrest was lodged with the

Privy Council on October 25, 1614.[47] In it he wrote (in Spanish) that Pallache was "a vassal of the king my lord who apostatized from the faith of Christ our Redeemer to become a Jew, then became a corsair as an ally of the Moors, and has now captured two ships from vassals of the king my lord." He also stated that he had attempted to have Pallache arrested in Plymouth, but that Pallache had managed to sail away from the town after bribing a number of people.

In a letter of November 4, 1614, John Chamberlain gave an account of Pallache's arrest, calling him

> a Jew pirat, that brought three prises of Spaniards into Plimmouth [Pallache had, in fact, only taken two ships, both of which had been sent to Holland, not Plymouth]. He was sent out by the King of Maroco, and useth Hollanders ships and for the most part theyre mariners. But yt is like he shall passe yt over well enough, for he pretendeth to have leave and licence under the King's hand for his free egresse and regresse, which he was not beleeved till he made proof of yt.[48]

Chamberlain thought it was likely that Pallache would be released, and in this he was eventually proved right. But for the time being, Pallache found himself in prison, and he was to remain there throughout October 1614, making desperate pleas for help from the Dutch via his brother Joseph and Noel de Caron, the Dutch ambassador in London. Caron wrote to the States General that "ledit sieur Palache ne cesse de me solliciter a toutes heures [the aforesaid Mr. Pallache importunes me incessantly at all hours]." Pallache complained to Caron about the length of his detention and the wretchedness of the prison cell he was forced to share with six of his Dutch sailors.[49]

Samuel Pallache gave his own account of events in a letter written in Dartmouth on November 2, 1614, and sent to the States General. Writing in Spanish, Pallache claimed that the aim of the Spaniards was to undermine the good understanding between Holland and Morocco and to discover details of the pacts between the two countries. Pallache also made veiled threats by suggesting that if the States General failed to help him and he were to fall into Spanish hands, certain Dutch state secrets might be at risk. He complained bitterly about his treatment by the Spaniards, and made reference to his condition as a diplomatic agent: "And the Spanish ambassador's wishes cannot take precedence over mine for I too am a public minister of my king and a person who treated for alliance with such a wise and noble republic [i.e., the Dutch]." He explained that amongst those who had arrested him there was "an Italian who treats me like an inquisitor; he has taken all my papers, which include copies and letters from His Highness [Prince Maurice] and from the king my master [Zaydan], because all his desire is to find out what goes on between them."[50] The seizure of Samuel's papers was confirmed by Joseph Pallache in The Hague, who insisted that details of the treaties between Holland and Morocco ran the risk of falling into enemy hands.[51]

According to Gondomar's official denunciation, Pallache was guilty of "Piracie, spoyle and outrage at sea upon subiects of the king [of Spain]."[52] Samuel's main line of defense was to argue that his arrest was illegal, and in this he was supported by his brother Joseph from The Hague.[53] Samuel claimed that there was nothing wrong with having conducted "licit war" on ships belonging to a nation hostile to his master, Muley Zaydan. As we have seen, this was tantamount to saying that although he was a privateer, he could not be considered a pirate. Samuel also continued to make reference to his alleged status as an ambassador of the sultan, and pointed out that he possessed a safe-conduct granted him by the king of England. (This was the document that he had taken the precaution of obtaining from John Harrison in 1612.)[54]

The States General called in a letter addressed to James I in November 1614 for Samuel's release and the return of his papers.[55] Prince Maurice intervened personally by writing to James on December 11.[56] Maurice's letter, written in French, speaks of the "sinister accusations made by the ambassador of the king of Spain," when, in fact, "the said Pallache has done no more than follow the orders of the king of Barbary his lord, with whom the States General have a treaty of peace and alliance." Thanks to these interventions and that of Noel de Caron, who managed to obtain the support of leading English lawyers,[57] Samuel began to enjoy fairly privileged treatment. Despite protests by Gondomar, he was released on bail and placed in the care of Sir William Craven, lord mayor of London.[58] Pallache lived in Craven's London home from this point on, and his papers were also returned to him.[59] In December, Pallache wrote to Maurice and thanked him for his help.[60]

The Privy Council referred the case to the Admiralty Court at the end of December, but an order for Pallache's immediate release was revoked just a few days later.[61] According to Caron, such setbacks were owing to the machinations of Gondomar, who took a personal interest in the case and even discussed it with James I in a special interview. The Spanish ambassador succeeded in bringing about a delay in the delivery of Pallache's release papers, and then tried to have Pallache rearrested within the framework of a new civil lawsuit. Gondomar's plan was to have Pallache forcibly restrained as he was walking out of the front door of Sir William Craven's house, but Caron intervened at the last moment and renewed Pallache's bail order, which was guaranteed by Craven himself.[62] According to Caron, his and Craven's actions served to protect Pallache from Gondomar, who was anxious to see Pallache hanged at the earliest opportunity.

Caron arranged a meeting with the members of the Privy Council, who informed him that Gondomar had told them that the brother or successor of the sultan of Morocco was an ally of Spain and had been supported by it. (Gondomar was referring to Muley al-Shaykh, who had, in fact, died in October 1613, although this news had yet to reach London). This was an important point. Gondomar was seeking to establish that Spain and Morocco could not be considered warring nations, because al-Shaykh was dependent on Spain. Acceptance of this point would make it impossible to regard Pallache's raids on Spanish ships as the actions of a privateer. He would have to be considered as nothing more than a pirate.

In the trial, which took place a few days later, Caron took it upon himself to defend Pallache in a speech that lasted more than an hour, without a single interruption. Caron's defense was based on the notion of state interest and the importance of maintaining international relations. Everyone was agreed, he said, that Pallache was "a Jew and a Barbarian [i.e., from Barbary]" and as such did not deserve to be treated any better than a dog. He himself would never have been willing to defend Pallache as an individual, because of his "non-divine" religion. Nonetheless, Pallache was the ambassador of an absolute king, and as such he traveled with a legal passport and an authentic and valid commission to make war on the nation of Spain. Caron argued that Pallache should therefore be respected for reasons of state, as had occurred under Queen Elizabeth, who had honored the sultan of Morocco and given respectful treatment to his ambassador at her court despite the fact that he was just as Jewish and just as Barbarous as Pallache. Caron's rousing but calculated speech was an apparent success and it stiffened English resolve to seek a political solution.

However, Samuel was still in London in January 1615, when he wrote to the States General to request them not to share out the booty from the two captured ships until he had arrived with the sailors who were imprisoned with him.[63] On January 20, the Privy Council determined that the case should be decided, not by the Admiralty court, as had been ex-pected, but by a special tribunal, which was to include the Lord Chief Justice of England and the Master of the Rolls.[64] In the meantime, Gon-domar submitted a written complaint to Admiral Sir Daniel Dun,[65] and Pallache himself showed signs of beginning to lose hope. In a letter dated February 20, 1615, to the States General, he wrote: "And so, since for-tune has decided that in fleeing from the Spaniards I should fall straight into their hands, there is no remedy left to me but that of God and Your Highnesses."[66]

On March 13, Noel de Caron sent a letter to Ralph Winwood, an Eng-lish agent in the Dutch Republic, in which he requested that the Privy Council pass sentence in the Pallache case, which remained pending.[67] He drew attention to Pallache's importance to the interests of the Dutch state and in certain unspecified matters that could be delayed no longer.[68] In The Hague, Moses Pallache also intervened by vouching for the authen-ticity of the commission granted to Pallache by Zaydan, a fact Gondomar continued to dispute. Moses declared that the sultan's authenticating sig-nature was genuine, and asked the States General to confirm this in writ-ing.[69] The latter complied with Moses' request in a letter dated March 16, and also acknowledged that all the Moroccan caids who had visited Pal-lache in The Hague had addressed him as Zaydan's "ambassador."[70]

The Privy Council finally communicated the sentence reached by the special tribunal on March 20.[71] Pallache was declared not guilty of the charges in Gondomar's criminal lawsuit, and the case was remitted to a civil court. During or after the ceremony, the Admiralty judge Sir Daniel Dun pointedly asked Pallache to sit beside him, provoking the consider-able ire of Gondomar, who made loud complaints that the English fa-vored Barbarians and Jews over Christians. However, a definitive resolu-tion of the case was impossible until the following month because of the continued absences from London of James I and the Lord Chief Justice. When James eventually returned to the capital, Caron arranged another personal audience with him to discuss the Pallache case. On arriving at court, Caron was delighted to observe that whereas he had been granted an audience with the king, Gondomar had to make do with speaking to members of the Privy Council. Gondomar's arrogance, haughtiness and savagery were favorite themes of Caron, who expounded upon them at great length in his letters. Caron told James that the Spaniards considered "people of religion" (i.e., Protestants) no better and no worse than Jews or Turks, and were in the habit of burning them at the stake, a reference to the Spanish Inquisition. Given that the Spaniards would soon complete the expulsion of the moriscos and the extermination of both Jews and Muslims, Caron argued that "we [i.e., the Dutch and English] have to defend ourselves against them." Gondomar was reduced to demanding that Pallache's release should only take place after he had made a bond payment of £30,000 sterling, an exorbitant sum, whose mention had a devastating effect on the spirits of Pallache and Caron. According to Caron, Gondomar had been certain that no one in England would be prepared to pay such a large sum of money to help Pallache. However, Caron managed to persuade a group of prominent Dutch merchants at the London Stock Exchange to pay up the full amount, and Pallache was at last released. He wasted no time in leaving for Holland.

However, the civil case remained pending, and before leaving England, Pallache named one of his own servants as his legal representative.[72] Pallache also initiated his own legal action against Gondomar, insisting that the Spanish ambassador should be made to pay the costs of his trial. This appeal was pursued by family members even after Pallache's own death in February 1616. On June 6, 1616, for example, the States General wrote to Noel de Caron with instructions to insist that Pallache's case be brought before James I.[73] Gondomar himself complained bitterly about how the affair had been conducted, protesting that it seemed to be a crime for Spaniards to ask for justice.[74] The whole episode must have been harmful to Gondomar, who requested an ambassadorial transfer to France soon after Pallache was released. It is interesting to note that although the Simancas archive[75] contains all of Gondomar's known official correspondence with the Spanish court, no mention of the Pallache affair appears in the record. Neither is there any reference to it in the published volumes of his letters.[76] Gondomar liked to paint a positive image of his successes as a diplomat and courtier, and although records of several of his actions against English and Dutch pirates have survived, they are always cases in which Gondomar himself plays a triumphant leading role. One obvious example is that of Sir Walter Raleigh, which occupies a large part of his published correspondence.[77] Gondomar probably decided that the Pallache case was less worthy of the interest of future generations.

SAMUEL HAD WON AN IMPORTANT LEGAL VICTORY, but he returned to Holland a ruined man. During his absence in detention, complaints had begun to pile up about the illegality of his activities, and several of these now came to the attention of the States General. A letter from the

Admiralty in Rotterdam protested about the capture of the *Winthont*,[78] and, most serious of all, there were further complaints about the captured Spanish vessels. As has been noted, Grotius was consulted on the legal aspects of the case.[79]

By the time Pallache returned to the Dutch Republic, the Rotterdam admiralty had already assessed the value of all of the ships.[80] This assessment included the ship that had limped into Veere harbor and the *Bonaventura*, on which Pallache had traveled under the command of Captain Jan Slobbe, which had been taken from Plymouth to Rotterdam on October 21, 1614.[81] Pallache expressed his opposition to this division of the spoils. Openly styling himself an "ambassador," he said that all the booty from the voyage belonged to the sultan of Morocco, who had given him letters of marque to act against the Spaniards.[82] The States General eventually decided to split the booty and gave a quarter of it to Bento and Pretto, the owners of the captured ships. The other three-quarters were divided equally between Muley Zaydan, Pallache, Slobbe, and the crew.[83] This left Pallache in a position of serious financial difficulty. Lawsuits had already been brought against him by members of his own crew because of the nonpayment of their wages, and when he sold his share of the booty, he was unable to raise enough money even to cover his debts. Virtually bankrupt, in disgrace with Muley Zaydan, and an increasing worry to the States General, Pallache must have realized that he would need to start looking for new employment.

CONTACTS WITH THE OTTOMAN EMPIRE

The Ottoman sultan, Ahmed I, was one possible employer. The Sublime Porte was seeking to improve its relations with Morocco,[84] and early in 1614, Moses Pallache had gone to Istanbul on behalf of Muley Zaydan on a largely unsuccessful mission to establish direct relations between the two countries.[85] Sultan Ahmed's chief admiral, Khalil Pasha, now hoped to use the Dutch as intermediaries in further negotiations.

An opportunity soon arose for Samuel Pallache to improve Moroccan relations with the Turks and at the same time to restore his own standing with Muley Zaydan and the Dutch. A woman from a wealthy Turkish family had been captured by the French and was released through the mediation of Pallache, who was asked to take charge of the ransom negotiations by the woman's family. Pallache traveled with her to Holland, where Prince Maurice took a direct interest in her case and ensured her safe journey home to Turkey.[86] She was accompanied by two French maid-servants, one of whom created a minor incident when, after arriving in Turkey, she escaped and sought refuge at the home of the French ambassador. (The other maidservant, in contrast, expressed a desire to convert to Islam.) Cornelis Haga, the Dutch ambassador in Istanbul, said that Samuel Pallache had intended both maidservants to be a personal gift from him to Khalil Pasha. Haga claimed that the women carried letters from Pallache, whose aim was to secure access for himself and his nephew Moses to the highest levels of Ottoman influence.[87]

The Turkish lady's family was initially very grateful to the Dutch for their help. According to Haga, however, Moses Pallache not only spread rumors that the Dutch were disappointed by the size of the reward for their kindness but had suggested that Haga himself was planning to murder a family member in revenge.[88] Haga also claimed that Moses had suggested that Haga no longer enjoyed the support of the States General, and that the Dutch had tried to block contacts between the Turks and the Moroccans by preventing the Pallaches from traveling to Istanbul.[89] Joseph Pallache, Muley Zaydan's agent in The Hague since Samuel's disgrace, was thereupon instructed by the States General to clear up the misunderstanding by attesting that it had never obstructed negotiations in any way,[90] and Joseph duly sent a written declaration to this effect. According to Joseph, Haga's suspicions derived from a misreading of a letter by Samuel about a projected embassy under Ahmad ben Abdallah al-Muruni that would carry precious gifts for the Ottoman sultan. Joseph asked for this letter to be translated correctly so that his brother Samuel could be seen to have intended no harm to Dutch interests.[91] Haga for his part was certain that the Pallaches' long-term aim was to move the entire family to Istanbul and take charge of both Dutch-Turkish and Moroccan-Spanish relations.[92] Haga believed that the Pallaches wanted him out of the way in order to achieve their plans.

In the event, Haga did everything in his power to prevent the Pallaches from playing the role they had intended in Istanbul. This led to a distancing between Haga and Khalil Pasha and a subsequent deterioration in Ottoman relations with the Dutch Republic. It also brought about a renewal of the old coldness between Ottomans and Moroccans. Neither did it help Samuel Pallache, who had become a confirmed source of trouble in the eyes of the Dutch.

By this stage, it should come as no surprise that Samuel Pallache, at the same time that he was involved in dealings with the Turks, also decided to open another chapter in the story of his relations with Spain. His contacts with the Spaniards, which led to a signed pact or contract in November 1615, were initiated in August of that year through Gregorio de Valencia, a friar of the Order of La Merced, and the Portuguese Jew Duarte Fernandes, who had known Pallache since his arrival in Amsterdam. According to the marquis of Guadaleste, the Spanish ambassador in Flanders, Fernandes was a "person of great opinion, listened to by the States," and it was Fernandes who had taken the initiative in this affair by assuring the friar that between them, they would be capable of "reducing [Pallache] to the royal service of His Majesty."[93] Fernandes himself had been working secretly for the Spaniards since the start of the year.

Once negotiations with Pallache were under way, Guadaleste turned for advice to the count of Gondomar. Gondomar, who only months before had opposed Pallache in such vehement and personal terms during his stay in London, did not now hesitate to come down firmly in favor of recruiting Pallache to work for the Spanish crown. Either because he regarded Pallache as a highly skilled opponent whom it was preferable to have on one's own side or because he appreciated the advantages to be derived from Pallache's talent for duplicity, Gondomar wholeheartedly recommended that Spain come to some sort of agreement with Pallache. No longer did Gondomar complain that Pallache was a dangerous Jew, a Barbarian, and an untrustworthy renegade. Samuel had obviously reached the stage where he was either a dangerous or a valuable individual, depending on whose side he was on, and who had the opportunity to use him.

Pallache's negotiations with the Spaniards proceeded rapidly, and by November 1615, the two sides had reached an agreement consisting of twelve contractual clauses.[94] This final agreement had been preceded by a series of interim versions, some of which have survived and enable us to trace the progress of the negotiations. One of these versions contains marginal glosses by Guadaleste outlining the possible favorable implications for Spain of each of the twelve clauses.[95]

The first clause stated that Samuel Pallache had undertaken to supply the Spanish crown with valuable and reliable information via Duarte Fernandes and his own nephew Moses. Pallache hoped to ensure that he would be paid promptly for whatever information he supplied, something that, he said, had not happened "in past years." The same clause stipulated that Pallache would be granted a passport and safe-conduct once he had demonstrated the usefulness and importance of his information. Clause 2 said that Pallache was to be assigned a salary of 200 escudos a month for as long as he continued to provide useful information to the crown, and that he would receive back pay for services previously rendered. Clause 3 committed him to keeping the crown up to date on Dutch secrets and the dangers to Spain resulting from Dutch political maneuvers. A marginal note specified that he would pass on information provided by "Arzeen," who may have been Cornelis Aersens, secretary to the States General, or even François van Aerssen, the former Dutch ambassador in France and one of the most powerful men in Holland. Clause 4 said Pallache was also to supply information on French and English relations with Morocco and the Turks. Furthermore (Clause 5), he would serve His Majesty the king of Spain by persuading the king of Morocco to cease all trading activity with France, Holland, and England, as a result of which the Strait of Gibraltar would be made safe for Spain and left under its exclusive control. (A marginal note pointed out that this was one of the most important clauses.) Clause 6 explained that Pallache was also to make direct contact with the Turks through Selim Pasha, a personal friend of Pallache's according to another marginal note. Clause 7 stated that all of Pallache's duties were to be carried out under his cover as a Moroccan ambassador and with unconditional loyalty and the utmost fidelity to the king of Spain. Clause 8 covered the conditions of Pallache's employment more generally: only if his services proved useful was he to be remunerated; a lack of results would lead to no payment. More precise payment details were to be discussed with Gregorio de Valencia. Clause 9 covered an issue described as very important "for our designs": the king of Spain would delay and frustrate the negotiations over Muley Zaydan's stolen books that were taking place between Morocco and France, for reasons Pallache would discuss personally with Gregorio de Valencia. We have already seen that Moses Pallache had taken part in 1612 in negotiations for the return of the books and was fully aware of their importance to Muley Zaydan. The Pallaches probably planned to take advantage of the affair of the stolen books to regain the sultan's favor in some way.

Clause 10 made Samuel's employment by Spain dependent on the withdrawal from Holland of Joseph Pallache and his family. In future, only Samuel and Moses would remain in the Dutch Republic, and it was repeatedly insisted that Moses was just "as important as Samuel." The reason for insisting that Joseph left Amsterdam is explained in the margin: Joseph was a declared enemy of Spain and would ruin all dealings between his brother and the Spanish crown. For his part, Samuel demanded 2,000 escudos in exchange for his brother moving to Istanbul. As well as helping to cover the costs of Joseph's move to Turkey, this was probably a way of obtaining money quickly in order to resolve the family's delicate financial situation. The contract stated, perhaps at Samuel's insistence, that Joseph's move to Istanbul was a matter of great urgency; time was of the essence (Clause 11). Clause 12 stated that Joseph's passport should be issued as soon as possible and "in the correct and proper way."

In a letter from Philip III to his brother Alberto, the king said that he had given his consent to the agreement and had asked to be kept informed of its progress.[96] However, very little ever came of Pallache's new pact with Spain, since he was already suffering from the illness that was soon to end his life.[97]

DEATH

Nothing is known of Pallache's final illness beyond the fact that when he applied to the States General for a loan of 200 pounds [*deux cent livres de gros*] on January 25, 1616, he wrote that he had been ill and bedridden for three months. When the loan was granted on February 5, it was in the knowledge that Samuel was mortally ill,[98] and he died the same day, his health perhaps undermined by his financial situation, as well as by his long detention in London. Samuel's age at the time of his death is also unknown, though he cannot have been particularly old. A States General resolution reveals that his corpse was escorted by Prince Maurice and members of the States General and of the Dutch Council of State as far as the Houtstraat bridge (now Waterlooplein), whence it was taken by sledge to the new Jewish cemetery in Ouderkerk aan de Amstel.[99] In this way, Maurice paid final homage to a man for whom he had felt an obvious personal sympathy, and whom he had supported on every possible occasion, sometimes even to the detriment of other parties and institutions in the republic. Despite this support, Samuel had died in poverty.

The Ouderkerk death register and the inscription on Pallache's tombstone both describe him as *baham*, or "reverend," and this gives some indication of his religious knowledge and participation in Jewish ceremonies.[100] Pallache's tombstone, which survives to this day, bears an oval shield with a lion and a count's crown. Above the shield is a Hebrew poem and beneath it are the words, also in Hebrew: "This is the monument that marks the resting place of the wise, pious, and noteworthy man who fulfilled his duties to God and men, the Haham Samuel Pallache, may he rest in peace, called to the bosom of God on Friday 16 Shebat of the year 5376."

Pallache's contractual obligations with Spain were at first assumed by his nephew Moses, who traveled to Brussels with Duarte Fernandes in order to speak with the marquis of Guadaleste and Ambrosio de Spinola. Moses explained his interest in contributing in some way to the planned Spanish occupation of Salé and Fedala in Morocco. The Spaniards eventually abandoned their intention to occupy these towns,[101] but Moses is known to have remained in contact with the duke of Medina Sidonia and other Spanish courtiers until at least 1627.

Meanwhile, the Pallache family continued to play a role on the international stage. In June 1616, Joseph, as Zaydan's agent in the Netherlands, requested that the States General cover the costs of a journey he was about to make to Morocco, from where he intended to accompany the Moroccan ambassador to Istanbul.[102] The Moroccan embassy, led by Ahmad ben Abdallah al-Muruni, arrived in Istanbul as planned, but the mission was largely unsuccessful, partly because the Turks were said to be disappointed by the gifts the Moroccans had presented to the Ottoman sultan.[103] Istanbul and Madrid gradually disappeared from the Pallache sphere of influence as the family devoted itself more and more exclusively to Moroccan and Dutch affairs. Samuel's death also marked the end for the family of the kind of adventurous risk-taking that had been characteristic of Samuel's career. The Pallaches were by now well established in their own specialized fields, and did not need to adopt the same hazardous strategies as their ground-breaking forerunner. The Pallaches who were left after Samuel's death are the subjects of the following, and final, chapter.

CHAPTER 5

AFTER SAMUEL

The Pallache Family

Several members of the Pallache family continued to live in the Dutch Republic after Samuel's death. A notarial document recording the purchase by the Neve Salom community of Samuel's Torah scrolls provides some details of the makeup of the family at this time. The document mentions, on the one hand, Samuel's widow Reina/Malca (equivalent names, since "Malca" or "Malika" means queen, i.e., Spanish "Reina," in both Arabic and Hebrew) and his son Isaac; it also refers to Samuel's brother Joseph, his wife Benvenida, and their several children. Joseph's children are not all named in this document, but we know from other sources that he had a total of five sons: Isaac, Moses, Joshua, David, and Abraham. Joseph Pallache may also have had a daughter by the name of Amalia: a tombstone bearing this name stands in the Ouderkerk cemetery alongside those of Samuel, Joseph, and David, but it is too seriously damaged to determine her exact relationship to them. Samuel Pallache also had at least one other son apart from Isaac, a certain Jacob-Carlos, of whom we know only that he was employed as an agent of the sultan of Morocco in Denmark in 1654.[1]

The most important members of the Pallache family, both before and after the death of Samuel, were undoubtedly his brother Joseph and Joseph's sons Moses and David. Joseph continued to live in Amsterdam as an agent of the Moroccan sultan until the end of his own life. Moses settled at the Moroccan court after 1618 and became a translator and interpreter to successive sultans, while David acted as deputy to both his father and Moses, especially at times when Joseph was forced to leave Holland for Morocco. Moses Pallache, who had already become known as Samuel's faithful assistant during the final years of his life, soon assumed the role of family head once his uncle had gone.

JOSEPH AND MOSES

Samuel's death left the family in a difficult position. When Joseph made a journey to Morocco in 1616, he was given a frosty reception by Muley Zaydan, whose subsequent letter to the States General failed to clarify whether he intended to give Joseph his continued support. Zaydan was concerned about the legitimacy of the Pallache family's activities in the Netherlands and asked to be shown accounts covering the final years of Samuel's life. The sultan was particularly interested in checking the records of incomes from the sales of various cargoes personally entrusted to Samuel, as well as seeing proof of expenditure on arms and munitions that Samuel had acquired on Zaydan's behalf. For this purpose, Zaydan sent a special commissioner, Jacques Jancart, to the Dutch Republic with instructions to carry out a thorough inquiry into possible Pallache misdemeanors. Jancart's brief also covered other issues, such as the best way to share out the booty from the ships Samuel had captured. Muley Zaydan took the view that he had sponsored Samuel and his crew, and that all the booty taken should therefore belong to him alone.[2] The States General informed Joseph Pallache of Jancart's arrival in The Hague in January 1617, and also wrote to the admiralties of Rotterdam and Middelburg to brief them on Jancart's mission and request them to place accounts books at Jancart's disposal, together with all the booty seized by Samuel Pallache. They also authorized Jancart to take legal action against Joseph Pallache if necessary.[3] With the Pallache family now in such a dubious position, Muley Zaydan started to turn to other Jewish servants to work for him in the Netherlands, and in February 1617, he sent Israel ben Cheloha and Muchy Levy to The Hague with merchandise and letters of recommendation to the States General.[4]

In the meantime, Joseph Pallache was forced to ask the States General for a loan of money. Although committed to assisting Jancart in the realization of his investigative work, it granted Joseph the loan, and officials also took it upon themselves to write a long letter to Muley Zaydan in July 1617 testifying to the constant devotion and loyalty that Samuel, Joseph, and Moses Pallache had always shown toward their sultan. The letter went on to claim that the Pallaches would never have been able to live in a manner befitting those of their station if it had not been for the financial assistance over the years of the States General.[5] Joseph requested and obtained further assistance from the States General on several occasions over the following months, and it again interceded directly on Joseph's behalf with Muley Zaydan. In addition, as we have seen, a group of Amsterdam businessmen signed a notarial document in 1617, at Joseph's request, in which they certified that Samuel Pallache had lost all his personal possessions to pirates at the time of his first journey to Holland. Joseph probably asked for this statement to be made as a means of justifying and explaining periods of bankruptcy mentioned in the accounts being examined by Jancart.

At the beginning of 1618, Joseph applied to the States General for letters of recommendation for his son Moses, who had decided to leave Holland to serve Muley Zaydan in Morocco. Once again, the States General had no hesitation in complying with Joseph's request, stating that it had always been highly satisfied with Moses' services.[6] Like his cousin Isaac, Moses had attended university in the Dutch Republic, studying Oriental languages at Leiden, where he became one of the candidates for a new chair in Arabic, which was eventually occupied by the famous Thomas Erpenius.[7] Once in Morocco, Moses was to work as a translator and interpreter of Spanish, Dutch, and French, firstly for Muley Zaydan and then, after his death in 1627, for Zaydan's three successors: Muley Abd al-Malik, who died in 1631 after a rebellion led by his own brothers; Muley al-Walid, who was assassinated in 1636; and Muley Muhammad al-Shaykh al-Saghir. Moses worked as a court secretary and often acted as an intermediary when Christian ambassadors arrived at the Moroccan court. His role was eventually close to that of a court "favorite," and he was able to occupy a delicate post and keep the trust of four different sultans without ever falling into disgrace. This was a particularly striking achievement when one considers the nature of the disputes for succession to the throne and the fact that each new sultan was often a direct enemy of the man who had preceded him. Moses married the daughter of Israel ben Cheloha,[8] also known as Shaykh Israel, the Jewish community *naguid*, who worked as a tax official and businessman for Muley Zaydan and had been sent to The Hague as Zaydan's agent after Samuel Pallache's death. He eventually succeeded his father-in-law as *naguid* when Cheloha died.

To a certain extent, Moses also represented Dutch interests in Morocco, at least so long as they did not clash with those of the sultan himself. (Albert Ruyl, whose visit to Morocco is discussed at greater length below, was to complain that Moses and his father Joseph always put the sultan's interests before those of the Dutch Republic.) In addition, Moses made sure he kept up his contacts with Spain: in a letter to the duke of Medina Sidonia written on April 4, 1627, Moses began by thanking him for "the favors received by us and by my ancestors, both my father and my uncle, at that house, both in the times of the late duke [the seventh] as in those of Your Highness [the eighth]," and he informed Medina Sidonia that he was about to depart for Spanish-held Mazagan in order to pass on secret information about Muley Zaydan to the governor of the town, Gonzalo Coutinho.[9] This was not the only such trip that Moses made, Coutinho later reporting that he had received information from Moses Pallache on several occasions.

Moses' importance within the Pallache family can be deduced from the fact that many of its members now drifted back to Morocco. It seems likely that he helped or urged his brothers to settle there. Joshua, who had earlier worked with his brother Isaac in Danzig and Hamburg, became another of Zaydan's many tax officials; and Abraham took up residence in Safi and became involved with Moses in several business ventures. Abraham worked as a supplier of water and provisions to ships visiting Moroccan ports, and his name also occurs in connection with other kinds of trade, especially the purchase and sale of precious stones. It was as such a trader that Abraham later found himself involved in a lawsuit similar to that which his own brother Isaac had once brought against Henrique Garces in Brussels. In 1623, Abraham Uziel, a Jew from Amsterdam, revoked and annulled a contract that he claimed Abraham Pallache, acting under the instructions of his brother Moses, had previously forced him to sign in the port of Safi. Uziel said that he had been preparing to sail for Amsterdam from Safi when Abraham Pallache had ordered him to be seized and held prisoner until he made a written promise to return two balas rubies that Abraham accused Uziel of intending to transport illegally from Morocco to Amsterdam. Uziel said that the rubies had been given to him by Moses Pallache as security against a loan of 260 ducats, a sum that he now requested be returned by Moses.[10] Moses Pallache's name also appears in many other Dutch notarial records, placing orders for sumptuary items or being mentioned as owing money for their purchase. It is impossible to know whether these transactions were carried out on the sultan's behalf or whether Moses bought jewels for his own use or trading purposes. What is clear is that the purchase and sale of jewels and precious stones continued to be an important field of activity for the Pallache family.[11]

Moses' cousin Isaac also returned to Morocco, settling at some time after 1623 in Rabat-Salé, where he made a living from the ransoming of Dutch prisoners.[12] Isaac's role in Rabat-Salé seems to have been close to that of a Dutch consul, and the States General expressed its written gratitude to him on several occasions.[13] Another brother, David, applied for his own official commission from the States General, paid or unpaid, to enable him to carry out his ransoming activities in Morocco with greater authority.[14] He is also mentioned as working directly for the "king of Barbary."[15] David Pallache was still in Morocco in 1630, and in 1634, he was involved in a business deal with Michael de Spinoza, father of the philosopher Baruch de Spinoza, apparently in an effort to clear some of his debts. David's name appears alongside that of Spinoza in a contract for the sale of merchandise from a vessel sailing from Salé.[16]

Several members of the family were thus involved in important work, but Moses emerges very clearly as the leading Pallache. He held the most stable and influential position at court, and he was powerful enough to assist his relatives when necessary. Moses' pivotal role was clearly accepted by the rest of the family. Isaac Pallache once wrote to the States General from Salé that "the man who is closest to the king is the lord Mose Pallache, my cousin."[17] Moses himself seems to have been aware of the family's dependence on him, judging by an anecdote from the time of Albert Ruyl's visit to Morocco, which is covered in greater detail below. Ruyl, who despised Moses, was once told by him that he was planning a journey to the Netherlands, and Ruyl pointed out that if this were the case, Moses' father and brother would have to stay behind in Morocco and take responsibility for certain negotiations. Moses' appalled reaction to this idea, Ruyl says, was to exclaim: "For God's sake! My father and brother would undo in three days what it has taken me five years to achieve!"[18]

From 1636 on, Moses' name also crops up in English records, and he put his signature to the Spanish translation of the ratification of the 1638 treaty between the English and Sultan Muhammad al-Shaykh al-Saghir.[19] English diplomats were obviously impressed by Moses' abilities, and official documents describe him thus:

> Mousa Peliachi, a Jew, Sheck [i.e., shaykh] of all the rest that live in the Judaria; he was borne in Amsterdam and hath seene the Courts of most Christian

princes; he is a good linguist and excellent speaker, used by the King as a necessary minister (secretary of State or interpreter) at audience of Embassadours and in other foraigne negotiations. He hath had the happiness, notwithstanding theis late changes, to be retained by all the fower Kings successively, now being very gratious with Mahamet Sheck.[20]

The last known reference to Moses Pallache dates from April 1650, when he must have been over seventy. In that month, a letter from the sultan to the States General in The Hague informed the Dutch that Joseph Pallache's eldest living son, Moses, had expressed his desire to marry leviratically the widow of his brother David, who had recently died. The letter openly explained that Moses intended to marry David's widow in order to take up his brother's inheritance. The States General replied, politely but succinctly, that the widow had no wish to move to Morocco.[21]

THE PALLACHES AND THE AIER PORT PROJECT

Joseph stayed behind in Amsterdam after Moses' departure for Morocco in 1618. Jancart concluded his inquiries without finding any telling evidence against the Pallaches, but this does not seem to have remedied Joseph's situation immediately. In June 1619, Muley Zaydan sent another special envoy to the Dutch Republic. This time, his representative was a Frenchman named Jacques Fabre. Zaydan entrusted Fabre with tasks that Joseph might have been expected to carry out himself in normal circumstances. Thus, for example, Fabre accompanied a group of ransomed Dutch captives to the Netherlands and collected the money that Zaydan had paid for them. He was also instructed to oversee the manufacture of a number of bronze cannons.[22]

Joseph Pallache was alarmed by Fabre's arrival, which seemed to threaten his role as official intermediary between the Dutch Republic and Morocco. In a memorandum addressed to the States General in which he proposed possible messages to be sent to Muley Zaydan and a series of arguments to be used in defense of his deceased brother Samuel,[23] Joseph asked the States General to support him in the face of Zaydan's unjustified complaints about the Pallaches, suggesting that the sultan had been poorly informed by Fabre. He specifically asked: "Your Highnesses, in order to please him [Muley Zaydan], to write to him in the Spanish language so that His Majesty may understand you well." Joseph had good reason to be concerned about his position: when, as the sultan's agent in

The Hague, he asked the States General to pay the rent on his official accommodation, its reply was that payments had been temporarily suspended pending confirmation from Zaydan that Joseph was to be retained in his post.

Joseph became even more agitated when Fabre began to make preparations to return to Morocco in 1620. Anxious that Fabre should not have exclusive access to Zaydan, Joseph applied for permission to go back to Morocco himself so that he could speak with the sultan.[24] The States General, preferring not to take sides, decided to write two separate letters to Zaydan, one to be carried by Jacques Fabre and the other by Joseph Pallache.

Joseph arrived in Safi in January 1621, and by the time he returned to the Netherlands in August of the same year,[25] he had fully regained Muley Zaydan's favor and was confirmed in his post as Moroccan agent, as can be seen from the letter from Zaydan to the States General that Joseph took back with him.[26] This recovery in Joseph's fortunes may have owed something to the States General's continued backing, but was probably also due to the influence of his son Moses, now a recognized favorite of the sultan. Joseph's restitution was also related to his involvement in a scheme to offer European powers concerned about pirate activity in the Salé region access to a new Moroccan port, which provides a great deal of useful information about the Pallache family after Samuel's death.

The idea of the creation of a completely new port went back to 1619, when an unnamed morisco, employed with troops sent by Muley Zaydan to the Dukkala region, close to Cape Cantin, had made an important discovery. The morisco soldier had followed the flight of a flock of geese inland along a previously uncharted channel, which turned out to lead directly into the Aier lagoon. The discovery of this passage, which opened the possibility of using the channel and lagoon for oceangoing shipping, was made known to the sultan, who ordered the area to be examined. In its earliest stages, the scheme was associated with the French agent in Morocco, Claude du Mas, and a Provençal knight by the name of Saint-Mandrier. Du Mas was in Morocco to negotiate over the Castelane affair of the sultan's stolen books, and Saint-Mandrier was employed at court. The two Frenchmen assumed responsibility for setting up a society in Paris for the creation of a new port at Aier, and they obtained an initial lease on it from the sultan in exchange for large sums of money. However, the project ran into serious difficulties when Du Mas, on his way to Paris, visited Admiral Don Fadrique de Toledo in Spain and secretly informed him of Zaydan's plans. Don Fadrique was shown confidential maps of the area, and ships were sent from La Mamora to make an inspection, but the Spaniards soon realized the impossibility of constructing a port at Aier and lost interest in the project. However, when Muley Zaydan learned that the Spaniards had been informed, he furiously ordered both Du Mas and Saint-Mandrier to be imprisoned.[27] Still resentful over what he regarded as French deceitfulness in the Castelane affair, Muley Zaydan had Saint-Mandrier convicted of treason and executed.

In 1621, Zaydan decided to take personal charge of the Aier port scheme, and there are signs that he was encouraged in this decision by either Joseph or Moses Pallache. Unable to undertake such a task without foreign capital and expertise, Zaydan turned to the Dutch for the technical assistance he needed, thus guaranteeing Pallache involvement in the project. In August, Joseph traveled back to the Netherlands with Captain Outger Claesz, and both men carried maps and plans, which they had been instructed to show to Maurice of Nassau. In order to encourage Dutch interest in the project, Muley Zaydan hinted that in exchange for its help, the States General would be authorized to mine unlimited quantities of saltpeter—an essential component of gunpowder—on Moroccan territory. Joseph Pallache also led the States General to believe that the Dutch would be allowed to exploit some of the region's natural resources, such as its salt marshes, and that they might eventually be given complete control of the Aier port itself.[28]

After a series of meetings and deliberations, the States General decided to send a special commissioner to Morocco to study the Aier lagoon region. The commissioner, Albert Ruyl, was accompanied on his journey to Morocco by Joseph Pallache and the Leiden professor of Arabic Jacobus Golius, as well as by a group of stoneworkers, whose presence had been specifically requested by Muley Zaydan. Unfortunately, the Dutch soon realized, like the Spanish before them, that a port could never be built at Aier because there was a massive rock barrier across the entrance to the channel. To make matters worse between the two sides, it was discovered that the Moroccan salt marshes offered to the Dutch in exchange for their assistance produced only tiny amounts of salt, hardly enough even to cover the needs of the local inhabitants. The Aier lagoon project was definitively shelved amid considerable acrimony, and Ruyl's whole mission came to be regarded as a disaster. Its failure would cast a shadow over relations between the Dutch and Morocco for several years to come.[29]

Nonetheless, Albert Ruyl's failed mission did have one fascinating by-product from our point of view, and that is Ruyl's detailed diary of his expedition, which has survived intact to this day. Ruyl's diary contains precious information on several members of the Pallache family and their considerable influence on Moroccan public affairs. In fact, the Pallaches are mentioned on almost every page. Firstly, there is Joseph, "the old man" with whom Ruyl traveled to Morocco and also made the emotionally fraught return journey to Holland at the end of the abortive mission. Also ever-present in the diary is Moses, the sultan's secretary and translator, who supervised and effectively thwarted Ruyl's contacts with Muley Zaydan throughout the time of the Dutchman's stay in Morocco. Abraham, Moses' younger brother, is mentioned by Ruyl for his work in the provision of foodstuffs and accommodation for the ships' crews and embassy. Finally, Isaac Pallache, described by Ruyl as "lame," also makes occasional appearances, although it is unclear whether he was in Morocco from the beginning of the mission or arrived later from Algeria in order to arrange ransom payments for a group of captives.

Ruyl's relations with the Pallaches were poor from the very beginning, and they deteriorated considerably as the months went by. It is clear from Ruyl's diary that the Pallaches did their utmost to prevent him from carrying out his work effectively, and deliberately blocked his movements at all times. Ruyl was in Morocco for a total of seven months without ever being allowed to leave the town of Safi, and he was never permitted either to speak with Muley Zaydan or even to inspect the Aier lagoon region. Unsurprisingly, Ruyl came to despise the Pallaches and blamed them for the failure of his mission.

ACCORDING TO RUYL, Joseph Pallache made it plain from the outset that he thought his own diplomatic status was far superior to that of the Dutchman and regarded the whole area of relations between Morocco and the Dutch Republic as the exclusive domain of the Pallache family: "The old man has had the effrontery to say that no one but he can maintain the alliance [between Holland and Morocco], and that there were no more than three or four people who could understand the mysteries of this alliance . . . the rest were all novices."[30] Joseph's attitude was extremely humiliating for Ruyl, who became increasingly frustrated as the mission dragged fruitlessly on and he realized the extent to which he was in Joseph's hands. Ruyl accused Joseph of acting in the sultan's interests and against those of the Dutch: "Old Pallache is doing much harm to these negotiations, for he wishes to please his king even when his conduct runs contrary to the interests and reputation of Your Lordships [of the States General]." According to Ruyl, Joseph Pallache had told him: "I am a servant of His Majesty [Muley Zaydan], and I am not at liberty to do anything that might prejudice him or go against his interests; but I assure you that if you do not carry out your duty in full, I shall lodge serious complaints about you with their Lordships of the States."[31] Ruyl wondered how such important state business could ever be entrusted to Jews, who were known to be entirely untrustworthy: "These Jews who seek nothing but to ruin the honor and reputation of Your Lordships"[32] were, as everybody knew, "vain and childish liars."[33] Moses had made it impossible for Ruyl to speak with Muley Zaydan, and Ruyl complained that it was obvious that he would never be allowed to do anything in Morocco. Moses' attitude toward Ruyl is made clear from his alleged reaction on first learning that his father Joseph was coming to Morocco with a Dutch commissioner. Ruyl had been informed that Moses had lost his temper on hearing the news and shouted, "What the devil does my father think he is doing in bringing a commissioner here? Can't we resolve these affairs ourselves?"[34]

Ruyl's diary is full of complaints about the Pallaches, but it also provides unique information on their relationship with Muley Zaydan. For example, it is fascinating to read Ruyl's descriptions of how "old Pallache" (i.e., Joseph) was in the habit of riding into the sultan's palace on horseback to greet his master. In theory, Jews were neither authorized to ride horses nor to flaunt their wealth and behave in such a way as to imply superiority to Muslims. This rule was sometimes ignored in practice, but only as a special mark of favor, and Joseph boasted to Ruyl that the sultan treated him with great familiarity, even seating him at his side and treating him like one of his grandest alcaydes.

Ruyl had dealings with other Jews, including two close friends of the Pallaches who were in charge of the saltpeter negotiations. Ruyl protested that the Moroccans were offering far less saltpeter than he had initially been led to expect by the Pallache family. "Thus these cunning Jews with their hypocritical manners have dragged Your Lordships into great expenditures, deceiving and defrauding you," he wrote back to The Hague. In fact, Ruyl's writings are one long litany of complaint against Jews, repeatedly described as a damned nation, or the perfidious, hypocritical, and deceitful enemies of all the world.[35] As negotiations dragged on, Ruyl became incensed by the Pallaches' delaying tactics and the way they prevented him from speaking to the sultan. Joseph Pallache claimed that Ruyl's instructions from the States General did not allow him to act without Pallache's own approval, which Ruyl disputed.[36] Ruyl accused Abraham, Joseph's youngest son, of cheating him in the supply of provisions and water. He also accused Isaac Pallache of spreading the false rumor that Ruyl had never laid eyes on the members of the States General or Maurice of Nassau and had never even set foot in the city of The Hague, whereas the Pallaches had been serving the States General loyally for sixteen years.[37]

There were several violent scenes between Joseph Pallache and Ruyl. Joseph publicly described Ruyl as "a drunk" (Spanish *borracho* in the original Dutch text) and at one time boasted proudly of his origins and said that the soles of his shoes were of greater worth than Albert Ruyl. Joseph even went so far as to say, in the presence of a group of the sultan's alcaydes, "By God, my family is of better origin than that of King Philip [of Spain] and my house of equal worth to that of Muley Zidan." The "house of Muley Zidan" was that of a sultan whose members prided themselves on descending directly from the Prophet Muhammad. Nevertheless, it should be remembered that leading families of Moroccan Jews also claimed direct descent from the prophets, and it was probably for this reason that, to the astonishment of Ruyl and other Christians who were in the room, none of the Moroccan alcaydes was outraged by Joseph's statement.[38] Their only reaction was to ask Joseph if he was not afraid that Ruyl would throw him overboard on the return journey, to which Joseph replied that in The Hague, he was powerful enough to have twenty men like Ruyl thrown overboard whenever he liked. As can be seen, Ruyl's diary illustrates perfectly the notion that the Pallaches had developed of their own importance and their opinion of those who surrounded them. It also gives an idea of the kind of power that the Pallaches were able to exercise.

In the course of another dispute, Ruyl went so far as to cause Isaac Pallache serious head injuries with a stick. Ruyl's frustrations had multiplied by this stage. Not only was it clear that his mission would be unsuccessful, but he had even been denied the sultan's permission to sail home. Ruyl's anxiety must have been exacerbated by the recent case of the unfortunate Saint-Mandrier, who had repeatedly applied for permission to leave Morocco only to suffer eventual execution. The truth was that Ruyl was entirely at the mercy of the Pallache family.

It was at this time that Ruyl learned of another disturbing rumor from the alcayde Toletoli (i.e., el Toledano, the Toledan), a morisco friend of the Pallaches. Toletoli told him that Muley Zaydan had discovered that

Ruyl had written to Holland to explain that only Marrakech and Safi were under the sultan's complete control, and that this had made the sultan furiously angry. Ruyl was horrified by this piece of news and wondered in writing how it was that the Jews were able to find out about everything, and how so many people could be so devoted to them. He was extremely afraid that this development would prevent him from ever obtaining the sultan's permission to leave Morocco.[39] Ruyl describes a comical meeting with Toletoli and other colleagues, at which a morisco described Holland as "a cowpat" (una caca de vaca) compared with Morocco and said that the Dutch had only ever been able to defend themselves against the Spaniards with the assistance of England and France. The alcayde Toletoli kept the jokes flowing by suggesting that Holland was called "The Low Country" because its inhabitants were of low extraction, weak understanding, and poor spirits. Ruyl indignantly asked the morisco how he knew this if he had never been to Holland himself, and the morisco's reply was that he had been informed by his close friend Joseph Pallache. Ruyl again wrote of the perfidious and unbearable nature of Jews and passed the story on to the States General.[40]

The hopeless Dutch mission eventually came to an end. Muley Zaydan sent Ruyl back to Holland on the same ship as Joseph and Isaac Pallache and the new Moroccan ambassador, the morisco Yussef Biscaino. Moses Pallache wrote a condescending letter to the States General in which he implied that responsibility for the failure of the mission lay with Ruyl, who had shown himself to be out of his depth. This letter is a good illustration of Moses' verbal dexterity: in it, he seems to absolve Ruyl of all personal blame, while simultaneously entirely discrediting him. Moses wrote that although it was impossible to deny Ruyl's good intentions, the Dutchman had spoken too much, committed several indiscretions, and offended the sensibilities of many Moroccans. Moses was at pains to suggest that Ruyl ought not to be held personally responsible, because he was probably incapable of acting in any other way, but it was equally clear that he should never be entrusted with further missions of such a delicate nature.[41]

Yussef Biscaino's report on Ruyl's conduct turned out to be much harsher. Immediately after arriving in The Hague in July 1624, one of the new ambassador's first actions was to write a letter of complaint to the States General about Ruyl's treatment of Joseph Pallache and his sons, who, Biscaino emphasized, were official agents of the sultan of Morocco.[42] Biscaino's letter provides us with revealing details about the return journey to Holland. Although Ruyl had not gone quite so far as to throw the Pallaches overboard, as the Moroccan alcaydes had jokingly predicted, he had certainly not fallen far short. Ruyl had ordered Joseph Pallache to be locked in a miserable cabin, where he had been given virtually nothing to eat for the fifty days that the journey had lasted, whereas Isaac Pallache had been physically beaten and clapped in irons. To make matters worse, Ruyl had struck David Pallache in the presence of Ambassador Biscaino upon their arrival in Rotterdam.

Yussef Biscaino called for justice to be done. In The Hague he also wrote a long memorandum on Ruyl's previous conduct in Morocco, which serves as a useful counterweight to the version of events contained in Ruyl's diary and describes several of the Dutchman's diplomatic blunders. Biscaino wrote that when Ruyl's ship first arrived at port in Safi, it was approached by a group of small skiffs bringing food and refreshments. One of these skiffs turned out to carry two Dutch renegades to Islam, and Ruyl took the illegal step of ordering his compatriots to be retained on board his ship, unconvinced by the argument that the renegades had converted voluntarily. In a separate incident, Ruyl had displayed great insolence and bravado in sheltering a pirate whom Muley Zaydan had ordered to be arrested, with the result that "His Majesty considers him a greater enemy than the Spaniard." According to Biscaino, Ruyl had committed several acts of considerable imprudence and indiscretion, had ignored all established legal procedures between the two countries, and had placed relations between them in grave danger. He had refused to understand that the Pallaches were agents of the sultan and as such deserving of his utmost respect.[43]

Joseph Pallache wrote his own report and legal petition to the States General, outlining the various kinds of mistreatment that he and his sons Isaac and David had suffered at Ruyl's hands. Joseph wrote that Ruyl had confiscated his luggage and had tried to force him to pay a fare for the return journey to Holland. He also described in great detail how Ruyl had struck his son David, leaving him with blood on his clothing, in the presence of the new ambassador to The Hague.[44] David Pallache wrote a separate letter of complaint in his own and his father's name.[45]

The States General was left with no choice but to take action against Albert Ruyl, who was placed under house arrest and forbidden to enter The Hague. Joseph and David Pallache's positions were considerably strengthened as a result.

As well as being assaulted by Albert Ruyl, David Pallache was at the center of another diplomatic incident that serves to illustrate still further the role and influence of the Pallache family in Morocco and the Netherlands after Samuel Pallache's death.

The incident had its origins in the actions of two Frenchmen, Razilly and Du Chalard, who paid out large sums of money in 1630 in order to ransom all the captive French slaves that they could find in the town of Salé. The Frenchmen later discovered that many more of their compatriots were being held captive in Marrakech, and Razilly wrote to the Moroccan sultan Muley Abd al-Malik, the successor to Muley Zaydan, to request the release of these captives in exchange for further payments. Razilly had three ships sent from France to transport the slaves home and traveled to Safi to supervise arrangements for the voyage. However, the arrival of the French captives in Safi was deliberately delayed by Abd al-Malik, whose intention seems to have been to prolong the affair until the winter weather forced Razilly's ships to leave for France without the Frenchmen. The stalemate was unexpectedly broken in October 1630, when Razilly organized an expedition off Safi that captured a Dutch ship chartered by the Pallaches and discovered large quantities of contraband matériel stored upon its decks.[46]

The value of the arms was estimated at one hundred thousand pounds and Moses Pallache, now a well-established secretary and translator at the sultan's court, acted swiftly to have the ship and its cargo returned to the Pallache family. Moses persuaded al-Malik to release the French captives in Marrakech, but by the time they had finally been taken to Safi, Razilly had already decided to sail for France, fearing the onset of bad weather. He left the booty from the captured ship behind him, together with instructions to the French consul to sell it off at the highest possible price.

Desperate to have the ship and its contents returned to the family, Moses decided to send his brother David to intercede on his behalf at the French court. He instructed David to remind Cardinal Richelieu of how conscientiously he had worked for the release of the French captives, and he sent his brother two letters to be presented to Louis XIII. One of these letters was written by al-Malik himself and the other by a representative of the French captives now stranded in Safi.

Following his brother's instructions, David Pallache left his home in

The Hague for Paris, where he arrived in March 1631 and delivered the two letters to the king. The French court was duly moved by the plight of the unfortunate captives abandoned to their fate by Razilly's impatience, and it was decided to send a new embassy to Morocco to take up their case and negotiate a peace treaty with the sultan. David succeeded in having the ship, though not its cargo, returned to the Pallaches, and he was given several splendid gifts and new franchises as a reward for his work.

The new French mission was headed by Razilly, Du Chalard, and a Monsieur Molères, who was given overall responsibility for negotiating with the sultan. Meanwhile, Abd al-Malik had died in March 1631 and been succeeded as sultan by his brother Muley al-Walid. Molères arrived in Safi and traveled with David Pallache to Marrakech, where, thanks largely to the efforts of Moses, a peace treaty between the two countries was negotiated at some speed, an unusual occurrence in dealings with the Moroccans. The treaty was signed in September 1631, and Molères took a French copy of the document with him to Safi, while Moroccan officials continued to work on their final draft of the Arabic version.

Molères waited with the French slaves in Safi for the arrival of this Arabic text, which had to be signed by Razilly and Du Chalard. The document was eventually brought by Moses Pallache himself, and the Frenchmen put their signatures to it, adding in French the proviso that their signatures would only be considered valid insofar as the Arabic text reflected the French one previously signed in Marrakech. Moses Pallache also signed the French text and certified that both versions said the same thing.

David Pallache then traveled back with the French party, taking with him the two versions of the treaty. He was received as a Moroccan ambassador in Paris and once more showered with valuable gifts. The treaty was ratified by Louis XIII in April 1632, and David was given the task of carrying the ratification back to Muley al-Walid in Morocco. Thus far, negotiations had proceeded rapidly and smoothly, but for reasons that are unclear, David now chose to delay his journey to Morocco and traveled first to The Hague, where he remained for some months, possibly on personal business.

After waiting in vain for the promised ratification to arrive, Muley al-Walid deduced that he had been slighted by the king of France. Corsair activity against French shipping resumed, and new slaves were captured. The French themselves remained unaware that David Pallache had still not arrived in Morocco and unwittingly sent a new ambassador, Du Puy, to the Moroccan court. Advised by Moses Pallache, al-Walid decided not to recognize David's responsibility for the misunderstanding and ordered the immediate imprisonment of Du Puy and the French consul, Pierre Mazet.

The French were informed of Du Puy's imprisonment and finally became aware of David Pallache's negligence or treachery. Instructions were swiftly sent to the French representative in the Dutch Republic, Alphonse, or Alfonso, López (discussed at greater length below), to petition the States General for David's immediate arrest and extradition. It is worth pointing out that records pertaining to the David Pallache case are so full of stereotypical characterizations of Jews that it is sometimes difficult to establish the precise course of events, let alone David's reasons for acting as he did. "Given that it is a well-known fact that the behavior of the Jews is always accompanied by fraudulence and their actions are full of fallacies and tricks, how can one trust a man who has no honor and whose nation is a sworn enemy of all other nations?" a typical example from the French archives asks.[47]

The members of the States General had been placed in a highly embarrassing situation. They were well aware that to arrest David Pallache and send him to the king of France would be tantamount to a violation of the immunity of a diplomatic agent, and they therefore decided to send excuses to Louis XIII and write to Sultan al-Walid requesting advice on what to do next. The sultan's response was very clear: he told them to arrest "the damned Jew," who had willfully disobeyed orders.[48] In the meantime, David himself had prudently withdrawn to the city of Cologne in the hope that the good offices of his father and brother Moses would resolve the situation and restore him to the sultan's favor.

Unfortunately, Moses Pallache now had troubles of his own. Muley al-Walid had been angered by the fact that Moses had signed the Arabic version of the peace treaty with the French representatives, and he accused his secretary of falsely translating letters in which he had given himself and his relatives honorific titles that did not appear in the original versions. Thus, for example, Moses had written "loyal and honorable deputy" where the Arabic simply said *dhimmi* (i.e., Jewish servant), to some extent a pejorative term.[49] Al-Walid also accused the Pallaches of posing as Moroccan ambassadors abroad. Moses Pallache was imprisoned and came very close to losing his life.[50]

However, events took yet another turn when Muley al-Walid was assassinated by French renegades in February 1636. Al-Walid was succeeded

A MAN OF THREE WORLDS

by his brother Muley Muhammad al-Shaykh al-Saghir, who emerged from the prison cell to which he had been confined by al-Walid in order to accede to the throne. The new sultan was much more sympathetic to the Pallaches than his deceased brother, perhaps partly because he was the son of a Spanish mother and had two Spanish wives. Like Muley Zaydan, al-Saghir spoke good Spanish, and he confirmed Joseph, Moses, and David Pallache in their respective posts shortly after becoming sultan.[51] Al-Saghir told the States General that he believed in the innocence of David Pallache, falsely accused of treachery by Du Chalard, and said that he wished to reinstate him as a Moroccan diplomatic and commercial agent in the Netherlands. Moses Pallache was also restored to his post and was able to continue his highly influential career at the Moroccan court.

ALPHONSE LÓPEZ

As noted, Alphonse López, a fascinating figure whose career has much in common with that of Samuel Pallache and deserves separate scrutiny, was given responsibility for the David Pallache affair in the Netherlands.[52] In The Hague, López asked the prince of Orange [Maurice of Nassau] to requisition David's possessions, as well as those of his father Joseph in Amsterdam, and formally requested David's extradition to France.[53]

The first biographical news of López dates from 1610, when he was in Agde, close to Montpellier, in order to supervise the reception and transit through France of large numbers of moriscos recently expelled from Spain. Marie de Medicis, mother of the young Louis XIII, had granted the moriscos permission to cross France and sail for North Africa from Agde,[54] where López seems to have been in charge of arrangements for embarcation.[55] López clearly exercised great influence over the morisco exiles, and he was entrusted by them with the task of collecting money to finance their transportation and protect them against possible tax levies by officers of the French king. It was in relation to his work for the moriscos that a legal dispute arose in 1611 that required López to go to Toulouse. When the case was referred to the king's Privy Council in 1612, he moved on to Paris to conduct his own defense.

López seems to have traveled to Paris with a circle of morisco friends, and shortly after arriving in the capital, he described himself as a thirty-year-old morisco native of Zaragoza. Once in Paris, López did not limit his activities to preparing his defense in the morisco legal case. He set up in business, acting as a commercial intermediary between French merchants and Turkey and establishing the first Paris workshop for the cutting and polishing of diamonds. López also became a moneylender and a seller of antiquities and works of art to the aristocracy. In fact, in a very short period of time, he became involved in trading in a whole range of luxury goods.[56] Despite his claim to be a morisco, López's professional activities in Paris were characteristically Jewish and seem to point to a Jewish background.

López found favor with the marquis of Rambouillet, who spoke or at least understood Spanish, and it was through Rambouillet that López was introduced at the Louvre palace, where he achieved immediate success as a jewel merchant. At the French court, López presented himself as a descendant of the last Abencerraje, but French contemporary records do not hesitate to describe him as Jewish (he is referred to as the "seigneur Hebreo"), and he is thought to have moved mainly in Jewish circles. Among his known acquaintances were Elias Montalto,[57] the well-known Jewish doctor to Marie de Medicis and Leonora de Galigaï, wife of Marie's personal favorite Concino Concini; López also knew the writer Carlos García, author of a curious treatise on the *Antipatía entre franceses y españoles*, published in Paris in 1617.[58] At one point, López found himself caught up in the events of Leonora's trial on charges of witchcraft, and he was also accused of spying for Spain, a country with which he certainly had at least commercial relations.

It was during this period that López first met Cardinal Richelieu, a renowned connoisseur of jewels and other luxury goods, whose rise to power subsequently provided López with a series of new openings. He advised Richelieu on the feasibility of the commercial development of the port of Le Havre, and was sent on several occasions to purchase naval equipment in Holland. López was always able to count on Richelieu's personal support, which generally gave him a status well above that of the French ambassador in the Dutch Republic. His role as a jeweler and art merchant gave him access to the leading noble houses, and this enabled him to carry out valuable work as a spy and informer for Richelieu. Not only did he manage to amass a great personal fortune, but his activities as a loyal servant of the cardinal earned him appointments as *maître d'hôtel* to the king and later as a *conseiller d'État*. His loyalty to Richelieu and Louis XIII do not ever appear to have been placed in doubt. Nevertheless, J. H. Elliott, in his book on Richelieu and Philip IV of Spain's favorite and chief minister Gaspar de Guzmán Olivares, mentions a private letter written by López to Olivares in 1638 in which López said that he wished to return to Spain. As Elliott says, "it is uncertain whose game López was playing: was he an agent of Richelieu in Olivares' camp, or an agent of Olivares in Richelieu's camp; or perhaps both at once?"[59] Whatever the explanation, López's complex general situation in France seems to bear a striking resemblance to that of Samuel Pallache in the Dutch Republic.

Somehow considered both a Spanish Jew and a Spanish morisco in France, Alphonse López embodies and represents the two main groups of exiles from their native land. In the outlines of his extraordinary career, it is possible to trace the ability and the desire of Jews and moriscos to lead lives of a certain cultural ambiguity. López's career has obvious parallels with that of Samuel Pallache, as well as with those of the Jewish Portuguese financiers employed by Philip IV and Olivares in Madrid.

ISAAC PALLACHE

Archive references to the Pallaches continue to occur for the years that followed. In November 1636, Moses Pallache persuaded Sultan Al-Saghir to write to the English king Charles I in favor of his father and brother David, who were due to carry out important business for the sultan in England and then travel on to Jerusalem.[60] However, it is not known whether Joseph Pallache ever reached the holy city. He died in 1638 and was buried in the Ouderkerk cemetery beside his more illustrious brother Samuel. David Pallache followed him only eleven years later and is buried beside Samuel and Joseph.

Moses continued to work at the Moroccan court, and some idea of the favors he enjoyed at Sultan Al-Saghir's side can be gained from the letter of April 1650, mentioned above, in which the sultan asked the States General to allow Moses to marry his brother David's widow:

> We make it known to you by this letter that the Jews Pallache, who from father to son have served and serve our illustrious house, beneath whose shade they have sheltered, have come to us and fallen at our feet begging us to write to you concerning David Pallache, who has died in your country. This man has left an immense fortune in his widow's hands and has no direct heir of either sex other than the said widow. And in his Faith, it is the elder brother of the deceased who should succeed him, marry the widow, and inherit his goods.

The sultan requested that the affair be resolved according to the dictates of Jewish law:

Do not cease to assist the elder Pallache until he obtains this inheritance without having to abandon his home. . . . In protecting Pallache, you will be fulfilling your duty toward them, for they have lived among you for a long time. Do not neglect the duties of one neighbor towards another, nor those of an employer toward his employee.[61]

Samuel Pallache, one of the sons of Joshua Pallache, was given responsibility for the affair in The Hague, Moses himself now being too old to travel.[62] The States General's respectful reply to the sultan's request was that David's widow refused to leave the Dutch Republic and that the laws of their country did not allow them to force her to go against her will.[63] There are no further mentions of Moses Pallache in the records.

Joseph's oldest son, Isaac, became involved in a series of events in the 1630s that also left their mark in Dutch records. Isaac, it will be remembered, was one of the two Pallache brothers (the other was Joshua) who had been prepared to convert to Catholicism when living in Spain in 1605. In 1610, it was Isaac who had denounced Henrique Garces for appropriating and then selling valuable merchandise taken to Holland by his uncle Samuel and the Moroccan ambassador Ahmad ben Abdallah al-Maruni. In 1610, Isaac had been at pains to present himself as an altruistic and respectable citizen, saying that his denunciation was solely motivated by his desire to serve "God and the king [of Spain]" against their enemies the States General and the king of Morocco. However, Isaac is generally portrayed in the early records as a rebellious young man, whose own father had ordered him to be imprisoned for some time at the castle of Purmerend near Amsterdam. In 1612, Isaac was involved in another lawsuit, this time against Joseph and Samuel Pallache, his own father and uncle, although the causes of this dispute are unknown.[64]

Another indication of a turbulent youth is perhaps to be found in the breaking-off of Isaac's engagement to Catalina Lopes, the daughter of the Portuguese couple Jerónimo and María Lopes, which became a cause of litigation. In fact, it is not entirely clear from the notarial records whether Isaac and Catalina may actually have married, but at all events, the relationship was certainly terminated, and probably against Isaac's wishes: in 1614, we find him applying to be compensated for the loss of Catalina's dowry.[65] In 1619, Catalina became engaged to Abram Alfarim, on condition that Alfarim forgave her for her previous pledge to marry Isaac Pallache.[66]

Despite his apparently rebellious nature, Isaac managed to complete his studies in Hebrew and oriental languages at the University of Leiden. In 1631, he even described himself as a professor of Hebrew at Leiden, but this was almost certainly a false claim.[67] He features as a student in the university's *Album Studiosorum*, but not as a professor, and in 1635, he is known to have sought work in Amsterdam as a broker, a much less elevated position than that of university professor.[68]

Isaac, like all other members of the Pallache family, was involved in various kinds of diplomatic and commercial activity. Between 1614 and 1616, he lived in Istanbul, where he attempted to negotiate the preconditions for the settlement there of his father or uncle as agents of the Moroccan sultan.[69] In 1624, he was in Morocco, where, like other members of his family, he clashed with Albert Ruyl. The Dutch commissioner recorded in his diary that Isaac Pallache had contemptuously told him, in the course of a violent discussion that took place in the presence of several caids, "that he was a better ambassador than me, for he had been sent as such by the Ottoman sultan to His Majesty of Morocco, whereas I came only on behalf of a mere republic."[70]

Isaac converted to Protestantism in about 1633.[71] His father Joseph was incensed by this decision and asked the States General to grant him the custody of Isaac's two-year-old son in consequence. A long legal process ensued over the child's custody, which eventually ruined Isaac, who had a total of six children to support and was also obliged to go through the courts to fight his father over his right to a share of his maternal inheritance. A group of theology professors at Leiden University organized a collection to alleviate Isaac's precarious financial situation,[72] and it may have been due to his monetary difficulties that Isaac decided to start working in the potentially lucrative but risky business of ransoming Christian captives in Morocco.

In 1639, Isaac asked the Dutch government to give him responsibility for negotiations with Sidi Ali ben Mussa, then in control of the Sous region to the south of Marrakech, who was known to be holding a group of Dutch captives. Isaac knew Ali ben Mussa well, because he had already bought arms and munitions on his behalf in Holland and had mediated for him in talks with the Dutch. It is interesting to note that while Isaac's father and brother Moses worked for the sultan, Isaac had thus positioned himself on the side of one of the several local leaders who had declared war on the Moroccan king. In April 1639, Isaac wrote to the States General to the effect that it had been misinformed by his brother David about recent events in Morocco. David Pallache had described Sidi Ali ben

Mussa as a military "rebel," but Isaac told the States General that he should not be considered as such because he had never been a subject of the sultan. Isaac concluded that there was therefore no reason for denying military aid to Ali ben Mussa.[73]

Before leaving for Morocco, Isaac collected money from the families of the captives and was given letters in Arabic for Ali ben Mussa, which were drafted by Jacobus Golius, the professor of Arabic at Leiden. Isaac traveled on a ship belonging to the East India Company, which took him first to Santa Cruz, where he failed to achieve the release of the captives, and then on to Brazil. He returned to the Netherlands a year later, and was invited by the States General to visit The Hague and give an account of his abortive mission. Isaac declined the offer, arguing poor health as a result of the long and arduous journey, and sent a written report instead, which gave a very full account of the unsuccessful mission and explained the various legal cases that had arisen out of it and remained pending. On the one hand, there were the demands of the families of the captives, who wanted the return of the money they had given Isaac to cover the ransom payments and who had also refused to pay Isaac his salary and the costs of his journey. In addition, Isaac was embroiled in a legal dispute with the Delft Chamber of the East India Company over merchandise he had brought back from Brazil that the Company claimed as its own. This dispute was still going on as late as 1647, and we do not know how it was eventually resolved, but at all events, it proved to have a devastating effect on Isaac's fortunes.[74]

Isaac's long report to the States General is a rich and illustrative source of information on the perpetually difficult situation of the Pallaches.[75] The family's difficulties tended to derive from their role as intermediaries from whom both sides demanded exclusive loyalty, but also from the tremendous disdain and suspicion with which they were treated by the Dutch as a consequence of their Jewishness. Although Dutch legislation guaranteed certain freedoms to Jews, and the Pallache family always enjoyed the unwavering support of the States General and Maurice of Nassau, general hostility toward Jews is as evident in the Dutch records that we have seen as it is in those of any other European nation at that time.

One example of the kind of prejudice encountered by Isaac Pallache can be found in the behavior of the ship's captain on Isaac's outward journey to Morocco. The captain refused outright to allow any Dutchman to serve Isaac, for the simple reason that he was a Jew. Another example, taken from later in Isaac's report, is provided by one of the Dutch captives, a man with whom Isaac had formed a certain friendship and on whom he had lavished great hospitality in Morocco. One day, arriving at Isaac's lodgings and observing how Isaac's servant removed his boots for him, this man turned to his fellow captives and openly lamented, "It breaks my heart to see a Christian serving a Jew like this."[76] Isaac Pallache, the Jew in question, was by this time a convert to the Protestant faith, but this seems to have had little effect on the widespread animosity toward him.

Isaac's report also makes it clear that there were many Christians who considered it perfectly legitimate to cheat Jews, or at least to take maximum advantage of them. When he saw the accounts presented by the woman innkeeper from Rotterdam for the days that he and his wife had lodged with her while waiting to sail for Morocco, Isaac's bitter reaction was to write, "Until now I had thought the only place where there were pirates was at sea, but now I see that in truth there are more to be found in this country, famed for its justice."[77] As we have seen, the Pallaches themselves were not averse to practicing deception when it suited them, but European Christians appeared to take the view that since Jews were a people "without honor," there was no reason to make much reference to principles of honor, or honesty, in dealings with them.

Isaac's text attempted to answer each of the accusations leveled at him by the Delft Chamber. Firstly, there was the general charge that, although considered a Christian in the Dutch Republic, Isaac had lived as a Jew in Morocco and had lodged among the Jews of Santa Cruz. The Delft chamber also claimed that Ali ben Mussa had been displeased that the envoy sent to him turned out to be a Jew. Isaac's answer to these charges was as follows: "How could I pretend to be a Jew, when I have abandoned my father and mother and my belongings and my home country, all for the love of the Christian religion?" Of course he had lodged with Jews, he wrote. All foreign envoys and ambassadors in Morocco lodged with Jews, because there were no inns in that country and it was the custom to accommodate guests in the Jewish quarter, as was tolerably well known. Professor Jacobus Golius could testify to this fact, given that he had done exactly the same when he traveled to Morocco with Albert Ruyl and Isaac's father Joseph. As for the insinuation that the Moors did not trust Jews, Isaac simply cited his own family as refutation, pointing out that Moses Pallache was employed by the sultan as his court secretary, and Joshua as a trusted tax official. As if this were not enough, his father Joseph had now been Moroccan ambassador to the States General for some thirty-two years, and his youngest brother, David, was also an agent of the sultan in the Dutch Republic. According to Isaac, responsibility for the failure of the mission lay with the ship's captain and the captives themselves, who had behaved imprudently.

Further on in his report, Isaac listed the goods he had brought back from Brazil, which included opium, cloves, rubber, lacquer, wood, coconuts, and Peruvian balsams. He also brought back what he described as a series of "rarities," some of them gifts from the governor of Dutch Brazil, Johan Maurits of Nassau, such as a spectacle case encrusted with mother-of-pearl. Isaac protested that he had not been permitted to keep any of these goods or the presents that the governor had given him. Clearly angered, he begged God to give him patience and swore by his "nine little grandchildren."

Finally, Isaac made reference to another issue, which is not easy to understand completely, claiming that he had been denounced in his absence by his own brother David, who had made false accusations about him to the Dutch Reformed Church. The basis of David's accusations is unknown—perhaps, like the Delft Chamber, David had alleged that his brother had been a practicing Jew in Morocco? Whatever the nature of David's accusations, Isaac and his family were denied access to Dutch churches as a result of them. In general, it is difficult not to feel sympathy for Isaac Pallache when reading his report, in which he comes across as an entirely embittered man who had been abandoned by everyone he knew.

However, this was not quite the end of Isaac's career. We know that in 1647, he carried letters "of great importance" from the Moroccan sultan to King Wladislaus VII of Poland,[78] and in the same year, he examined a copper mine in Morocco with his brother Moses and wrote to the States General to propose its exploitation.[79] Further traces of his life do not seem to have survived, but one curious piece of evidence about Isaac Pallache dates from several years after his death and may provide a final posthumous insight into the true nature of his religious convictions. The reference is contained in a pamphlet first published in London in 1680, which relates the story of Eva Cohen, a granddaughter of Isaac Pallache, born in 1658. Eva's father was Abram Cohen, a wealthy merchant and overseer of Dutch plantations in Brazil, and Eva's mother was one of Isaac's daughters. Eva had received a Jewish education from her parents, but around 1680, she expressed a sudden desire to convert to Christianity. Eva's mother was strongly opposed to the idea and tried to lock the girl up at home, but Eva escaped and fled to London, where she converted under the name of Elizabeth and married Michael Verboon, a former ser-

A MAN OF THREE WORLDS

vant of her father. A pamphlet publicizing the story assumed Eva's love for Verboon to have been the main reason for her wish to become a Christian and also said that her grandfather Isaac Pallache was widely known to have been a Jew at heart despite having lived as a Christian for many years.[80]

JACOB PALLACHE AND SABBATEANISM

At least one member of the Pallache family was also involved in the so-called Sabbatean movement of the mid seventeenth century. Sabbatai Tsevi, born in Smyrna in 1626, was the mystical leader of one of the most noteworthy messianic movements in the history of Judaism, and Jacob Pallache was a rabbi from Marrakech who later lived in Egypt, where he was a distinguished supporter of the Sabbateans. Jacob Pallache was excommunicated and expelled from the Cairo community by local rabbis after Sabbatai's final apostasy, but is known to have remained a fervent Sabbatean for many years after these events.[81]

Sabbatai's ideas, which caused unprecedented excitement in Jewish and even Christian circles, spread outward from their point of origin in the Ottoman empire to Yemen, Hungary, and Poland, and their effects were felt as far afield as Morocco, Holland, and Britain. Sabbatai Tsevi proclaimed himself Messiah in about the year 1648, and as a result, he and his supporters were expelled from Smyrna in 1651. After periods spent in Salonika and Cairo, Sabbatai later moved to Jerusalem, where he was associated with a nucleus of mystic cabbalists, followers of Isaac Luria, and where he met his future disciple Nathan of Gaza. Nathan proclaimed himself the emerging prophet Elijah whose mission was to clear the way for his Messiah and, led by Sabbatai and the energetic Nathan, the movement spread rapidly. In 1666, widely announced as the messianic year, Sabbatai made a triumphant march on Istanbul, which was followed by his forced conversion to Islam and deportation to Albania, where he died in 1676. Many of Sabbatai's followers converted to Islam like their leader, and Nathan of Gaza struggled to keep the movement alive.[82]

Sabbateanism had important repercussions in Amsterdam, home to both adherents and opponents of the new Messiah. Less well known are the effects of the movement in Morocco, where Salé became an important center for transmission of the Sabbatean word between Amsterdam and the East. Germain de Mouette, a Frenchman captured by pirates in 1670, who lived in Salé for many years and wrote an account of his captivity and life in Morocco, described the enthusiastic scenes in 1671 when a ship arrived in Salé from Amsterdam bringing news of Jewish prophecies concerning a Messiah who would reveal himself the following year.[83] Mouette wrote that the Jewish population reacted to this news by rejoicing wildly and celebrating a second Feast of the Tabernacle that lasted for eight days. According to Mouette, these Jews gathered in the house of one Jacob Bueno de Mesquita, a converso who had fled from the Spanish Inquisition. Mouette's account reveals several significant points. Firstly, we can see from it that Salé was an important Sabbatean stronghold, and that it received news about Sabbatai from Amsterdam. Secondly, it shows the tremendous widespread expectation over the arrival of the Messiah, now scheduled for 1672. Finally, it reveals the interesting fact that converso exiles from Spain also took part in the Sabbatean movement.

A search for further information on Jacob Bueno de Mesquita has proved unsuccessful, but several other members of the Bueno de Mesquita or Amezquita family do appear in Spanish inquisitorial records.[84] Originally natives of Vilaflor in Portugal, the Mezquita family included several important traders who settled in Amsterdam and exported goods to the Iberian Peninsula. In Amsterdam, in 1670, a group of devout Jews set up a yeshiva with the official name of Tif'eret Bahurîm, but commonly known as the yeshiva of Mesquita, because one of its *parnasim*, or community leaders, was Abraham David Bueno de Mezquita, who gave up his home for meetings and meditation. In this, he was followed by his sons and their descendants. The well-known Jacob Sasportas was a part of this yeshiva,[85] and Sasportas's polemical work *Tsitsat novel Tsevi* turns out to be the best source of information on the impact of Sabbateanism in Morocco. Sasportas had been born in Spanish Oran in 1610 and belonged to one of the leading families of the *judería*. He was apparently banished from Oran after a dispute between the Sasportas family and the other powerful Jewish clan in the city, the Cansinos.[86] Jacob became a rabbi in Tlemcen and later in Fez and in Salé. He emigrated with his family to Amsterdam in 1653, and later became grand rabbi in Hamburg, where he wrote the *Tsitsat novel Tsevi*, one of the most significant of all works written in opposition to the Sabbatean movement. Sasportas had an attitude of militant antagonism toward the Sabbateans, as can be seen from his correspondence with Jewish community leaders in many parts of Europe and North Africa. Some of these letters, written to and from Morocco, are reproduced in his *Tsitsat novel Tsevi*. Sasportas expressed astonishment that Sabbatai should have such a huge number of Jewish followers even after his conversion to

Islam and imprisonment, but he makes no explicit mention of Jacob Pallache in this connection.[87]

THE PALLACHES CONTINUED to play key roles in relations between Morocco and the Dutch Republic throughout the duration of the Sa'adian dynasty. As Sultan Muley al-Shaykh al-Saghir had said in his letter to the States General, the Pallaches lived "beneath the shade of his house," and it was the disappearance of that house in the 1660s that brought an end to the Pallaches' influence. After al-Saghir's death in 1663, the Pallache family is hardly mentioned again. During the reign of the following Filali dynasty, which still rules Morocco, other Jewish merchant families came to dominate relations with the Dutch. The Maymoran, Toledano, and Sasportas families all rose to prominence in the decades that followed.[88]

The Pallache family dispersed over several countries. A few years after the disappearance of the Sa'adians, Rabbi Jacob Sasportas sent an epistle to one Isaac Pallache in Livorno, and a short time later he learned that Isaac now lived in Smyrna, where he worked for the protection of Portuguese Jews. In 1695, the same Isaac Pallache wrote a letter to the Dutch consul in Smyrna to request protection for one Salomón Mendes.[89]

One family branch remained in the Netherlands. The subsequent history of the Dutch Palaches (as most family members spell the name today) would require a separate study to do it full justice. However, mention can be made of two well-known bearers of the family name who played a significant role in Jewish life. Isaac van Juda Palache (1858–1927) was grand rabbi of the Portuguese congregation in Amsterdam, and Juda Lion Palache was a professor of Semitic languages in the theology faculty of the University of Amsterdam and chairman of the Portuguese Talmud Torah congregation. During World War II, Juda was deported to Auschwitz, where he died in 1944.[90] Members of the Palache family continue to live in Amsterdam, where they participate actively in the city's Sephardic traditions.

CONCLUSION

This book has sought to trace the story of Samuel Pallache's life as accurately as extant records will allow. Beyond that, we have also tried to make sense of his Moroccan and Dutch contexts by examining his work in the fields of commercial and diplomatic relations between Europe and the Islamic world. Now that we have described Pallache's career and those of the members of his family who came after him, it is time to summarize and draw conclusions. Samuel Pallache needs to be reinterpreted in the light of what we now know about him.

There are several possible ways in which to consider Pallache. First and foremost, he should probably be seen as an adventurer, a man who was forced to resort to highly dangerous strategies in his search for a means of supporting himself and his family. As far as we know, Pallache's adventures began in 1603, when he gave up an extremely precarious existence in Morocco for an almost impossible one in Spain. The Pallaches traveled to Spain as barely tolerated *judíos de permiso*, and in doing so they were certainly not unique or exceptional, as we have tried to show. It did, however, place them in an awkward situation, which turned out to be untenable in the long term. In Spain, judíos de permiso were regarded as passing and fairly unwelcome guests, and the Pallaches' attempts to break this mold were always doomed to failure. They were never able to obtain the kind of acceptance they craved from Spanish society, however willing they may have been to comply with what was demanded of them, and however prepared they were to renounce their religious identity.

The situation was more complex in the Dutch Republic, where Pallache's sense of adventure took him next. Relations between the "New Jews" of Amsterdam and those, like the Pallaches, who were heirs to an older Sephardic tradition were probably more strained than has traditionally been thought. Samuel was deemed a man of some religious knowledge, and he certainly became a member of the Neve Salom community, but he was always excluded from the kinship ties that formed the basis of the commercial networks run by Portuguese Jews. *Los portugueses* were a close, tightly knit group and probably regarded "Barbary Jews" like Samuel Pallache with a certain wariness. In addition, Samuel's work as an official agent of Morocco required him to take up residence in The Hague, not Amsterdam, and the nature of this work restricted his movements within the Dutch Republic, as well as forcing him to make frequent trips abroad. All of this must have limited the extent of his relations with the Jewish communities of Amsterdam.

Throughout his career, the adventuring Pallache never ceased to sound out options in other European countries, and even in Istanbul. He exploited his talent for self-promotion, sold information, and generally went to great lengths to find countries and individuals who were prepared to pay for his services. It can hardly have been an easy way to make a living, and there is something admirable about the way in which Pallache was able to build up his own private sphere of influence and pugnaciously defend it from all those who tried to snatch it from him. Thanks to Samuel, the entire field of diplomatic and commercial relations between Holland and Morocco became Pallache family territory, as was soon discovered by anyone who tried to encroach upon it, from van Lippeloo to Ruyl. Once this private territory had been pieced together with considerable risk, effort, and skill, the following generation of Pallaches found themselves in a position where they did not need to take so many chances. They had no need for Samuel Pallache's founding violence or his boundless questing energy. They did not have to travel as incessantly as he had, or to become involved in acts of privateering or piracy. The Pallaches had become members of the bourgeoisie in an almost literal sense of the term: they attended university, enjoyed the benefits of a stable professional role, which had been created mainly by Samuel, and made the most of an expertise that guaranteed them useful and rewarding employment. Once set, the Pallaches were able to serve Morocco loyally and work for the Dutch government at one and the same time.

THERE ARE OTHER WAYS of interpreting Samuel Pallache's career. One of the most rewarding is surely to see him as a clear predecessor of the European "court Jews" who came to prominence around 1670 and exerted an important influence on European politics until the early eighteenth century.[1] "Court Jews" were employed as representatives and military suppliers to European states and occupied high-ranking posts, mainly in Germany, Austria, and Holland, but also in Poland, Denmark, Hungary, and Italy after the Thirty Years' War. They handled the payment of wages to troops, managed the provisioning of armies and the delivery of fodder for their horses, and, above all, supplied gunpowder. On occasions, such Jews showed a strong commitment to one particular government, but this was not frequent or characteristic. As Jonathan Israel has shown, Jews acting as court agents usually lived well away from the court itself and often even resided outside the states they were serving, since it was common for them to work for more than one government at a time. European governments used Jewish agents as regular suppliers of political and economic information, and many of them worked in big cities like Amsterdam and Hamburg, where munitions and naval equipment were chiefly bought and sold. Many court Jews were expert jewelers, as in the well-known cases of the Oppenheimer and Gomperz families.

Nevertheless, it is worth noting that "court Jews" were never employed as diplomats by European monarchs. This was perhaps the biggest difference between court Jews in Europe and Jews serving at the Moroccan and Ottoman courts, and it underlines the extraordinary character of the work performed for over three-quarters of a century by the Pallache family. It also goes some way toward explaining the antagonism encountered by the Pallaches among their European colleagues, who were completely unaccustomed to dealing with Jews in a diplomatic milieu.

ANOTHER WAY TO INTERPRET the figure of Samuel Pallache is to view him as a typical representative of the burgeoning spirit of mercantilism. Mercantilism was not a new set of principles or economic theories, but rather a concerted attempt to promote states' economic interests over and above questions of privilege, tradition, or religion. Originating in the late sixteenth century, it combined with a politics based on reasons of state to drive what has been called the first great European emancipation. In fact, mercantilism has been described by one of its best-known historians as necessarily involving the processes of "emancipation," "secularization," and "amoralization."[2] The importance of all three aspects emerges very clearly from our study of Pallache's life, as do the pragmatic "reasons of state" so explicitly invoked by his Dutch defenders at his trial in London. Reasons of state were undoubtedly also a crucial factor in Gondomar's subsequent decision to recommend Pallache's recruitment by the Spanish crown. In the light of these facts, it becomes very difficult to uphold the traditional idea of Pallache as a symbol of loyalty to the Dutch struggle against Spain. As we have seen, Pallache's loyalties were in fact multiple and extremely flexible. In this, he was not alone; what makes him exceptional is the work he carried out for Muley Zaydan, the degree of his commitment to the sultan's cause, and the long time during which he was employed.

FINALLY, CERTAIN DETAILS in Pallache's career also seem to hint at the presence of another important factor, namely, the kind of religious skepticism that scholars have suggested was crucial to the creation of modern Western identity. The period has been described as an "Age of Dissimulation."[3] In the sixteenth and seventeenth centuries, many people were forced by religious wars and persecution both to dissimulate their beliefs and to find ways to legitimize the dissimulation, often with a skepticism that may have led to the first stirrings of atheism. It is certainly the case that dissimulation was the cornerstone of countless ethical and political activities in the seventeenth century. These could be maneuvers of a spiraling baroque complexity in which one lied in order to affirm or concealed in order to reveal.[4] It is tempting to detect the pressure of a skeptical attitude in the words of Pallache's parting letter to Philip III in 1608, when he wrote that "as for affairs of the soul, God can be found everywhere." It is an idea that seems almost to echo the work of Spinoza, and a claim that seems to reveal the existence of a highly personal faith that is the sole concern of the one who professes it. It also brings to mind Vaz de Azevedo, whose reply when urged by his interrogators to confess was that he had already "confessed in his heart." Or Isaac Pallache, whose laconic comment on the Jews of Antwerp was: "Who knows how each of them prays?"

In his well-known study of the European Renaissance, Jakob Burckhardt suggested that the origins of modern identity were to be found in the figure of the Renaissance adventurer. Lucetta Scaraffia, in a study of the construction of modern Western identity based on the case of the "renegade," presents such individuals as very different from the stereotyped figure of the simple "traitor" to Christianity. In Scaraffia's view, renegades' lives throw light on an important moment in the development of modern Western man. Renegades were individuals with multiple allegiances who were capable of "choosing" the elements with which to build their own identities in accordance with changing circumstances or the various stages of their lives. One of these many elements was religion, as it was interiorized and experienced within a single personal conscience. People like this dispensed with their roots and first allegiances and worked toward a position where they were in dialogue with themselves alone.[5] It is in the light of reflections like these that Samuel Pallache comes to seem such a complex, and such a modern, individual.

NOTES

ABBREVIATIONS

ADM   Archivo Ducal de Medinasidonia, Sanlúcar de Barrameda (Cádiz)
AGS   Archivo General de Simancas, Simancas
AHN   Archivo Histórico Nacional, Madrid
AN/TT   Arquivo Nacional da Torre do Tombo, Lisbon
BNM   Biblioteca Nacional de Madrid
SIHM *Les sources inédites de l'histoire du Maroc, de 1530 à 1845,* 1st ser., *Dynas-tie Sa'adienne, 1530–1660, Archives et bibliothèques de France, Pays-Bas, Angleterre, Espagne,* edited by Henry de Castries; *Archives et biblio-thèques de Portugal,* edited by Pierre de Cenival, David Lopes, Robert Ricard, and Chantal de La Véronne

CHAPTER I. FROM FEZ TO MADRID

1. See Pieterse, "Daniel Levi de Barrios."
2. Ibid., p. 53.
3. Zwarts, "De eerste rabbijnen," p. 200.
4. See, e.g., Corcos Abulafia, "Samuel Pallache and His London Trial"; Heeringa, "Een bondgenootschap"; Gans, "Don Samuel Palache als moré en zeerover"; Gans, *Memorboek,* pp. 34–35; Hirschberg, *History of the Jews of North Africa,* 2: 212 ff.
5. See Swetschinski, "Un refus de mémoire."
6. Wilke, "Conversion ou retour?"; Salomon, "'De Pinto' Manuscript."
7. Israel, "Spain and the Dutch Sephardim, 1609–1660."
8. AGS, Estado, Leg. 208. In 1607, the brothers stated that they had been at court for four years.
9. ADM, Leg. 2405.

10. AGS, Estado, Leg. 2636, Oct., Nov., and Dec. 1602; ADM, Leg. 2405.

11. ADM, Leg. 2405, letter from the king to Medina Sidonia, Jan. 12, 1603.

12. ADM, Leg. 2405, Mar. 6, 1603.

13. ADM, Leg. 2407.

14. AGS, Estado, Leg. 2636, letter dated Dec. 18, 1602. Several authors—e.g., Hirschberg, *History of the Jews of North Africa*, 2: 213, where no sources are cited—have claimed that Sultan al-Mansur had already used the services of Samuel and his brother Joseph in 1579–80. However, the Pallaches' names do not appear in any of the Spanish records referring to negotiations with al-Mansur, and the Pallaches themselves made no allusion to such experience when they sought to establish their merits in 1605.

15. On the merchant Juan de Marchena, see Rojas, *Relación de algunos sucesos postreros de Berbería*, f. 11. Juanetín Mortara became a Spanish agent at the court of Muley al-Shaykh (see Guadalajara y Javier, *Prodición y destierro*, f. 96 ff.).

16. AGS, Estado, Leg. 493. This is a summary of the session. An entire *acta* for it can be found in AGS, Estado, Leg. 2637, but the papers presented by Pallache do not figure among the surviving records of this meeting.

17. AGS, Estado, Leg. 208.

18. AGS, Estado, Leg. 2637, no. 59, June 19, 1605.

19. Ibid., no. 159, June 13, 1605.

20. Ibid., no. 60, Aug. 16, 1605.

21. AGS, Estado, Leg. 2637 bis, Sept. 6, 1605.

22. AGS, Estado, Leg. 200.

23. ADM, Leg. 2406, Sept. 20, 1605.

24. Ibid., Nov. 15, 1605.

25. AGS, Estado, Leg. 200.

26. ADM, Leg. 2757.

27. Juanetín Mortara seems to have first gone to Fez, "with the idea of trading in diamonds and fine jewels with Muleyxeque, who, as we have said, never tired of them and prided himself on searching them out and knowing them and paying well for them" (Rojas, *Relación de algunos sucesos postreros de Berbería*, f. 11).

28. This was commonly the case with contemporary Jewish families and is usually interpreted in the context of their commercial networks (see Swetschinski, "Kinship and Commerce").

29. This according to documents from the ADM, though no references are given, in Álvarez de Toledo, *Alonso Pérez de Gúzman*, 2: 65.

30. AGS, Estado, Leg. 200.

31. AGS, Estado, Leg. 208. Joseph and Samuel Pallache received money for "just causes." On the Larache affair, see García Figueras and Rodríguez Juliá Saint-Cyr, *Larache*.

32. *Colección de documentos inéditos para la historia de España*, 81: 478.

33. Letter from de Jaubert in Madrid, Sept. 29, 1606, *SIHM, France*, 2: 343–44.

34. Letter from de Jaubert to Henri IV, Nov. 26, 1606, *SIHM, France*, 2: 352–54.

35. AGS, Estado, Leg. 208.

36. AGS, Guerra y Marina, Leg. 679.

37. *SIHM, France*, 2: 375.

38. Ibid., p. 433.

39. See letter from de Jaubert to Henri IV, Apr. 16, 1608, ibid., and also AGS, Guerra y Marina, Leg. 679.

40. The Inquisition is known to have grown wary on such occasions. In 1671, when Solomon and Samuel Sasportas of the Oran Jewry sought to take advantage of their services to the Spanish crown and be baptized with their whole family in order to settle permanently in Spain, the Holy Office swiftly intervened. It ordered each of them to be interrogated separately, "asking them for the story of their lives since leaving Oran, by what route they had come and by whose license . . . for what reasons they had put aside their proper Jewish clothing, through which ports they had entered, with whom they had had dealings, and what reasons they had for desiring to be baptized and live as Christians."

41. The planned conversion of the Pallaches should also be considered from the point of view of Jewish law. See, e.g., Zimmels, *Die Marranen in der rabbinischen Literatur*. Full justice cannot be done to this point here, but we hope to return to it in a separate study.

42. Samuel and Joseph Pallache, letter to Philip III, Sept. 9, 1607, AGS, Estado, Leg. 208.

43. AGS, Estado, Leg. 208.

44. Ibid., p. 206.

45. AGS, Guerra y Marina, Leg. 679.

46. According to a notarial document dated Sept. 23, 1616, no. 1000 in *Studia Rosenthaliana* 10 (1976): 221.

47. *SIHM, Pays-Bas*, 2: 269.

48. Ibn Daud, *Book of Tradition*, pp. 48, 52, mentions a Jewish family in Córdoba in the tenth century with a similar surname, the Ibn Falija, but this identification is highly implausible. According to Laredo, *Les noms des juifs au Maroc*, p. 966, they emigrated to Morocco after the expulsion of 1492, but no sources are cited to support this claim.

49. Laredo, *Les noms des juifs au Maroc*, p. 967. For more on Isaac Uziel, see Chapter 3.

50. Roth, "Strange Case of Hector Mendes Bravo," p. 243.

51. See Chapter 3.

52. "Reduction de cinco Erches renegados de Verversía y sus confesiones," AHN, Inquisición, Leg. 1821, no. 15. See Mediano, "Portugueses en Marruecos."

53. ADM, Leg. 2409, letter from Philip III to Medina Sidonia, Sept 23, 1614.

54. *SIHM, Pays-Bas*, 2: 170.

55. See esp. the letters of Pallache edited in *SIHM, Pays-Bas*, vol. 2, passim.

56. AHN, Inquisición, Toledo, Leg. 134, no. 18, fol. 8.

57. This trial is analyzed in Beinart, "Halijatam shel yehudim."

58. Cf. the papers sent by the Lisbon Inquisition to that of Toledo, AHN, Inquisición, Leg. 134, no. 18 f. 13r.

59. AHN, Inquisición, Toledo, Leg. 145, no 13.

60. AHN, Inquisición, Leg. 156, no 4.

61. Mendoça, *Jornada de África*, fol. 68v.

62. Tavim, *Os judeus e a expansão portuguesa em Marrocos*, pp. 107 ff. and documentary appendix.

63. López Belinchón, "Aventureros, negociantes y maestros dogmatizadores."

64. See Beinart, "Halijatam shel yehudim."

65. But it must be remembered that not all Jews returning to the Peninsula actually converted. See Yerushalmi, "Professing Jews in Post-Expulsion Spain and Portugal."

CHAPTER 2. JEWS IN MOROCCO

1. In the application made by the Pallaches on Apr. 8, 1608, for a passport to enter the Netherlands, it is explicitly stated that they were "van natie ende professie der Hebreeuwen, geboren te Fees in Barbarije," i.e., "Hebrews by nation and profession, born at Fez in Barbary" (*SIHM, Pays-Bas*, 1: 273–75).

2. Bernáldez, "Historia de los Reyes Católicos," p. 601a. See also Ibn Verga, *Chebet Yehudá*, pp. 53 ff.

3. Genot-Bismuth, "Le mythe de l'Orient"; Ruderman, "Hope against Hope."

4. See Sasson, "Exile and Redemption." Saba, *Tseror ha-mor* describes the Jewish exiles' general attitude to Muslims, in contrast to their attitude to Christians; see esp. fol. 47 (Genot-Bismuth, "Le mythe de l'Orient," p. 820).

5. Laredo, "Les 'Purim' de Tánger"; Cantera Burgos, "El 'Purim' del Rey Don Sebastián." For further coverage of this subject, see Valensi, *Fables de la mémoire*, ch. 4.

6. Torrutiel, *El Libro de la Cabala*, pp. 42–43. The fire is also discussed in Bernáldez, "Historia de los Reyes Católicos," p. 391, who describes the misery suffered by those who emigrated to Morocco, and claims that many of them returned to Spain between 1493 and 1496: "All those Jews who passed over to the kingdom of Fez and returned here came naked, barefoot, and covered in lice, starving to death and very misadventured, it was painful to see them."

7. Sémach, "Une chronique juive de Fès."

8. These garrison towns had always been home to Jewish conversos: in October 1488, João II had found it necessary to decree the death penalty for conversos traveling inland from the ports with the purpose of returning to their previous faith. See Tavim, *Judeos e a expansão portuguesa em Marrocos*, p. 75.

9. See, e.g., Torres, *Relación del origen y suceso*, pp. 192–94, and Mendoça, *Jornada de África*. And see also Le Tourneau, "Notes sur les lettres latines de Nicholas de Clénard," and Koningsveld, "'Mijn Kharûf'," passim, on Nicolaas Cleynaerts (Nicolas Clénard), who lived in the Jewish quarter in 1541.

10. Mármol, *Descripción general de África*, f. 91 r. and v.

11. Mendoça, *Jornada de África*, fol. 11v.

12. Ibid., fol. 11r.

13. Cruz, *Chronica*, p. 371.

14. Clénard, *Correspondence*, 3: 73, letter of Aug. 21, 1541.

15. Glick, "Moriscos and Marranos," p. 119. See Tedghi, "Books, Manuscripts and Hebrew Printing in Fez," which gives the titles of nine books printed in Fez during these years. The Sassoon Library in London contains three copies of Hebrew books printed in Fez in 1521. After 1524, Fez scholars were forced to print their books in Italy, Istanbul, or Salonika (Thessaloníki).

16. Cf. Beinart, "Fas, merkaz le-giur we-la-sibat anusim la-yahadut," pp. 319–24, which studies some of the Inquisition sources cited here.

17. Juan Núñez, a tailor from Toledo, left for Fez with those expelled and later returned to Toledo. His trial took place in 1521–23 (AHN, Inquisición, Toledo, Leg. 171, n. 12). At the trial of Pedro Serrano, a statement was made by a converso who had gone to Fez with his parents and after remaining there for sixteen years, had returned to Spain and converted. See Baer, *Die Juden im Christlichen Spanien*, 2: 544. García Fuentes, *La Inquisición en Granada*, p. 180, speaks of a defendant who "wanted to pass to Barbary . . . there was a decision to go with some Moors to their land . . . and keep the law of the Jews [there]."

18. Wolf, *Jews in the Canary Islands*, p. 90.

19. AHN, Inquisición, Leg. 176, no. 11, says of Juan Robles [Abraham Aguer]: "He is in the Jewry of Fez and he wears the signal of the Jew upon his cap and he was circumcised by the rabbi of the Jews . . . and he learnt the Hebraic tongue in order to know better the law and pray with the other Jews, he was full of cheer and very glad to have become a Jew. . . . He would go to read and pray in the synagogue of the Jews, and he would take to the synagogue some straps that they call *tafelis*, . . . and he had made a narrow strip of leather like a bandage on his forehead, which hung down his back as far as the waist and was tied there, and which in the glass-making furnace he wore gathered up."

20. Tavim, *Judeus e a expansão portuguesa em Marrocos*, pp. 108 ff.

21. Saldanha, *Crónica de Almançor*, pp. 70 ff.

22. Ibid., p. 183.

23. Ibid., p. 85.

24. Ibid., p. 84.

25. In the Inquisition proceedings against Vicente Lourenço (AN/TT, Inquisição de Lisboa no. 12562, ff. 8–20), six Portuguese Jews were mentioned as working in the Sous sugar refineries. See also Saldanha, *Crónica de Almançor*, p. 78.

26. *Crónica de Almançor*, p. 82.

27. Ibid., pp. 402 ff.

28. "Avisos de Berbería de Juan Agustín de la Torre," cited by Boronat y Barrachina, *Los moriscos españoles y su expulsión*, 2: 516.

29. Vajda, "Un recueil de textes historiques judéo-marocaines," p. 326.

30. García-Arenal, "Les *bildiyyin* de Fes."

31. See Gerber, *Jewish Society in Fez*, ch. 7, "Jews in Commerce," pp. 159 ff.

32. See, e.g., *SIHM, Angleterre*, vol. 2, doc. 38, p. 117, where Sir Christopher Parkins gives advice concerning the protocol to be observed at the Moroccan court and says that the English ambassador should address the sultan as *emperador* ("emperor" in Castilian) and his son as *alteza* ("Your Highness").

33. For the reign of al-Mansur, see Yahya, *Morocco in the Sixteenth Century*.

34. *SIHM, Angleterre,* 2: 11 n. 2.

35. See, e.g., correspondence between "Xeque Rutt" and Baltasar Polo in 1595, in AGS, Estado, Leg. 492, passim.

36. R. Ricard, "Notice sur Bastião de Vargas, agent de Jean III au Portugal," in *SIHM, Portugal,* 3: 176–90.

37. *SIHM, Portugal,* vol. 2, passim.

38. Gozálbes Busto, *Los moriscos en Marruecos,* p. 103.

39. For instance, *SIHM, Portugal,* vol. 3, docs. 19, 21.

40. Bastião de Vargas often referred to Portuguese conversos trading in wheat with Morocco and complained that many of them took advantage of their travels to deal in forbidden merchandise, such as arms.

41. *SIHM, Portugal,* 5: 50, 52–54.

42. Laredo, *Les noms des juifs au Maroc,* p. 552.

43. Ricard, "Baptême d'un Juif de Fès."

44. Mármol, *Descripción general de África,* 2: 54r.

45. According to Mármol (ibid. 2: 55v), there were four hundred Jewish households in Azemmour when the town was occupied by the king of Portugal.

46. *SIHM, Espagne,* 1: 246; *Portugal,* 2: 562, 583.

47. *SIHM, Portugal,* 4: 239.

48. Laredo, *Les noms des juifs du Maroc*: Senanes, pp. 906 ff.; Pariente, pp. 980 ff.; Rute, pp. 375 ff.; Ben Zemiro, pp. 550 ff.

49. Israel, "Jews of Spanish North Africa," pp. 71–72.

50. ADM, Leg. 2411, Dec. 1614.

51. Ibid., Dec. 1619.

52. See Jacob Cansino, "Relación de los servicios de Iacob Cansino y los de su padre," published as an introduction to id., *Extremos y grandezas de Constantinopla compuesto por Rabi Moysen Almosnino.*

53. See, e.g., ADM, Leg. 2407, letter from the king to Medina Sidonia, Dec. 7, 1612.

54. According to documents from 1623 and 1624, Juda Levi was later a tax official of the sultan in Safi: *SIHM, Angleterre,* 2: 233–63, 441, 468; *Pays-Bas,* 1: 297–300, 341, 441, 445, 500; *Pays-Bas,* 2: 283, 286, 288, 525.

55. *SIHM, Angleterre,* 2: 501, *Pays-Bas,* 3: 14.

56. "Ibn Ways is the kings [Abu Farīs] merchant" (*SIHM, Angleterre,* 2: 233, 363).

57. *SIHM, Angleterre,* 2: 490.

58. *SIHM, Pays-Bas,* 3: 532, and vol. 4, passim.

59. Gozálbes Busto, *Los moriscos en Marruecos,* p. 131. Abraham Gibre made several journeys to Portugal in connection with ransom negotiations for captives, and ended up settling in Tangiers as another Christian convert. See Mendoça, *Jornada de África,* bk. 1, ch. 1; bk. 2, ch. 5.

60. AGS, Guerra y Marina, Leg. 662.

61. AGS, Estado, Leg. 493. Juanetín Mortara requested a safe-conduct for Natán Benterny, a servant and special protégé of Muley al-Shaykh, and for Benterny's family, asking that they be permitted to pass into Spain and all its territo-

ries. In Mortara's opinion, Benterny was extremely important and it was impossible to deal with Muley al-Shaykh unless through him.

62. Rojas, *Relación de algunos sucesos postreros de Berbería*, fol. 67v.

63. Mendoça, *Jornada de África*, is particularly explicit in this respect; see f. 153v. See also Dakhlia, "Réinscriptions linagères et redéfinitions sexuelles des convertis."

64. AGS, Estado, Leg. 494.

65. *SIHM, Pays-Bas*, 4: 352 ff., 355, 482 ff., 513 ff., etc.

66. AGS, Guerra y Marina, Leg. 660, 1606.

67. AGS, Guerra y Marina, Leg. 645, 1505: Juan Alonso de Moscoso, by nation a Moor and native of the mountains of Melilla, passed over with arms and horse; AGS, Guerra y Marina, Leg. 670, 1607: Juan Henríquez, a convert from Melilla, went to Spain with his family and ten children.

68. Rojas, *Relación de algunos sucesos postreros de Berbería*, ff. 60–61, ranges widely over this problem, and mentions cases where moriscos were even prepared to return as slaves.

69. AGS, Estado, Leg. 495.

70. Boyajian, "New Christians Reconsidered."

71. Tavim, "Os judeus e a expansão portuguesa na India."

72. For more on this, see Saraiva, *Inquisição e cristãos-novos*.

73. Tavares, "Judeus de sinal."

74. See Ricard, "Bastião de Vargas, agent de Jean III" and "Datos complementarios."

75. *SIHM, Portugal*, 4: 55 ff.

76. Domínguez Ortiz, *La clase social de los conversos de Castilla*, pp. 84–87; Kaplan, *From Christianity to Judaism*, ch. 1, "From Portugal to Spain"; Yerushalmi, *From Spanish Court to Italian Ghetto*, pp. 8 ff.

77. Domínguez Ortiz, *La clase social de los conversos de Castilla*, p. 114.

78. Ibid., n. 21.79. AN/TT, Inquisição, no. 4356, extracts published in Tavim, *Os judeus na expansão portuguesa em Marrocos*, pp. 569–72.

80. *SIHM, France*, 1: 178–81.

81. *SIHM, Angleterre*, 1: 48–49.

82. AN/TT, Inquisição, Leg. 5393. See García-Arenal, "Entre Oriente y Occidente."

83. Robert Shirley had first traveled to Persia with his brother Anthony, and in 1599, when Anthony was sent to Moscow by Shah Abbas on a diplomatic mission, Robert stayed behind in Persia as a hostage. He then served for several years in the Persian army and tried to gain the confidence of the shah, who eventually sent him as his ambassador to Spain in 1610, and then to England, from where he returned to Persia in 1613. Robert dressed in the Persian style and was married to a Catholic Circasian by the name of Teresia Khan. Robert's brother Anthony was sent by Rudolf II of Germany on a commercial and diplomatic mission to Morocco in 1605. For more on the Shirleys, see Ross, *Sir Anthony Sherley*.

84. The baptism certificate from El Escorial, dated Apr. 3, 1589, presents "a man of forty years of age, a Jew by nation, native of Fez, and called Moisén ben

Zamerro in Judaism and in the baptism he is called Pablo de Santa María." In Ricard, "Baptême d'un juif de Fès."

85. Modena, *Autobiography of a Seventeenth-Century Venetian Rabbi*, pp. 14–15.

86. See Gerber, *Jewish Society in Fez*, pp. 78–80.

87. al-Fishtali, *Manahil al-safa*, p. 42. The moriscos settled in a district beside the Alcazaba known as Riyad al-Zaytun. According to Mármol, *Descripción general de África*, 2: f. 33, they gave it the name Órgiva la Nueva, or New Órgiva.

88. See, e.g., Wiegers, "Learned Moriscos."

89. This fascinating subject has been covered in several studies. A general summary can be found in Caro Baroja, *Las falsificaciones de la historia*, ch. 3.

90. al-Hajari, *Kitab nasir al-din 'ala l-qawm al-kafirin*.

91. *SIHM, Angleterre*, 2: 166, 203.

92. *SIHM, Angleterre*, 2: 214–15; *Pays-Bas*, 1: 644. Owing to strict prohibition of their entry into the country after the Expulsion of 1609–14, Moroccan sultans found it impossible to use morisco agents for missions to Spain. Orders were also issued repeatedly for moriscos not to be allowed to enter Tangiers, Ceuta, or Larache. See ADM, Leg. 2409, letter from the king to the governors of these towns, May 9, 1613.

93. García-Arenal, "Vidas ejemplares."

CHAPTER 3. BETWEEN THE DUTCH REPUBLIC AND MOROCCO

1. See Webster, "Hebraizantes portugueses."

2. Hirschberg, *History of the Jews of North Africa*, 2: 213, claims that Samuel and Joseph Pallache worked as merchants in Amsterdam as early as 1596, stating that they are both mentioned in the list of the first Portuguese *minyan*, which met at Samuel's home to celebrate the first public service of Yom Kippur. But Hirschberg's only source for this information is the *Historia Universal Judayca* of Miguel de Barrios, now shown by several scholars to be extremely unreliable, as was explained in Chapter 1 (see, e.g., Zwarts, "De eerste rabbijnen," p. 200). The most that can be said is that the Pallaches may have taken part in the foundation of the second community, Neve Salom, in about 1610, although there is as yet no documentary evidence to support this.

3. Nahon, "Les rapports des communautés judéo-portugaises avec celle d'Amsterdam," p. 39.

4. Israel, *European Jewry in the Age of Mercantilism*.

5. AGS, Estado, Leg. 627. See Lapeyre, *Géographie de l'Espagne morisque*, esp. pp. 184–87. Juan Núñez Saraiva, a future royal contractor, and other Portuguese men were accused by a French merchant of removing the money of moriscos from the area of Almagro and Daimiel. AHN, Inquisición, Leg. 171, according to López Belinchón, "Estudio de la minoría judeoconversa en Castilla," p. 39.

6. AGS, Estado, Leg. 629.

7. *SIHM, Pays-Bas*, 1: 273–75.

8. There are hints in the records that while Samuel was on his way back to

Morocco, his brother Joseph may have made some sort of approach to the duke of Tuscany. See letter from Descartes to Puisieux, *SIHM, France,* 2: 475–76.

9. Koen, "Notarial Records," no. 1184.

10. See Bouzineb and Wiegers, "Tetuán y la expulsión de los moriscos."

11. Letter from Coy to the States General, Oct. 6, 1608, *SIHM, Pays-Bas,* 1: 302.

12. *SIHM, France,* 1: 299.

13. *SIHM, Angleterre,* 3: 606.

14. The merchants were Jan Janz, Carel de Jonge, and Symon Willemsz Nooms and his associates. See notary doc. no. 368, published in *Studia Rosenthaliana* 5 (1971): 112.

15. Contreras, "Cristianos de España y judíos de Amsterdam."

16. Israel, *European Jewry in the Age of Mercantilism,* introduction.

17. Kaplan, *Judíos nuevos en Amsterdam,* introduction.

18. Israel, *European Jewry in the Age of Mercantilism.*

19. See Salomon, *Portrait of a New Christian,* p. 46.

20. In Kaplan's terms, in *Judíos nuevos en Amsterdam,* p. 13.

21. Opinions differ on the reasons for the founding of a second community. According to Kaplan in "De joden in de Republiek," p. 130, these reasons were mainly demographic, and had to do with the growth of the Jewish population. Bodian, *Hebrews of the Portuguese Nation,* p. 46, maintains that there were religious motives related to differences between the Ashkenazim and the Sephardim. See Vlessing, "New Light," pp. 48–49.

22. See the 1612 contract published in *Studia Rosenthaliana* 5 (1971): 240–42 and the references given there. Also Bodian, *Hebrews of the Portuguese Nation,* p. 59.

23. Kaplan, "De joden in de Republiek," p. 144.

24. For Uziel, see note 39 below.

25. Bodian, *Hebrews of the Portuguese Nation,* pp. 47–48.

26. See Kaplan, *Judíos nuevos en Amsterdam,* passim.

27. Bodian, *Hebrews of the Portuguese Nation,* pp. 147–48.

28. Fruin, "Uittreksel uit Francisci Dusseldorpii Annales," pp. 387–88: "Aliquot eorum continuo Amstelredamum appulerunt; quibus concessa fuit ibidem synagoga, in quam ex praecipius istius civitatis hereticis nonnulli, circumciso inguine, nomen dederunt. Usque adeo calvinismo et turcismo convenit"; cf. Zwarts, "De eerste rabbijnen," p. 203 n.

29. Groot, "Ottoman Empire and the Dutch Republic," pp. 11, 300, n. 20; Heeringa, *Bronnen tot de geschiedenis van den Levantschen handel,* 1: 206 ff.

30. ADM, Leg. 2408.

31. Kaplan, *Judíos nuevos en Amsterdam,* p. 67. The prohibition on the conversion of non-Jews may partly explain this refusal.

32. AGS, Estado, Leg. 2291.

33. See Roth, "Strange Case of Hector Mendes Bravo."

34. Duarte Fernandes was also denounced by Hector Mendes Bravo in 1617 (ibid., p. 237). In fact, Mendes Bravo mentioned two men with the name Duarte Fernandes: one was the Portuguese Jew from Amsterdam who assisted the Pal-

laches, and the other, Duarte Fernandes Veiga, was a merchant from Antwerp. On the first, see Koen, "Duarte Fernandes."

35. "Deux Juifz freres [Samuel et Joseph Pallache] . . . sont allez vers Messieurs des Estatz . . . trompans les ungs et les autres pour en tirer par leurs artiffices l'argent qu'ilz peuvent." Letter from Descartes to Puisieux, Oct. 12, 1609, *SIHM, France,* 2: 475.

36. Ibid., Oct. 25, 1609, *SIHM, France,* 3: 478–79.

37. Pieterse, ed., *Livro de Beth Haim do Kahal Kados de Bet Yahacob,* pp. 26, 27, 31, 65, 101, 130.

38. *Studia Rosenthaliana* 10 (1976): 221, doc. no. 1000.

39. Isaac Uziel had married Bella Vida in Istanbul. Although a rabbi, he was not Portuguese; neither did he marry a Portuguese woman. He died in 1622. See Bodian, *Hebrews of the Portuguese Nation,* p. 48; Pieterse, "Daniel Levi de Barrios," p. 63; Zwarts, "De eerste rabbijnen," pp. 233–35, appendix 25: "e nascido em a cidade de Fez." Uziel's grave can be found in the Ouderkerk cemetery, see Alvares Vega, *Het Beth Haim van Ouderkerk aan de Amstel,* p. 28.

40. On April 13, 1613, Dr. Pieter Wittendael, the surgeons Johan Quartelaer and Herman Borsman, and the pharmacist Dirk Verdoes, all citizens of The Hague, requested payment of their bills for the cure of Samuel Pallache's sons Isaac and Ya'qub (or Jacob) Carlos. The States General ordered Pallache to pay his debts (*Resolutiën der Staten Generaal,* n.s., *1610–1760,* 2 [1613–16], resolution of Apr. 13, 1613).

41. Joshua, Joseph's son, married a Jewish woman from Rotterdam who was buried in Ouderkerk, according to the *Livro de Bet Haim,* p. 137. It is not known whether she was a Portuguese Jew, although it seems probable.

42. Not. Arch. nos. 1682 and 781, cited in *Studia Rosenthaliana* 14 (1980): 91, and 18 (1984): 160.

43. The States General paid the rent on Pallache's accommodation: on June 4, 1615, it paid Jacob Willemsz of Voorburg the sum of 350 florins for half a year's rent (*SIHM, Pays-Bas,* 2: 166, 214, 688). Joseph Pallache lived in Amsterdam (ibid., 1: 462).

44. Samuel, "Portuguese Jews in Jacobean London," p. 175: Antwerp, Oct. 10, 1610, "Isacq Pallache here present said and affirmed he had seen him [Simão de Mercado] and had been seated with him in the house of Gimes Lopez who is also called by another name, Jacob Thirado, where all the Portuguese Jews assemble for prayers." See also ibid., pp. 209–10.

45. Archives générales du Royaume, Brussels, Office fiscal de Brabant, Porte-feuilles, W 131, no. 924a and b.

46. Bodian, *Hebrews of the Portuguese Nation,* p. 33 and references.

47. Balas rubies (in Arabic, *balakhsh*) come from Badhakhshan, a region in Central Asia which gives them their name. They differ from oriental rubies in that they are pinkish-red with blue spots and often have a generally milky tone.

48. Isaac Pallache's testimony against Juan Mendes Henriques, Aug. 1610, Archives générales du Royaume, Brussels, Office fiscal de Brabant, Portefeuilles, kl. n. 131 gr. n. 924 [A], f. 22v: "y recontrandolo en caille abierta y prinçipale

d'esta dicha villa lo dixo y lo amenaso en esta manera tomando las pocitas de barba a la man, trahidor, perro, judio y infame."

49. This is probably the same Fray Martín del Spíritu Santo, a Portuguese Benedictine monk and converso, who gave information to the Inquisition of Granada in 1607 in order to save his brother, who had been detained. Martín gave the tribunal details about the colony of conversos in Rouen and the colony was broken up as a direct result of his information. A few months later, the governor of Bayonne ordered Martín to be arrested and charged with spying for Spain after he had been denounced by the Portuguese Manuel Mendes. See Pelorson, "Le docteur Carlos García."

50. Archives générales du Royaume, Brussels, Office fiscal de Brabant, Portefeuilles, kl. n. 131 gr. n. 924A, ff. 281r–284r.

51. The use by Amsterdam Jews in the early seventeenth century of Jewish names in the synagogues and Christian names in daily life was discussed in the *responsa*. See Zimmels, *Die Marranen in der rabbinischen Literatur*, pp. 55, 155.

52. Archives générales du Royaume, Brussels, Office fiscal de Brabant, Portefeuilles, kl. n. 131 gr. n. 924A, ff. 281r–284r.

53. AN/TT, Inquisição Lisboa, no. 3292.

54. *SIHM, Pays-Bas*, 1: 311.

55. For this mission, see *SIHM, Pays-Bas*, 1: 357–499; *France*, 2: 485–86, 490–91.

56. *SIHM, Angleterre*, 2: 426–27.

57. *SIHM, Pays-Bas*, 1: 577.

58. Ibid., pp. 369–70, n. 3.

59. For more, see Wiegers, "Andalusi Heritage in the Maghrib."

60. Al-Maruni was probably the Moroccan ambassador whom Henrique Garces traveled to see in 1610.

61. *SIHM, Pays-Bas*, 1: 519–22.

62. Ibid., pp. 591–93.

63. See J. de Henin, "Descripción de los reinos de Marruecos (1603–1613). Memorial de Jorge de Henin," BNM, MS 17645, p. 121. An edition of this text was published by T. Pérez de Guzmán in Rabat 1997, but our references are to the manuscript itself.

64. Henin, "Descripción de los reinos de Marruecos," p. 121.

65. Ibid., pp. 107–8, 333.

66. Records of captures of Christian prisoners and ransom payments for captives in Tétouan in the early decades of the seventeenth century show similar kinds of collaboration between Jews and moriscos. See Gozálbes Busto, *Los moriscos en Marruecos*, esp. ch. 5, "La convivencia judeo-morisca en el exilio."

67. Cabrera de Córdoba, *Relaciones de las cosas sucedidas*, f. 367.

68. *SIHM, Pays-Bas*, 1: 690. Samuel went back to Morocco in 1609, 1610, 1611, 1612–13, and 1614–15.

69. Ibid., 2: 75, 115.

70. Ibid., 1: 353.

71. Ibid., 2: 141 ff.

72. Ibid., pp. 201, 269, autograph letter from Samuel Pallache to Prince Mau-

rice of Nassau, Dec. 20, 1614 (M. H. Gans collection, fol. 11a). Nearly all the documents in this collection were purchased by M. H. Gans on the occasion of an exhibition in London; see Victoria and Albert Museum, *Catalogue of an Exhibition of Anglo-Jewish Art and History*, p. 17, no. 54: *Samuel Palache, a Jewish Privateer.* Bound volume of twenty MS papers relating to the exploits and arrest of Samuel Palache, the ambassador of Morocco at The Hague, lent by H. Eisemann and C. Abramsky. For more on Maurice and Pallache, see Deursen, *Maurits van Nassau*, p. 217; Zandvliet, "Het Hof van een dienaar."

73. *SIHM, Pays-Bas*, 2: 8 ff.

74. Ibid., p. 15.

75. Ibid., pp. 12, 75.

76. Ibid., p. 41, Mar. 1612.

77. Ibid., p. 85.

78. Ibid., p. 172.

79. Ibid., 1: 623.

80. John Harrison, *The Messiah already come or profes of Christianitie . . . to convince the Jewes, written in Barbarie in the year 1610* (Amsterdam, 1619). The first edition, also published in Amsterdam, is dated 1612 and carries a dedication to the States General.

81. *SIHM, Angleterre*, vol. 3, John Harrison's Relation, pp. 27 ff.

82. *SIHM, Pays-Bas*, 1: 299, 309.

83. Ibid., pp. 526–27.

84. Ibid., pp. 545–46.

85. Henin, BNM, MS 17645, pp. 171–72.

86. Ibid., p. 185.

87. AGS, Estado, Leg. 495.

88. *SIHM, Pays-Bas*, 1: 624–27, cf. letter from Zaydan, Sept. 28, 1611, ibid., p. 673.

89. See, e.g., Kaddouri, "Ibn Abi Mahalli."

90. *SIHM, Pays-Bas*, 2: 21.

91. Ibid., p. 23.

92. See, e.g., ibid., pp. 182, 186.

93. See ibid., pp. 117 ff.

94. Reference was made to these two Moroccan Jews in Chapter 1. For the conflicts, due to commercial competition, see *SIHM, Pays-Bas*, 1: 381, 500.

95. Ibid., p. 384.

96. *SIHM, Angleterre*, 2: 469 ff.

97. Mose Palatse, *Een waerachtige beschryvinghe vant ghene datter geschiet is int lant van Barbarien* (Rotterdam, 1614), French translation and Dutch original in *SIHM, Pays-Bas*, 2: 440–45.

98. *SIHM, Pays-Bas*, 2: 215.

99. Ibid., p. 391.

100. Ibid., p. 245.

101. Ibid., p. 22, n. 7.

102. See letter from Muley Zaydan to Samuel Pallache, Feb. 13, 1612, ibid.,

p. 20ff. Samuel met Castelane in Safi before his own departure for Holland, ibid., p. 23.

103. See Justel, *La Real Biblioteca de El Escorial*.

104. *SIHM, Angleterre*, 3: 67.

105. For the letter, see *SIHM, Pays-Bas*, 2: 106.

106. Ibid., p. 131.

107. Ibid., p. 138.

108. In August 1612, the States General wrote to Louis XIII: "Prions atant, Sire, bien humblement, qu'il plaise à Vostre Majesté octroyer auxdicts sieurs alcayde, eunuque et Moyse Pallache benigne audience et donner tel ordre à ceulx qu'il conviendra" (ibid., p. 139).

109. Ibid., p. 192.

110. Ibid., p. 262.

111. See Marín, "Captive Word"; Koningsveld, "Andalusian-Arabic Manuscripts from Christian Spain," pp. 78–80.

112. In a letter of June 1615 to the States General, Louis XIII insisted that Castelane had never been given responsibility for official French business in Morocco, "qui ne fut oncques nostre ambassadeur, ny recommandé d'autre titre que de marchand." See *SIHM, Pays-Bas*, 2: 592–93.

113. Ibid.

CHAPTER 4. PRIVATEERING, PRISON, AND DEATH

1. *Resolutïen der Staten Generaal*, n.s., *1610–1670*, 2 (1613–16), Oct. 17, 1613 (*SIHM, Pays-Bas*, 2: 202) and no. 803, Oct. 25, 1613 (2: 201); cf. Nov. 30, 1613 (2: 209).

2. The two captains, Jan Slobb and Gerbrant Jansz, were required to state under oath that they would not harm the States General or its subjects (*SIHM, Pays-Bas*, 2: 205–6). The other officers did the same shortly afterward (ibid., pp. 209–10).

3. Ibid., pp. 207–8.

4. Ibid., p. 243. A yacht, or *jaght* (short for *jaghtschip*, literally, "hunting ship"), could be used for victualing; see also ibid., p. 279. M. H. Gans Collection, doc. 2, letter of Mar. 3, 1614 by Cornelis Aerssens (1545–1627), secretary to the States General between 1584 and 1623, on whom, see A. J. van der Aa, *Biographisch Woordenboek der Nederlanden* (Haarlem, [1852–]78), s.v.

5. Amsterdam, Municipal Archive, Notarial Records, no. 2323, Not. Arch. 199, fs 202–205v (1617), cited in *Studia Rosenthaliana* 18 (1984): 161.

6. Pallache was authorized to purchase ships in England to be used in privateering expeditions on Zaydan's behalf, cf. Joseph Pallache to the States General, Nov. 29, 1614, *SIHM, Pays-Bas*, 2: 423.

7. M. H. Gans Collection, doc. 9; *SIHM, Pays-Bas*, 2: 203.

8. *SIHM, Pays-Bas*, 2: 425.

9. Ibid., pp. 272–74.

10. On La Mamora (Al-Maᶜmûra), see E. Levi-Provençal in *Encyclopaedia of Islam*, 2d ed., s.v. al-Mahdiyya. It is about twelve miles north of Salé.

11. *SIHM, Pays-Bas*, 1: 624 ff.; 2: 3 ff.

12. Ibid., p. 43.

13. *SIHM, Pays-Bas*, 2: 46.

14. See Pallache's memorandum dated Jan. 20, 1612, in *SIHM, Pays-Bas*, 2: 3–4, repeated and amplified on Mar. 27, 1614, ibid., pp. 256–58.

15. Cf. "Requête de Joseph Pallache aux Etats Généraux," Nov. 29, 1614, *SIHM, Pays-Bas*, 2: 423. M. H. Gans Collection, docs. 2 and 10.

16. Letter from the Rotterdam admiralty to the States General, Nov. 21, 1614, *SIHM, Pays-Bas*, 2: 410–15.

17. "T'welcke doch meest voor date hen met zeeroven hadden geneert, daarvan de voorschreven generaal oock genoechsaem is gewaerschout."

18. These events suggest that a mutiny had taken place but the yacht's captain, Gerbrant Jansz, later (on July 1, 1615) presented a petition to the States General regarding this voyage.

19. "Endommager et faire la guerre aux Espaignolz, et aultres les enemis auec lesquels il estoit en guerre"; cf. Gans Collection, docs. 9 and 10. Joseph Pallache to the States General, Apr. 29, 1615, *SIHM, Pays-Bas*, 2: 546.

20. Ibid., p. 282.

21. Ibid., p. 288.

22. Ibid., p. 320.

23. Ibid., pp. 311–12, 339.

24. Ibid., pp. 305, 311.

25. When the Spaniards entered La Mamora, they found seventeen corsair ships in the harbor and a large hulk weighing more than three hundred tons, as well as 500 corsairs of various nationalities (Orozco, *Discurso historial*, p. 216).

26. *SIHM, Pays-Bas*, 2: 317.

27. ADM, Leg. 2408. Letter from Medina Sidonia to Philip III, Sept. 11, 1610.

28. ADM, Leg. 2409, letters from Mar. to Apr. 1614.

29. Ibid., Apr. 1614.

30. ADM, letter from Philip III to Medina Sidonia, Aug. 20, 1613.

31. ADM, Leg. 2409, letter from Philip III to Medina Sidonia, Mar. 2, 1614.

32. Álvarez de Toledo, *Alonso Pérez de Guzmán*, 2: 96.

33. See, e.g., the letter from Medina Sidonia to Philip III, Mar. 15, 1614, AGS, Estado, Leg. 495.

34. *SIHM, Pays-Bas*, 2: 339.

35. Ibid., p. 328.

36. M. H. Gans Collection, doc. 9c; *SIHM, Pays-Bas*, 2: 378.

37. *Resolutiën der Staten Generaal*, n.s., *1610–1670*, 2 (1613–16), no. 826 (not in *SIHM*). The reference to several ships being under Pallache's command is puzzling, given that the yacht had already been scuttled.

38. Cf. Pallache's protest in "Requête," Apr. 28, 1615, *SIHM, Pays-Bas*, 2: 540–42.

39. Cf. Swetchinski, "Portuguese Jewish Merchants of Seventeenth-Century Amsterdam," pp. 117–18, 173–74.

40. *SIHM, Pays-Bas*, 2: 547: "Ende is geschiet, dat wy twee buyten genomen hebbende, en conden in de havenen van Barbarien nyet arriveren deur belet van de armade van Spaignen, die op de custe was."

41. M. H. Gans Collection, doc. 10, letter from the States General to King James I of England.

42. *SIHM, Pays-Bas*, 2: 373.

43. Ibid., p. 382.

44. *Resolutiën der Staten Generaal*, n.s., *1610–1670*, 2 (1613–16), Nov. 4, 1614 (no. 913b).

45. *SIHM, Pays-Bas*, 2: 533, resolution of Apr. 22, 1615.

46. Letter from Samuel Pallache to the States General from Dartmouth, Nov. 2, 1614, *SIHM, Pays-Bas*, 2: 407–9.

47. *SIHM, Pays-Bas*, 2: 395.

48. *SIHM, Angleterre*, 2: 477, John Chamberlain to Dudley Carleton, Nov. 4, 1614; and see also M. H. Gans Collection, doc. 20, States General to King James I, Nov. 22, 1614.

49. *SIHM, Angleterre*, 2: 489.

50. *SIHM, Pays-Bas*, 2: 407–9.

51. Ibid., p. 422.

52. M. H. Gans Collection, doc. 3, Mar. 20, 1615. The same document has been published in Abrahams, "Two Jews," pp. 356–57.

53. Cf. Joseph Pallache, application to the States General, Nov. 29, 1614, *SIHM, Pays-Bas*, 2: 420–24.

54. Pallache obtained the safe-conduct through the mediation of John Harrison in 1612. Harrison to the States General from Safi, Sept. 12, 1614, *SIHM, Pays-Bas*, 2: 326–27.

55. Letter from the States General to King James I, Nov. 29, 1614, *SIHM, Pays-Bas*, 2: 425–28, Gans Collection, doc. 10.

56. Letter from Maurice to King James I, Dec. 11, 1614, *SIHM, Angleterre*, 2: 486–87.

57. Cf. Caron to the States General, Apr. 4–5, 1615, *SIHM, Pays-Bas*, 2: 521–29.

58. Samuel Pallache to the States General, end of Nov. 1614, *SIHM, Pays-Bas*, 2: 429–30.

59. Joseph Pallache to the States General, Dec. 4 1614, *SIHM, Pays-Bas*, 2: 433–34.

60. Autograph letter in the M. H. Gans Collection, doc. 11.

61. Abrahams, "Two Jews," p. 355; Acts of the Privy Council, Dec. 23, 1614, Jan. 2, 1615.

62. Caron to the States General, Jan. 8, 1615, *SIHM, Pays-Bas*, 2: 446ff.

63. Samuel Pallache to the States General, Jan. 26, 1615, *SIHM, Pays-Bas*, 2: 471.

64. Abrahams, "Two Jews," p. 356.

65. Diego Sarmiento de Acuña to Admiral Daniel Dun, Feb. 8, 1615, M. H. Gans Collection, doc. 14.

66. *SIHM, Pays-Bas*, 2: 473.

67. Ralph Winwood, a fervent Protestant, was an English agent in The Hague in 1613 and at the beginning of 1614, although he traveled frequently between England and Holland. He was named secretary of state on March 29, 1614. See *Dictionary of National Biography.*

68. *SIHM, Angleterre*, 2: 488–89.

69. Moses Pallache to the States General, Mar. 13, 1615, *SIHM, Pays-Bas*, 2: 500–502.

70. *SIHM, Pays-Bas*, 2: 504–5. It is a pity that the original copy of this commission has been lost. The M. H. Gans Collection contains a copy of one of Pallache's commissions from Muley Zaydan, but it cannot possibly be that granted by Zaydan in June 1614, given that it is dated the last day of *jumada* of 1021, i.e., July 1611 (Gans, *Memorboek*, p. 34). This would have to be the commission Pallache was given before his first mission as a privateer, when he made a short journey to the coasts of Spain with Ahmad ben Abdallah and the Rijsbergen flotilla.

71. Mar. 20 = Mar. 10, Old Style. See M. H. Gans Collection, doc. no. 3; another version of this document has been published in Abrahams, "Two Jews," pp. 356–57.

72. Caron to the States General, Apr. 9, 1615, *SIHM, Pays-Bas*, 2: 530–32.

73. Resolution 1615, no. 389, *SIHM, Pays-Bas*, 2: 682.

74. *SIHM, Pays-Bas*, 2: 531.

75. AGS, Estado, bk. 366, 1613–14.

76. *Correspondencia oficial de Don Diego Sarmiento de Acuña, conde de Gondomar*, vols. 1–4 in *Documentos Inéditos para la historia de España.*

77. Ibid., vol. 1.

78. Rotterdam admiralty to the States General, Nov. 21, 1614, *SIHM, Pays-Bas*, 2: 410–15.

79. Hirschberg's assertion, in *History of the Jews of North Africa*, that according to Grotius, Samuel Pallache tried to save a Dutch cargo on a ship seized by the Portuguese in 1604 is incorrect. See Universiteit van Amsterdam, Bibliotheek, *Catalogus der handschriften*, 7: 274–76, no. 555, Hugo de Groot [Grotius], "Tracten ende questien" (7 III–C-3, ff. 275–77).

80. *SIHM, Pays-Bas*, 2: 513.

81. Letter from the Rotterdam admiralty to the States General, Oct. 29, 1614, Ibid., pp. 398–402.

82. Resolution of Apr. 28, 1615, *SIHM, Pays-Bas*, 2: 540–42.

83. Resolution of Apr. 30, 1615, Ibid., pp. 548–50.

84. Ambassador Cornelis Haga to the States General, Feb. 9, 1616 (*SIHM, Pays-Bas*, 2: 629–31), i.e., four days after Samuel's death (ibid., p. 623). See also Groot, "Ottoman Empire and the Dutch Republic," p. 143. The Sublime Porte, or the Porte: the government of the Ottoman empire; the name alludes to the Bab-i-Hümayun (in French "la Sublime Porte") of the Topkapi Saray in Istanbul.

85. *SIHM, Pays-Bas*, 2: 643.

86. See ibid., pp. 578–83. Translation of a letter in Turkish written by Pallache to Khalil Pasha, probably at some time between May 29 and June 7, 1615: "Voorts sall Uwe Exellentie weeten, hoe dat alhier is gearriveert een man genaemt Abdulla van wegen den eersamen Ismael Aga tot verlossinge van een suster van dito Ismel Aga, die slaeff was in Vranckryck, ende ick Uwe Exellentie slave habbe alle mogelycke devoiren aengewendt om dito slavinne vuyt de handen van de Francoeysen te libereren, ende heb haer in myn huys ontfangen, betoenende jegens haer alle eer ende vrundtschap, ende ick heb haer daer nae gebracht by Syn Excellentie graff Maurits, dwelcke wel genegen zynde om haer met eenige gelegentheyt van scheepen wech te schicken."

87. Haga to the States General, ibid., pp. 655–58.

88. Haga to the States General, Apr. 16, 1616, ibid., p. 658.

89. Haga to the States General, Mar. 5, 1616, ibid., p. 644.

90. Resolution of May 4, 1616, ibid., pp. 672–75.

91. Ibid., pp. 672–75.

92. Ibid., p. 656.

93. Another friar, Gabriel de Oye of Cologne, had already tried to make contacts with the Spanish crown on Samuel Pallache's behalf. AGS, Estado, Leg. 629, no. 117.

94. AGS, Estado, Leg. 629, nos. 116–19, no. 119: "Samuel Pallache has been given these chapters in his own hand and signed by Duarte Fernandes, and I [Gregorio de Valencia] have seen them and had them in my hands."

95. These marginal notes do not appear in AGS, Estado, Leg. 2300.

96. Document in the M. H. Gans Collection, dated Dec. 14, 1615.

97. *SIHM, Pays-Bas*, 2: 621–22.

98. Ibid.

99. Ibid., pp. 623–24.

100. Pieterse, "Daniel Levi de Barrios," p. 55; Henriques de Castro, *Keur van Grafsteenen*, Samuel Pallache's tombstone, no. 15, pp. 91–94; trans. of the text on the stone, pp. 91–92; Hirschberg, *History of the Jews of North Africa*, 2: 219. See *Encyclopaedia Judaica*, s.v., *hakham*.

101. For the attempts by the moriscos of Salé to hand the town over to the Spaniards, see Bouzineb, "'Plática' en torno de la entrega de Salé."

102. *Resolutiën der Staten Generaal*, June 24, 1616, *SIHM, Pays-Bas*, 2: 690–91; letter from Joseph Pallache to the States General, June 25, 1616, Ibid., pp. 692–93.

103. Heeringa, *Bronnen tot de geschiedenis van den Levantschen handel*, 1: 119; Groot, "Ottoman Empire and the Dutch Republic," pp. 147–49. The Moroccans gave Sultan Ahmed a sumptuous caftan, a sword, and a scepter. See Groot, p. 148, citing Rijksarchief, Staten-Generaal, States General 6891, a letter from Haga to the States General, Mar. 4, 1617.

CHAPTER 5. AFTER SAMUEL: THE PALLACHE FAMILY

1. *SIHM, Pays-Bas*, 3: 244–45, 4: 399.

2. Ibid., 3: 5 ff.

3. Ibid., p. 7.

4. Ibid., pp. 13, 18.

5. Ibid., pp. 62 ff.

6. Ibid., pp. 4, 5.

7. Juynboll, *Zeventiende-eeuwsche Beoefenaars*, p. 52.

8. *SIHM, Pays-Bas*, 3: 426.

9. AGS, Estado, Leg. 2646.

10. *Studia Rosenthaliana* 24 (1990): 69, notarial doc. no. 2857.

11. Ibid., 16 (1982): 218, notarial doc. no. 2125.

12. *SIHM, Pays-Bas*, 3: 244.

13. Ibid., p. 388. Salé was the quasi-independent morisco pirate "republic" that had sprung up close to Rabat in the years after 1610.

14. Ibid., p. 367.

15. *Studia Rosenthaliana* 31 (1997): 146, doc. no. 3357.

16. Nadler, *Spinoza*, p. 39. We owe this reference to our colleague Guy Stroumsa (Jerusalem).

17. *SIHM, Pays-Bas*, 3: 246.

18. Ibid., p. 410.

19. *SIHM, Angleterre*, 3: 401.

20. Ibid., p. 483.

21. *SIHM, Pays-Bas*, 5: 192 ff

22. Ibid., 3: 88, 109.

23. Ibid., p. 112 ff.

24. Ibid., pp. 145, 148.

25. Ibid., pp. 163, 179.

26. Ibid., p. 172.

27. For all this, see ibid., pp. 571–78, and *France*, vol. 3.

28. *SIHM, Pays-Bas*, 3: 220 ff.

29. Sultan Muley al-Walid later built a fort known as Walidiya at the mouth of the lagoon.

30. *SIHM, Pays-Bas*, 3: 289.

31. Ibid., pp. 274–75.

32. Ibid., p. 411.

33. Ibid., p. 534.

34. Ibid., p. 412.

35. Ibid., p. 427.

36. Ibid., p. 427.

37. Ibid., p. 510.

38. Ibid., p. 507.

39. Ibid., p. 511.

40. Ibid., p. 527.

41. Ibid., p. 499.

42. Ibid., p. 564.

43. *SIHM, Pays-Bas*, 4: 4–5.

44. *SIHM, Pays-Bas*, 3: 566, and vol. 4, memorandum from Joseph Pallache, Aug. 28, 1624.

45. *SIHM, Pays-Bas*, 3: 567.

46. *SIHM, France*, 3: 325.

47. *SIHM, Angleterre*, 3: 209.

48. *SIHM, Pays-Bas*, 4: 373.

49. *SIHM, Angleterre*, 3: 157.

50. Ibid., pp. 208, 256.

51. *SIHM, Pays-Bas*, 4: 406.

52. On Alfonso López, see Caro Baroja, "El último Abencerraje," which mistakenly combines the biographies of two different men, Alfonso López and one Manuel Donlope, who is named in the correspondence of La Force. See also Hildesheimer, "Une créature de Richelieu.". The fullest account of López's life is to be found in Pelorson, "Le docteur Carlos García." We would like to thank Martin Beagles for pointing out Caro Baroja's error and for providing us with this last reference.

53. *SIHM, France*, 3: 471–72.

54. See Guadalajara y Javier, *Prodición y destierro*, pp. 124ff.

55. Santoni, "Le passage des Morisques en Provence," esp. p. 366ff.

56. Pelorson, "Le docteur Carlos García," p. 525.

57. On this interesting figure, see Roth, "Quatre lettres d'Elie de Montalte."

58. On García, see Pelorson, "Le docteur Carlos García."

59. Elliott, *Richelieu and Olivares*, p. 116.

60. *SIHM, Angleterre*, 3: 255; *Pays-Bas*, 4: 428.

61. *SIHM, Pays-Bas*, 5: 197–98.

62. Ibid., p. 234.

63. Ibid., p. 261.

64. *Resolutiën der Staten Generaal*, n.s., *1610–1670*, 1 (1610–12), no. 1178, Oct. 19, 1612.

65. *Studia Rosenthaliana* 7 (1973), notarial documents nos. 781, 784–90.

66. Ibid., 14 (1980), p. 91, no. 1682.

67. *Resolutiën der Staten Generaal*, Jan. 6, 1631, cited by Henriques de Castro, *Keur*, p. 93.

68. *Resolutiën der Staten Generaal*, Sept. 25, 1635.

69. *SIHM*, 2: 627, 639.

70. Ibid., 3: 507.

71. *Resolutiën der Staten Generaal*, Mar. 22 and June 3, 1633, cited by Henriques de Castro, *Keur*.

72. Eekhof, *De Theologische Faculteit te Leiden*, pp. 94, 129–32.

73. *SIHM, Pays-Bas*, 4: 492.

74. Ibid., 5: 108.

75. Ibid., 4: 530–50.

76. Ibid., p. 553; translation from Dutch to French, p. 535.

77. Ibid., p. 544.

78. *SIHM, Pays-Bas*, 5: 124.

79. Ibid., p. 128.

80. Burnet, *Die ware bekeringe en violente vervolgingen van Eva Cohen*, f. 4.

81. G. Scholem, *Sabaatai Sevi: The Mystical Messiah, 1626–1676.*

82. Ibid.

83. "Dans le temps que j'étois à Salé, il arriva un Vaisseau Hollandois d'Amsterdam, qui apporta aux Juifs de cette ville, de certaines Prédictions que ceux de Hollande leur envoyoient. Elles contenoient, entr'autres choses, que le Messie qu'ils attendoient depuis tant de siecles, naitroit en Hollande au commencement de l'année suivante, qui étoit celle de 1672" (Mouette, *Relation de la captivite*, p. 31).

84. Trial of Francisco de Amezquita, AHN, Inquisición, Leg. 134 exp. 13.

85. David Franco Mendes, in *Os judeus portugueses em Amesterdão*, p. 71.

86. Schaub, *Les juifs du roi d'Espagne*, esp. ch. 2, "Les Cansino contre les Sasportas."

87. Sasportas, *Tsitsat novel Tsevi*, p. 354.

88. See Bakker, "Slaves, Arms, and Holy War."

89. Hirschberg, *History of the Jews of North Africa*, 2: 212.

90. See, e.g., Gans, *Memorboek;* Vaz Dias, "Bijdrage tot de geschiedenis der Portugees Israëlietische gemeente te Amsterdam"; Blom et al., eds., *Geschiedenis van de Joden in Nederland.*

CONCLUSION

1. See, e.g., Israel, *European Jewry in the Age of Mercantilism*, ch. 6, "Court Jews."

2. Coleman, *Revisions in Mercantilism.*

3. Perez Zagorin, *Ways of Lying.*

4. Berti, "At the Roots of Unbelief," 562.

5. Scaraffia, *Rinnegati*, p. 187.

GLOSSARY

aljama	Jewish or Muslim quarter or section of a city or town. In the case of Jews, practically synonymous with *judería*
cristiano nuevo	*see* New Christian, *converso*
cristiano viejo	*see* Old Christian
converso	a Jew who was baptized and thus became, at least nominally, a Christian. Refers also to descendants of converts
dhimma(-i)	in Muslim society, a protected people. Generally refers to Christians or Jews who, in exchange for paying a tax and observing a number of restrictions, could practice their own religion
judería	Jewish quarter. Generally organized around a synagogue
judío de permiso	a practicing Jew who, following the Expulsion of 1492, had permission to live in Spain, provided he or she wear a distinctive sign
judaizante	a New Christian who secretly practiced, or is at least accused of practicing, Judaism
megorashim	term used by "native" Jews for Jewish immigrants from Spain following the Expulsion Order of 1492
Moro(-s)	literally, a Moor. Specifically refers to Berbers, Muslim peoples residing in North Africa, but more generally to all Muslims
morisco	a Muslim who converted, if only nominally, to Christianity. As with *converso*, it can also refer to a convert's descendants

New Christian	English term for *converso*
Old Christian	authocthonous (or native) Christians as distinguished from recent converts or descendants of converts, who were called New Christians
shaykh	literally, old man; a tribal chief or religious leader
Taqqanot	ordinances for Jewish community governance
toshavim	authocthonous Jews as distinguished from *megorashim*

BIBLIOGRAPHY

ARCHIVES

Former M. H. Gans Collection, Amsterdam
Archives générales du Royaume, Brussels
Archivo Ducal de Medinasidonia, Sanlúcar de Barrameda (Cádiz)
Arquivo Nacional da Torre do Tombo, Lisbon
Archivo Histórico Nacional, Madrid
Archivo General de Simancas, Simancas

PRINTED SOURCES

Abrahams, L. B. "A Jew in the Service of the East India Company in 1601." *Jewish Quarterly Review* 9 (1897): 173–75.
———. "Two Jews before the Privy Council and an English Law Court." *Jewish Quarterly Review* 14 (1902): 354–58.
Agt, J. F. van. *Synagogen in Amsterdam*. The Hague, 1974.
Alvar, A., ed. *Relaciones y cartas de Antonio Pérez*. 2 vols. Madrid, 1986.
Alvares Vega, L. *Het Beth Haim van Ouderkerk: Beelden van een Portugees-Joodse Begraafplaats*. Ouderkerk aan de Amstel, 1994.
Álvarez de Toledo, L. I. *Alonso Pérez de Guzmán, general de la Invencible*. 2 vols. Cádiz, 1994.
Baer, F. *Die Juden im christlichen Spanien*. Berlin, 1936.
Bakker, J. C. de. "Slaves, Arms, and Holy War: Moroccan Policy vis-à-vis the Dutch Republic during the Establishment of the ᶜAlawî Dynasty (1660–1727)." Ph.D. thesis, Amsterdam, 1991.
Barrios, Miguel de. *Triumpho del govierno popular judayco* [Triumph of Jewish Popular Government]. Amsterdam, 1683. Includes the author's *Historia universal judayca*.

Beinart, H. "Fas, merkaz le-giur we-la-sibat anusim la-yahadut" (Fez as a Center of Emigration and Return of Anusim to Judaism in the Sixteenth Century). In Hebrew. *Sefunot* 8 (1963–64): 319–24.

———. "Halijatam shel yehudim mi Maroco li-Sefarad bereshit hameá ha17" (Jewish Routes from Morocco to Spain in the Early Seventeenth Century). In Hebrew. In *Salo Wittmayer Baron: Jubilee Volume on the Occasion of His Eightieth Birthday*. New York, 1974.

Benbassa, E., ed. *Memoires juives d'Espagne et du Portugal*. Paris, 1996.

Ben Sasson, H. "Exile and Redemption in the Eyes of the Generation of Exiles from Sepharad." In Hebrew. In *Yitzhaek Baer Jubilee Volume*, pp. 216–27. Jerusalem, 1961.

Bernáldez, A. "Historia de los Reyes Católicos." In *Crónicas de los reyes de Castilla*, ed. Cayetano Rosell, vol. 3. Biblioteca de Autores Españoles, 70. Madrid, 1953.

Berti, S. "At the Roots of Unbelief." *Journal of the History of Ideas* 56 (1995): 555–75.

Blom, J. H. C., R. G. Fuks-Mansfeld, and I. Schöffer, eds. *Geschiedenis van de Joden in Nederland*. Amsterdam, 1995. Translated by Arnold J. Pomerans and Erica Pomerans under the title *The History of the Jews in the Netherlands* (Portland, Or.: Littman Library of Jewish Civilization, 2002).

Bodian, M. *Hebrews of the Portuguese Nation: Conversos and Community in Early Modern Amsterdam*. Bloomington, Ind., 1997.

Boronat y Barrachina, P. *Los moriscos españoles y su expulsión*. Valencia, 1901.

Bouzineb, H. "'Plática' en torno de la entrega de Salé en el siglo XVII." *Al-Qantara* 15 (1994): 47–73.

Bouzineb, H., and Wiegers, G. A. "Tétouan and the Expulsion of the Moriscos." In *Titwân jilâl al-qarnayn 16 wa 17*, pp. 73–108. Tétouan, Morocco, 1996.

Boyajian, J. C. "The New Christians Reconsidered: Evidence from Lisbon's Portuguese Bankers, 1497–1647." *Studia Rosenthaliana* 13 (1979): 129–56.

Burnet, Gilbert. *Die ware bekeringe en violente vervolgingen van Eva Cohen, nu genaemt Elisabeth. Zijnde een persoon van qualiteyt van de joodsche gesintheyt geweest . . . dewelcke gedoopt is den 10. october, 1680 in St. Martins Kerck . . . van Whitehall*. London, 1681.

Cabanelas, D. "El problema de Larache en tiempos de Felipe II." *Miscelánea de Estudios Árabes y Hebraicos* 9 (1960): 19–53.

Cabrera de Córdoba, H. *Relaciones de las cosas sucedidas en la corte de España desde 1595 hasta 1614*. Madrid, 1857.

Cansino, J. "Relación de los servicios de Iacob Cansino y los de sus padre." In *Extremos y grandezas de Constantinopla compuesto por Rabi Moysen Almosnino*. Madrid, 1638.

Cantera Burgos, F. "El 'Purim' del Rey Don Sebastián." *Sefarad* 5 (1945): 219–25.

Caro Baroja, J. *Los judíos en la España moderna y contemporánea*. 2d ed. 3 vols. Madrid, 1978.

——— "El último Abencerraje." In id., *Vidas poco paralelas (con perdón de Plutarco)*, pp. 51–68. Madrid, 1981.

———. *Las falsificaciones de la historia (en relación con la de España)*. Madrid, 1991.

Castries, H. de, ed. *Les sources inédites de l'histoire du Maroc, de 1530 à 1845.* 1st ser. *Dynastie Sa'adienne, 1530–1660. Archives et bibliothèques de France.* 4 vols. Paris: Éditions Ernest Leroux, 1905–28.

———. "Les relations de la France avec le Maroc de 1631 à 1635. Les Pallache. Introduction critique." In *Les sources inédites de l'histoire du Maroc, de 1530 à 1845*, 1st ser., *Dynastie Sa'adienne, 1530–1660. Archives et bibliothèques de France*, 3: 391–97. Paris: Éditions Ernest Leroux, 1911.

———. *Les sources inédites de l'histoire du Maroc, de 1530 à 1845.* 1st ser. *Dynastie Sa'adienne, 1530–1660. Archives et bibliothèques des Pays-Bas.* 6 vols. Paris: Éditions Ernest Leroux, 1906–23.

———. *Les sources inédites de l'histoire du Maroc, de 1530 à 1845.* 1st ser. *Dynastie Sa'adienne, 1530–1660. Archives et bibliothèques d'Angleterre.* 3 vols. Paris: Éditions Ernest Leroux, 1918–35.

———. *Les sources inédites de l'histoire du Maroc, de 1530 à 1845.* 1st ser. *Dynastie Sa'adienne, 1530–1660. Archives et bibliothèques d'Espagne, 1530–1660.* Paris: Éditions Ernest Leroux, 1921.

Cenival, Pierre de, David Lopes, Robert Ricard, and Chantal de La Véronne, eds. *Les Sources inédites de l'histoire du Maroc.* 1st ser. *Dynastie Sa'dienne, 1530–1660. Archives et bibliothèques de Portugal.* 5 vols. Paris: P. Geuthner 1934–53.

Clénard, Nicolas [Clenardus]. *Correspondence*. Translated by A. Roersch. 3 vols. Brussels, 1941.

Coleman, D. C. *Revisions in Mercantilism*. London, 1969.

Contreras, J. "Cristianos de España y judíos de Amsterdam: Emigración, familia y negocios." In J. Lechner and H. den Boer, eds., *España y Holanda: Ponencias leídas durante durante el Quinto Coloquio Hispanoholandés de Historiadores, celebrado en la Universidad de Leiden del 17 al 20 de noviembre de 1993*, pp. 187–213. Amsterdam, 1995.

Corcos Abulafia, D. "Samuel Pallache and His London Trial." In Hebrew. In *Studies in the History of the Jews of Morocco*, pp. 122–33. Jerusalem, 1973.

Correspondencia oficial de Don Diego Sarmiento de Acuña, conde de Gondomar. Vols. 1–4 in *Documentos inéditos para la historia de España.* Madrid, 1936–45.

Cruz, Bernardo da. *Chronica de El Rei D. Sebastião.* Lisbon, 1837.

Dakhlia, J. "Réinscriptions linagères et redéfinitions sexuelles des convertis dans les cours maghrébines (XVIe–XVIIe siècles)." In M. García-Arenal, ed., *Conversion religieuse en Islam Mediterranéen*, pp. 151–71. Paris, 2001.

Dánvila y Collado, M. *La expulsión de los moriscos españoles.* Madrid, 1889.

Deursen, A. T. van. *Maurits van Nassau: De Winnaar die faalde.* Amsterdam, 2000.

Domínguez Ortiz, A. *La clase social de los conversos en Castilla en la Edad Moderna.* Madrid, 1955.

Eekhof, A. *De Theologische Faculteit te Leiden in de 17e eeuw.* Utrecht, 1921.

Elliott, J. H. *Richelieu and Olivares.* Cambridge, 1984.

Exhibición de facsímiles de libros de autores judíos y judaizantes españoles (s. XVI–XVIII), realizado por Fernando Díaz Esteban con los fondos de la Biblioteca Nacional de Madrid. Annotated catalogue. Madrid, 1992.

Fischel, W. J. "Abraham Navarro, Jewish Interpreter and Diplomat in the Service of the English East India Company (1682–1692)." *Proceedings of the American Academy for Jewish Research* 25 (1956): 39–62.

Al-Fishtali. *Manahil al-safa fi akhbar mawali-na al-shurafa'*. Tétouan, Morocco, 1964.

Fruin, R., ed. "Uittreksel uit Francisci Dusseldorpii Annales." In *Werken uitgegeven door het historisch genootschap gevestigd te Utrecht*, 3d ser., no. 1. The Hague, 1893.

Gans, M. H. "Don Samuel Pallache als moré en zeerover, grondlegger onzer gemeenschap." In *Opstellen opperrabbijn L. Vorst aangeboden*, pp. 15–23. Rotterdam, 1959.

———. *Memorboek: Platenatlas van het leven der joden in Nederland van de middeleeuwen tot 1940*. Baarn, 1971.

García-Arenal, M. *Inquisición y Moriscos: Los procesos del Tribunal de Cuenca*. Madrid, 1978. Reprinted 1982 and 1988.

———. "Les *bildiyyin* de Fes: Un groupe de neo-musulmans d'origine juive." *Studia Islamica* 66 (1987): 113–44.

———. "Vidas ejemplares: Sa'îd Ibn Faray al-Dugâlî (m. 987/1579), un granadino en Marruecos." In M. García-Arenal and M. J. Viguera, eds. *Relaciones de la Península Ibérica con el Magreb, siglos XIII–XVI*, pp. 453–86. Madrid, 1988.

———. "Entre Oriente y Occidente: Los hermanos Almosnino, judíos de Fez." In R. M. Loureivo and S. Gruzinski, eds., *Passar as fronteiras*, pp. 313–38. Lagos, 1999.

———. "Los judíos de Fez a través del proceso inquisitorial de los Almosnino (1621)." In *Judíos en tierras de Islam*, vol. 2: *Entre el Islam y Occidente: Los judíos magrebíes en la edad moderna*. Forthcoming.

García-Arenal, M., and M. de Bunes. *Los españoles y el Norte de África, siglos XV–XVIII*. Madrid, 1992.

García-Arenal, M., and Beatrice Leroy. *Moros y judíos en Navarra en la Baja Edad Media*. Madrid, 1984.

García-Arenal, M., and M. J. Viguera, eds. *Relaciones de la Península Ibérica con el Magreb (siglos XIII–XVI)*. Madrid, 1988.

García Figueras, T., and C. Rodríguez Jouliá Saint-Cyr. *Larache: Datos para su historia en el siglo XVII*. Madrid, 1973.

García Fuentes, J. M. *La Inquisición en Granada en el siglo XVI: Fuentes para su estudio*. Granada, 1981.

Genot-Bismuth, J. "Le mythe de l'Orient dans l'eschatologie des Juifs d'Espagne à l'époque des conversions forcées et de l'expulsion." *Annales E.S.C.* 45, no. 4 (1990): 819–38.

Gerber, J. S. *Jewish Society in Fez, 1450–1700*. Leiden, 1980.

Glick, T. F. "Moriscos and Marranos as Agents of Technological Diffusion." *History of Technology* 17 (1995): 113–25.

Gozálbes Busto, G. *Los moriscos en Marruecos*. Maracena, Granada, 1992.

Groot, A. H. de. "The Ottoman Empire and the Dutch Republic: A History of the Earliest Diplomatic Relations, 1610–1630." Ph.D. thesis, Leiden, 1978.

Guadalajara y Javier, Marcos de. *Prodición y destierro de los moriscos hasta el valle de Ricote con las disensiones de los hermanos Xarifes y presa en Berbería de la fuerça y puerto de Alarache.* Pamplona, 1614.

Al-Hajarî, Ahmad b. Qâsim. *Kitâb nâsir al-dîn ʿalâ l-qawm al-kâfirîn (The Supporter of Religion against the Infidels).* Translated and edited by P. S. van Koningsveld, Q. al-Samarrai, and G. A. Wiegers. Madrid, 1997.

Heeringa, K. "Een bondgenootschap tusschen Nederland en Marokko." *Onze Eeuw* 7, no. 3 (1907): 81–119.

———. *Bronnen tot de geschiedenis van den Levantschen handel.* 2 vols. Rijks Geschiedkundige Publicatiën, 9, 10. The Hague, 1910.

Henriques de Castro, D. *Keur van Grafsteenen op de Nederl.-Portug.-Israël Begraafplaats te Ouderkerk aan de Amstel.* Leiden, 1833.

Hildesheimer, F. "Une créature de Richelieu: Alphonse López, le 'seigneur Hebreo.'" In *Les juifs au regard de l'histoire: Mélanges en l'honneur de Bernhard Blumenkranz,* pp. 293–99. Paris, 1985.

Hirschberg, H. Z. *A History of the Jews of North Africa.* Leiden, 1974–81.

Huussen, A. J. "The Legal Position of Sephardi Jews in Holland circa 1600." In *Dutch Jewish History,* ed. J. Michman, 3: 19–41. Jerusalem and Maastricht, 1993.

Ibn Daud, Abraham ben David, Halevi. *The Book of Tradition (Sefer ha-qabbalah).* Translated and edited by G. D. Cohen. Philadelphia, 1967.

Ibn Verga, Solomon. *Chébet Jehuda: La vara de Judá.* Translated into Spanish by F. Cantera Burgos. Granada, 1927.

Israel, J. I. "A Conflict of Empires: Spain and the Netherlands, 1618–1648." *Past and Present* 76 (1977): 34–74.

———. "Spain and the Dutch Sephardim, 1609–1660." *Studia Rosenthaliana* 12 (1978): 1–61.

———. "The Jews of Spanish North Africa, 1600–1669." *Transactions of the Jewish Historical Society of England* 26 (1979): 71–86.

———. *European Jewry in the Age of Mercantilism, 1550–1750.* 2d ed. Oxford, 1989.

———. *Empires and Entrepots: The Dutch, the Spanish Monarchy and the Jews, 1585–1713.* London, 1990.

Justel, B. *La Real Biblioteca de El Escorial y sus manuscritos árabes.* Madrid, 1978.

Juynboll, W. M. C. *Zeventiende-eeuwsche Beoefenaars van het Arabisch in Nederland.* Utrecht, 1931.

Kaddouri, A. "Ibn Abi Mahalli: a propos de l'itinéraire psycho-social d'un mahdi." In A. Kaddouri, ed., *Mahdisme, crise et changement dans l'histoire du Maroc,* pp. 119–25. Rabat, 1994.

Kaplan, Y. *From Christianity to Judaism: Isaac Orobio de Castro.* Oxford, 1989.

———. "De Joden in de Republiek tot omstreeks, 1750. Religieus, cultureel en sociaal leven." In J. H. C. Blom et al., eds., *Geschiedenis van de Joden in Nederland,* pp. 129–73. Amsterdam, 1995.

———. *Judíos nuevos en Amsterdam*. Madrid, 1996.

Koen, E. M. "Duarte Fernandes, Koopman van de Portugese Natie." *Studia Rosenthaliana* 2 (1968): 178–93.

———. "Waar en voor wie werd de synagoge van 1612 gebouwd?" *Amstelodamum* 57 (1970): 209–11.

———. "Notarial Records Relating to the Portuguese Jews in Amsterdam up to 1639." *Studia Rosenthaliana* 11 (1977): 95, no. 1184. Frequent articles in volumes from 1970 to the present.

Koningsveld, P. S. van. "Andalusian-Arabic Manuscripts from Christian Spain: A Comparative, Intercultural Approach." *Israel Oriental Studies* 12 (1992): 75–110.

———. "'Mijn Kharûf': Over de Arabische leermeester van Nicolaas Cleynaerts." *Sharqiyyât* 9, no. 2 (1997): 139–61.

———. "'Mon Kharûf': Quelques remarques sur le maître tunisien du premier arabisant néerlandais, Nicolas Clénard (1493–1542)." In *Nouvelles approches des relations islamo-chrétiennes à l'époque de la Renaissance (Actes de la troisième rencontre scientifique tenue du 14 au 16 mars 1998)*, pp. 123–41. Zaghouan, Tunisia, 2000.

Lapeyre, H. *Géographie de l'Espagne morisque*. Paris, 1959.

Laredo, A. "Les 'Purim' de Tanger." *Hespéris* 35 (1948): 193–203.

———. *Les noms des juifs au Maroc*. Madrid, 1978.

Lechner, J., and H. den Boer. *España y Holanda: Ponencias leídas durante el Quinto Coloquio Hispanoholandés de Historiadores, celebrado en la Universidad de Leiden del 17 al 20 de noviembre de 1993*. Amsterdam, 1995.

Le Tourneau, R. "Notes sur les lettres latines de Nicholas de Clenard relatant son sejour dans le royaume de Fès (1540–1541)." *Hespéris* 19 (1934): 45–63.

López Belinchón, B. "Estudio de la minoría judeoconversa en Castilla en el siglo XVII: El caso de Fernando Montesinos." Ph.D. thesis, Universidad de Alcalá de Henares, 1995.

———. "Aventureros, negociantes y maestros dogmatizadores: Judíos norteafricanos y judeoconversos ibéricos en la España del siglo XVII." In *Judíos en tierras de Islam*, vol. 2: *Entre el Islam y Occidente: Los judíos magrebíes en la edad moderna*. Forthcoming.

Marín, M. "The Captive Word: A Note on Arabic Manuscripts in Spain." *Al-Masaq* 8 (1995): 155–69.

Mármol, Luis del. *Descripción general de África*. 2 vols. Málaga, 1599.

Mediano, F. R. "Portugueses en Marruecos: cautivos de la batalla de Alcazarquivir." In M. García-Arenal, ed., *Conversión islamiques. Identités religieuse en Islam méditerranéen*, pp. 173–90. Paris, 2001.

Mendoça, J. de. *Jornada de África del rey Don Sebastián*. Lisbon, 1613.

Modena, L. *The Autobiography of a Seventeenth-Century Venetian Rabbi: Leon Modena's Life of Judah*. Translated and edited by M. R. Cohen. Princeton, N.J. 1988.

Mouette, G. de. *Relation de la captivite du sr. Moüette dans les Royaumes de Fez et de Maroc*. Paris, 1683.

BIBLIOGRAPHY

Nadler, S. *Spinoza: A Life*. Cambridge, 1999.

Nahon, G. "Les rapports des communautés judéo-portugaises avec celle d'Amsterdam au XVIIe siècle." *Studia Rosenthaliana* 10 (1976): 37–78.

———. *Métropoles et périferies sefarades d'Occident: Kairouan, Amsterdam, Bordeaux, Jérusalem*. Paris, 1993.

Offenberg, A. K. "Spanish and Portuguese Sephardi Books Published in the Northern Netherlands before Menasseh Ben Israel (1584–1627)." In *Dutch Jewish History*, ed. J. Michman, 3: 7–90, 82–83. Jerusalem and Maastricht, 1993.

Os judeus portugueses em Amesterdão. Colecção Monumenta Iudaica Portucalensia, 1. Lisbon, 1990. Reprint of *Memorias do estabelecimento e progresso dos judeus portuguezes e espanhoes nesta famosa cidade de Amsterdam* by David Franco Mendes (1772; Assen, 1975) and *Os judeus portugueses em Amsterdam* by J. Mendes dos Remédios (Coimbra, 1911).

Orozco, A. *Discurso historial de la presa que del puerto de la Maamora hizo el armada real de España en el año 1614*. Biblioteca de Autores Españoles, 36. Madrid, 1615.

Pelorson, J. M. "Le docteur Carlos García et la colonie hispano-portugaise de Paris (1613–1619)." *Bulletin Hispanique* 71 (1969): 518–76.

Perez Zagorin, J. *Ways of Lying: Dissimulation, Persecution and Conformity in Early Modern Europe*. Cambridge, Mass., 1990.

Pieterse, W. C. "Daniel Levi de Barrios als geschiedschrijver van de Portugees-Israelietische gemeente te Amsterdam in zijn 'Triumpho del govierno popular.'" Ph.D. thesis, Amsterdam, 1968.

———, ed. *Livro de Beth Haim do Kahal Kados de Bet Yahacob*. Assen, 1970.

Ravid, B. "The First Charter of the Jewish Merchants in Venice, 1589." *ASJ Review* 1 (1976): 187–222.

Resolutiën der Staten-Generaal van 1576 tot 1609, 17 (1607–1609). Edited by H. H. P. Rijperman. The Hague, 1970.

Resolutiën der Staten-Generaal. N.s. *1610–1670*, 1 (1610–1612). Edited by A. T. van Deursen. The Hague, 1971.

Resolutiën der Staten-Generaal. N.s. *1610–1670*, 2 (1613–1616). Edited by A. T. van Deursen. The Hague, 1984.

Révah, I. S. "Autobiographie d'un marrane." *Revue des études juives* 119 (1961): 41–130.

Ricard, R. "Baptême d'un Juif de Fès à l'Escorial (1589)." *Hespéris* 24 (1937): 136.

———. "Bastião de Vargas, agent de Jean III de Portugal au Maroc." *Al-Andalus* 10 (1945): 53–77.

———. "Datos complementarios sobre Bastião de Vargas, agente de Juan III en Portugal en la corte de Fez." *Al-Andalus* 10 (1945): 383–86.

Rojas, J. L. de. *Relación de algunos sucesos postreros de Berbería, salida de los moriscos de España y entrega de Alarache*. Lisbon, 1613.

Ross, E. D. *Sir Anthony Sherley and His Persian Adventure*. London, 1933.

Roth, C. "Quatre lettres d'Elie de Montalte: Contribution à l'histoire des Marranes." *Revue des Etudes juives* 87 (1929): 137–65.

————. "The Strange Case of Hector Mendes Bravo." *Hebrew Union College Annual* 18 (1944): 221–45.

Ruderman, D. B. "Hope against Hope: Jewish and Christian Messianic Expectations in the Late Middle Ages." In *Exilio y Diáspora: Estudio sobre la historia del pueblo judío en homenaje al profesor Haim Beinart*, pp. 185–202. Madrid, 1991.

Saba, Abraham ben Jacob. *Tseror ha-mor.* 1522. Reprint. 5 vols in 1. New York, 1960–61.

Saldanha, António de. *Crónica de Almançor, sultão de Marrocos (1578–1603)*. Edited by A. Dias Farinha. Lisbon, 1997. This chronicle is anonymous but is attributed to Saldanha by its editor.

Salomon, H. P. "The 'De Pinto' Manuscript: A Seventeenth-Century Marrano Family History." *Studia Rosenthaliana* 9 (1975): 1–62.

————. "Portrait of a New Christian, Fernão Álvares Melo (1569–1632)." *Fontes documentais portuguesas* 18 (1982): 333–46.

————. *Os primeiros Portugueses de Amesterdão: Documentos do Arquivo Nacional da Torre do Tombo, 1595–1606*. Braga, 1983.

————. "Une lettre jusqu'ici inédite du docteur Felipe Rodrigues Montalto (Castelo Branco, 1567–Tours, 1616)." In *Les rapports culturels et littéraires entre le Portugal et la France: Actes du colloque, Paris*. Paris, 1983.

————. "Mendes, Benveniste, de Luna, Micas, Nasci: The State of the Art (1532–1558)." *Jewish Quarterly Review* 88 (1998): 135–211.

————. *Het Portugees in de Esnoga van Amsterdam*. Amsterdam, 2000.

Samuel, E. R. "Portuguese Jews in Jacobean London." *Transactions of the Jewish Historical Society of England* 18 (1958): 177–230.

Santoni, P. "Le passage des Morisques en Provence (1610–1613)." *Provence Historique* 185 (1996): 333–83.

Saraiva, A. J. *Inquisição e cristãos-novos.* Oporto, 1969.

Sasportas, Jacob. *Tsitsat novel Tsevi.* Edited by Isaiah Tishby. Jerusalem, 1954.

Scaraffia, L. *Rinnegati: Per una storia dell'identità occidentale.* Rome, 1993.

Schaub, J. F. *Les juifs du roi d'Espagne, Oran, 1509–1669.* Paris, 1999.

Scholem, G. G. *Sabbatai Sevi, the Mystical Messiah, 1626–1676.* Translated by R. J. Zwi Werblowsky. Princeton, N.J., 1973.

Schreiber, M. *Marranen in Madrid, 1600–1670.* Vierteljahrschrift für Sozial-und Wirtschaftgeschichte, 117. Stuttgart, 1994.

Sémach, Y. D. "Une chronique juive de Fès: Le Yahas Fes de Ribbi Abner Hassafaty." *Hespéris* 19 (1934): 79–94.

Swetschinski, D. M. "The Portuguese Jewish Merchants of Seventeenth-Century Amsterdam: A Social Profile." Ph.D. thesis, Brandeis University, 1979.

————. "Kinship and Commerce: The Foundations of Portuguese Jewish Life in Seventeenth-Century Holland." *Studia Rosenthaliana* 15 (1981): 52–74.

————. "Tussen Middeleeuwen en Gouden Eeuw, 1516–1621." In J. H. C. Blom et al., eds., *Geschiedenis van de Joden in Nederland*, pp. 53–94. Amsterdam, 1995.

————. "Un refus de mémoire: Les juifs portugais d'Amsterdam et leur passé marrane." In E. Benbassa, ed., *Memoires juives d'Espagne et du Portugal*, pp. 69–79. Paris, 1996.

Tavares, M. J. Pimenta Ferro. "Judeus de sinal em Portugal no século XVI." *Cultura-História e Filosofia* 5 (1986): 339–63.

———. *Los judíos en Portugal*. Madrid, 1992.

Tavim, J. A. Rodríguez da Silva. "Os judeus e a expansão portuguesa na India durante o século XVI. O exemplo de Isaac do Cairo." *Arquivos do Centro Cultural Calouste Gulbenkian* 33 (1994): 137–260.

———. *Os judeus na expansão portuguesa em Marrocos durante el século XVI. Origens e actividades duma comunidade*. Braga, 1997.

———. "Uma 'estranha' tolerância da Inquisição Portuguesa: Belchior Vaz de Acevedo e o interesse das potências europeias no Marrocos, na segunda metade do século XVI." In *Judíos en tierras de Islam*, vol. 2: *Entre el Islam y Occidente: Los judíos magrebíes en la edad moderna*. Forthcoming.

Tedghi, J. "Books, Manuscripts and Hebrew Printing in Fez." In Hebrew. *Pe'amim* 52 (1992): 47–74.

Torres, Diego de. *Relación del origen y suceso de los xarifes y del estado de los reinos de Marruecos, Fez y Tarudante. Sevilla, 1578*. Edited by M. García-Arenal. Madrid, 1980.

Torrutiel, Abraham ben Salomon de. *El Libro de la Cabala*. Translated into Spanish by F. Cantera Burgos. Salamanca, 1928.

Universiteit van Amsterdam. Bibliotheek. *Catalogus der handschriften*. Vol. 7: *De handschriften, krachtens bruikleencontract in de Universiteitsbibliotheek berustende*. Part 1: "De handschriften van de Remonstrantsche Kerk beschreven door . . . M. B. Mendes da Costa." Amsterdam, 1923.

Valensi, L. *Fables de la mémoire: La glorieuse bataille des Trois Rois*. Paris, 1992.

Vajda, G. "Un recueil de textes historiques judéo-marocaines." *Hespéris* 35 (1978).

Van Deursen, A. Th. Maurits van Nassau. De Winnaar die faaldeVaz Dias, S. "Bijdrage tot de geschiedenis der Portugees Israëlietische gemeente te Amsterdam tijdens de tweede wereldoorlog." *Studia Rosenthaliana* 29, no. 1 (1995): 29–70.

Victoria and Albert Museum. *Catalogue of an Exhibition of Anglo-Jewish Art and History in Commemoration of the Tercentenary of the Resettlement of the Jews in the British Isles, Held at the Victoria and Albert Museum, 6 January to 29 February 1956*. London, 1956.

Vlessing, O. "New Light on the Earliest History of the Amsterdam Portuguese Jews." In *Dutch Jewish History*, ed. J. Michman, 3: 43–75. Jerusalem and Maastricht, 1993.

De Ware Bekeringe en Violent vervolgingen Van Eva Cohen, Nu genaemt Elixabeth. Nu getranslateert in het Nederduyts, etc., 1681.

Webster, W. "Hebraizantes portugueses en San Juan de Luz en 1619." *Boletín de la Real Academia de la Historia* 15 (1889): 347–60.

Weiner, J. M. "Fitna, Corsairs, and Diplomacy: Morocco and the Maritime States of Western Europe, 1603–1672." Ph.D. thesis, Columbia University, 1976.

Wiegers, G. A. *A Learned Muslim Acquaintance of Erpenius and Golius: Ahmad b. Kâsim al-Andalusî and Arabic Studies in the Netherlands.* Leiden, 1988.

———. *Islamic Literature in Spanish and Aljamiado: Yça of Segovia (fl. 1450), His Antecedents and Successors.* Leiden, 1993.

———. "Learned Moriscos and Arabic Studies in the Netherlands, 1609–1624." In J. Lüdtke, ed., *Romania Arabica: Festschrift für Reinhold Kontzi zum 70. Geburtstag,* pp. 405–17. Tübingen, 1996.

———. "The Andalusi Heritage in the Maghrib: The Polemical Work of Muhammad Alguazir (d. 1610)." *Orientations* 4 (1997): 107–32.

———. "European Converts to Islam in the Maghrib and the Polemical Writings of the Moriscos," in M. Garcia-Arenal (ed.), *Conversions islamiques. Identites religieuses en Islam Mediterraneen,* pp. 207–23. Paris, 2001.

Wilke, C. L. "Conversion ou retour? La métamorphose du nouveau chrétien en juif portugais dans l'imaginaire sépharade du XVII siècle." In E. Benbassa, ed., *Memoires juives d'Espagnes et du Portugal,* pp. 53–67. Paris, 1996.

Wolf, L. *The Jews in the Canary Islands.* London, 1926.

Yahya, D. *Morocco in the Sixteenth Century: Problems and Patterns in African Foreign Policy.* London, 1981.

Yerushalmi, Y. H. *From Spanish Court to Italian Ghetto: Isaac Cardoso, a Study in Seventeenth-Century Marranism and Jewish Apologetics.* London, 1971.

———. "Professing Jews in Post-Expulsion Spain and Portugal." In *Salo Wittmayer Baron: Jubilee Volume on the Occasion of His Eightieth Birthday,* English section, 2: 1023–58. New York, 1974.

Zandvliet, K. "Het hof van een dienaar met vorstelijke allure." In id., ed., *Maurits, Prins van Oranje,* pp. 37–63. Zwolle, Netherlands, 2000.

Zantkuyl, H. J. "Reconstructie van een vroeg 17ᵉ eeuwse synagoge." *Amstelodamum* 57 (1970): 199–207.

Zimmels, H. J. *Die Marranen in der rabbinischen Literatur: Forschungen und Quellen zur Geschichte und Kulturgeschichte der Anussim.* Berlin, 1932.

Zwarts, J. "De eerste rabbijnen en synagogen van Amsterdam naar archivalische bronnen." *Bijdragen en Mededeelingen van het genootschap voor de joodsche wetenschap in Nederland* 4 (1928): 147–271.

INDEX

loyalties, viii, ix, xx, 131
Luria, Isaac, 125

Madrid: Moroccan Jews in, 18; Pallache brothers in, 4–10
Málaga, 19, 72
al-Malik, Abd (sultan of Morocco), 51, 103, 114, 115
Manoel I (king of Portugal), 40
al-Mansur, Ahmad (sultan of Morocco): Jewish employees of, 33; library of, 80; and moriscos, 50, 51–52; Pallache brothers' service to, 4, 134n. 14; reign of, 27–29
Marchena, Juan de, 5
Mármol, Luis del, 22, 24–25
Marrakech, 27–28, 29, 50, 140n. 87
al-Maruni, Ahmad ben Abdallah al-Hayti (Ahmed Elhaitia Biscaino), 51, 71, 72, 76, 77, 96, 100
Maurice of Nassau (prince of Orange), 1, 2, 35, 51, 55, 73–74, 91, 95–96, 117
Mazet, Pierre, 116
Medicis, Marie de, 81, 117
Medina Sidonia, duke of (Alonso Pérez de Guzmán): and La Mamora, 87; and moriscos, 59; and Moses Pallache, 100, 104; and Samuel Pallache, 4–9, 11, 87–88; and Pariente, 34–35
Mellahs. See Jewish quarters
Mendes Bravo, Hector, 12, 60
Mendes Henriques, Juan, 65, 66
Méndez, Simón, 13
Mendoça, Jerónimo de, 25, 26
Mercado, Simao de, 64
mercantilism, 130–31; Samuel Pallache as exemplar of, 74–75, 130–31
merchants, Jewish: in Dutch Republic, 35–36, 57–59; in France, 53–54
messianic movements: Jewish, 23, 125–26; Muslim, 77
Mezquita (Mesquita) family, 126
military activities: Moroccan Jews' involvement in, 38; Pallache's involvement in, 55, 73, 76–77. See also arms trade
Molères (Frenchman), 115
Montalto, Elias, 118

moriscos, x, xxii; alliances with Jews, 72; in Amsterdam, 59; Andalusian, dress of, 13; in Aragon, 9; in France, 53–54, 117; Harrison's contact with, 75; and Morocco, x–xi, 30, 50–52, 140nn. 87 & 92; Samuel Pallache's contact with, xi, 9, 51, 52, 72; in Salé, 75, 150n. 13; and Spain, 11, 39, 62, 139n. 68; and Muley Zaydan, 50–51, 72–73
Moroccan Jews: Azevedo's life story, 42–44; diplomatic activities of, 32–38; emigration to Iberia, 37, 38, 39, 49–50, 136n. 65; immigration from Europe, 22, 23–24, 40–41, 49; "judaizing" by, 5, 16, 18–19; languages of, 47, 49–50; in Lisbon, 5, 15, 18; and Spanish Inquisition, 18; trade activities of, 32, 35–36; treatment of, in Morocco, 24–25. See also Fez Jews; North African Jews
Morocco: civil war, 5, 6, 29–32; Dutch relations, Samuel Pallache as envoy for, 55–56, 71–75, 84–85, 102, 129; French peace treaty affair, 114–17; Ibn Abu Mahalli uprising, 77–79; Jewish immigration to, 22, 23–24, 40–41, 49, 136n. 6; al-Mansur's reign, 27–29; moriscos in, x–xi, 50–52; Ottoman relations, Pallaches and, 95–96, 100, 149n. 103; of Pallaches' time, viii; and Muley Zaydan's stolen books, 79–82
Mortara, Juanetín, 5, 36, 134nn. 15 & 27, 138–39n. 61
Moscoso, Juan Alonso de, 139n. 67
Mouette, Germain de, 125–26
Muslims: conversions of, 38–39, 139n. 67; converted (see moriscos)

al-Naqsis, Ahmad, 31, 55, 60, 76
Natán Ulet. See Benterny, Nathan
Nathan of Gaza, 125
Navarre, 43
Neve Salom community, 58, 63, 140n. 2, 141n. 21
"New Christians." See conversos; Portuguese Jews/conversos
"New Jews," 3, 58, 71

Nooms, Symon Willemsz, 73, 141n. 14
Noronha, Alfonso de, 34
Noronha, Manoel de. *See* Ben Zamirro, Salomón
North Africa, links with Iberia, 52
North African Jews: attitude toward Islam, 22–23; dress of, 5; in Málaga, 19; migration to Spain, 41–42; Spanish Inquisition and, 18–19. *See also* Moroccan Jews; *specific cities of origin*
Novoa, Matías de, 42
Núñez, Juan, 137n. 17

Olivares, Gaspar de Guzmán, 41, 18–19
Orán, Baltasar de, 19
Oran, Jewish families of, 13, 35, 126, 135n. 40
Otter (ship), 85
Ottoman Empire, 95–96, 100, 149nn. 86 & 103
Oye, Gabriel de, 149n. 93

Paes, Domingo, 44
Paes, Sebastião, 13
Palache, Isaac van Juda, 127
Palache, Juda Lion, 127
Palache family (descendants), 127
Pallache, Abraham (nephew), 12, 104, 109, 111
Pallache, Benvenida (sister-in-law), 12, 101
Pallache, David (nephew), 12, 101–2, 105, 113, 119, 121–22, 124; and French-Moroccan peace treaty, 114–17; widow of, 106, 119–20
Pallache, Isaac (descendant), 127
Pallache, Isaac (father), 12
Pallache, Isaac (nephew), 12, 61, 62, 64, 120–25; and Aier port scheme/conflict with Ruyl, 109, 111, 112–13, 121; lawsuit *vs.* Garces, 64–71; religious convictions of, x, 121, 123, 124–25
Pallache, Isaac (son), 12, 101, 103, 105, 142n. 40
Pallache, Jacob, 125, 127
Pallache, Jacob (Ya'qub) Carlos (son), 12, 101, 142n. 40
Pallache, Joseph (brother): Aier port scheme/conflict with Ruyl and, 108,

109–11, 112–13; conflicts with Isaac, 120, 121; death of, 119; and duke of Tuscany, 140–41n. 8; in Dutch Republic, 1–2, 54–56, 72, 73, 74, 140n. 2; family of, 11–12, 101; in France, 10, 11, 54; Garces affair and, 65, 67; inquiry after Samuel's death and, 102–3; in Istanbul, 100; and Joshua's approach to Spain, 60, 61–62; and Moses' approach to France, 62, 63; and Samuel and Moses' pact with Spain, 98–99; in Samuel Pallache legend, 1, 2; and Samuel's arrest and trial, 90, 91; after Samuel's death, 100, 101, 106–7; as Samuel's deputy, 72, 73, 74, 86; and Samuel's privateering, 89; service: —to al-Mansur, 4–5, 134n. 14; —to al-Saghir, 117; —to Muley Zaydan, 96, 100, 102–3, 106–7; in Spain, 4–10, 11, 133n. 8, 134n. 31
Pallache, Joshua (nephew), 12, 60–62, 104, 142n. 41; son of, 120
Pallache, Moses (nephew), viii, xvii, 3, 12, 60, 62–63, 72, 73, 74, 81, 103–6, 124; and Aier port scheme/conflict with Ruyl, 109, 110, 112; and David's widow, 106, 119–20; and French-Moroccan peace treaty, 114, 115, 116, 117; and Ibn Abu Mahalli uprising, 78–79; at Moroccan court, 101–2, 103–4, 105, 117, 119–20; and Ottoman Empire, 95, 96; and Samuel's trial, 93; service to Spain, 97, 98–99, 100, 104
Pallache, Reina/Malca (wife), 12, 101
Pallache, Samuel, xix–xxi; and Amsterdam Jewish community, 1–2, 63–64, 71, 129; arrest and trial of, 89–94; burial of, 1, 2, 59, 99–100; career summary, vii–viii, xix–xx; childhood milieu of, vii, 24; death of, 99; in Dutch Republic, 2, 54–56, 71–75, 76–77, 84–85, 94–95, 140n. 2; in England, 73, 75, 89–94; family of, 11–12, 101; in France, 10, 11, 54; and Garces affair, 65, 67, 68, 69–70; inquiry into, after death, 102–3, 106; interpretations of, 128–32; and La Mamora

affair, 84–88; languages of, 14; lawsuits involving, 74, 142n. 40; legend of, 1–4; loyalties of, viii, ix, xx, 131; as mercantilist, 74–75, 130–31; and moriscos, xi, 9, 51, 52, 72; and Moroccan civil war, 5, 6, 31–32; and nephews' approaches to France and Spain, 60, 61–62, 62, 63; and Ottoman Empire, 95–96, 149n. 86; physical appearance of, 12–13; privateering by, 72, 75, 83, 84, 88, 94–95, 145n. 6; religiosity of, 3, 63, 99–100, 131; and Rijsbergen expedition, 76–77; service: —to al-Mansur, 4–5, 134n. 14; —to Muley Zaydan, 54, 55–56, 69, 71–75, 76, 77–79, 84–88, 131; and Spain: —attempts to resettle in, 4–10, 11, 19, 61, 128, 133n. 8, 134n. 31; —pact with, 97–99; —secret dealings with, 86–88; times of, vii, viii; trading activity of, 29, 55–56, 65, 72, 73–75; and Muley Zaydan's stolen books, 1, 3, 98, 144–45n. 102

Pallache, Samuel (grandnephew), 120

Pallache family, 11–12; and Aier port scheme, 108–13; and Amsterdam Jewish community, 2, 64, 71; attempts to resettle in Spain, 9–10, 11, 128; conversion offers by, 10, 62; descendants of, 127; in Dutch Republic, 54, 101, 136n. 1; and Ibn Abu Mahalli uprising, 78–79; and jewel trade, 104–5; lawsuits of, 74; loyalties of, viii, ix; as mediators between Europe and North Africa, viii–ix; Moroccan branch, 104, 105, 127; origins of, 12, 49, 135n. 48; Ruyl's diary on, 109–13; after Samuel's death, 100, 101–2, 104, 127, 129; spelling of name, xvii, 12

Pardo, Joseph, 69

Pariente, Salomón, 34–35

Pariente family, 34, 48

Parkins, Christopher, 137n. 32

Penelope (ship), 88

Peralta, Juan de, 80

Pérez, Antonio, 8

Pérez de Guzmán, Alonso. *See* Medina Sidonia, duke of

Philip II (king of Spain and Portugal), 13, 35, 43

Philip III (king of Spain): Jewish policy of, 41; and Morocco, 30, 31, 87; and Samuel Pallache, 4–11, 87, 98, 99; and Muley Zaydan's stolen books, 1, 3, 80–82, 98

Philip IV (king of Spain), Jewish policy of, 41–42

Pinto, Cristóbal, 65

Pinto, Isaac, 3

piracy, 83–84; Samuel Pallache's arrest and trial for, 89–94. *See also* privateering

Polo, Baltasar, 7–8

Portugal: captives from, held in Fez, 25–26, 29; Jewish policies, 40–41; Moroccan Jews in, 18

Portuguese Inquisition, 18, 40, 41, 60; Jews tried by, 13, 15, 42, 44, 45–49, 68–71

Portuguese Jews/conversos: in Amsterdam, 3, 53, 56–59, 64, 129; in Antwerp, 57; arms trading by, 138n. 40; compulsory conversion of, 40; denunciations of, 60–61, 64–66, 70, 141–42n. 34; diaspora of, 40–41, 42; dress of, 13; in French trade, 53–54; migration to Morocco, 40–41, 49; Pallache family and, 64, 66, 71; Portuguese policies toward, 40–41

Prado, Juan de, 82

Pretto, Hierónimo Fernandes, 89, 95

privateering: *vs.* piracy, 83–84; by Said ben Foraj al-Dugali, 51–52; by Samuel Pallache, 72, 75, 83, 84, 88, 94–95, 145n. 6; Samuel Pallache's arrest and trial for, 89–94

Puñonrrostro, count of, 5, 6, 8

purim, 23

Querido, Aaron, 38

Rambouillet, marquis of, 118

Razilly (Frenchman), 114, 115

"Relación sobre Berbería y Muley Xeque" (Domínguez), 7

religious skepticism, 56, 131

Remmokh, Yamin ben, 35–36